The First Book of

Unix

First Book of
Unix

Douglas Topham

alpha
books

A Division of Prentice Hall Computer Publishing
201 West 103rd Street, Indianapolis, Indiana 46290 USA

International Standard Book Number: 1-56761-398-5
Library of Congress Catalog Card Number: 93-73054

95 94 9 8 7 6 5 4 3 2 1

Interpretation of the printing code: the rightmost number of the first series of numbers is the year of the book's printing; the rightmost number of the second series of numbers is the number of the book's printing. For example, a printing code of 94-1 shows that the first printing of the book occurred in 1994.

Screen reproductions in this book were created by means of the program Collage Plus from Inner Media, Inc., Hollis, NH.

Printed in the United States of America

Publisher
Marie Butler-Knight

Product Development Manager
Faithe Wempen

Managing Editor
Elizabeth Keaffaber

Aquisitions Editor
Seta Frantz

Development Editor
Ella Davis

Cover Designer
Michele Laseau

Designer
Kevin Spear

Indexer
C. A. Small

Production Team
Gary Adair, Katy Bodenmiller,
Brad Chinn, Kim Cofer,
Meshell Dinn, Mark Enochs,
Stephanie Gregory,
Jenny Kucera, Beth Rago,
Marc Shecter, Carol Stamile

Special thanks to Scott Parker for assuring the technical accuracy of this book.

Contents

1 Introduction to UNIX   3

What Is an Operating System? 3
How Does UNIX Differ from DOS? 4
   Common Characteristics 4
   Text Processing and Formatting 6
   Programming Tools 6
   System Administration 6
UNIX and Standards 7
   The Three Versions 7
   Other Standards 8
Getting Started 9
   Preliminary Setup 9
   Logging into the System 11
   Entering Commands 13
   Changing Your Password 14
   Entering a Command Line 15
   Logging Out of the System 17
Chapter 1 Quiz...18

2 The File System   21

An Overview of the File System 21
   Naming Files...23
   Types of Files 24
Handling Directories 24
   Looking at Directories 25
   Changing Directories 26
   Creating a Directory 27
   Deleting a Directory 28
Handling Files 29
   Copying Files 29
   Examining Files 30
   Renaming and Moving Files 31
   Deleting Files 33
   Linking Files 33
   Matching Characters 35

File Permissions 37
  Reading Permissions 37
  Changing Permissions 39
Chapter 2 Quiz 41

3 Processing Commands   45

The Different Shell Programs 45
Commands and Command Lines 46
  The Shell Prompt 46
  Entering a Command Line 47
  Command Arguments 48
  Commands and Processes 49
Redirection of Input and Output 49
  Redirection of Input 50
  Redirection of Output 51
Connecting Processes 53
  Using Pipes 53
  Using Tees 54
Background Processing 56
  Requesting a Background Process 57
  Checking on Background Processes 58
  Terminating a Background Process 59
Executing Commands from Files 60
  Obtaining Directory Information 60
  Adding Another Function 61
The Initialization Files 63
  Using the Shell Start-Up File 63
  Changing the Environment from the
    Command Line 66
Chapter 3 Quiz 66

4 Some Utility Programs   71

Displaying a Calendar 71
Displaying Text on the Screen 73
  Entering Text Manually 74
  Displaying Large Files 75

Printing 76
    Printing Options 77
    Requesting a Specific Printer 78
    Displaying the Printing Queue 79
Finding Files 80
    Search Criteria 82
    Action Statements 84
Searching for Text in a File 85
    Searching More Than One File 86
    Using Regular Expressions 88
Sorting Lines in Files 90
    Selecting Fields 90
    Using Sort Options 92
    Sorting More Than One File 93
    Sending the Output to a File 93
Performing Calculations 94
    Using the Desk Calculator 94
Using the High-Precision Calculator 96
Chapter 4 Quiz 97

5 Editing with vi   101

Beginning and Ending an Editing Session 101
    Comments on the Session 103
    Command Mode and Text-Entry Mode 104
Moving the Cursor 104
    Moving One Position at a Time 105
    Repeating and Undoing Keystrokes 107
    Moving to the End of the Line 109
    Moving a Word at a Time 109
    Moving a Sentence at a Time 110
    Moving a Paragraph at a Time 111
    Moving Around the Screen 111
    Moving to a Specific Line Number 112
Adjusting the Screen Display 112
    Scrolling 113
    Controlling the Screen Display 114
    Clearing System Messages 115

Entering New Text 115
  Inserting Text 116
  Appending Text 117
Opening a New Line 118
Deleting Text 120
  Deleting Characters 120
  Deleting Words 120
  Deleting Lines 122
  Deleting Sentences 123
  Deleting Paragraphs.....................................124
Moving Text 125
  Moving Sentences 125
  Moving Other Units of Text 127
Finding and Replacing Text 128
  Searching for Text 128
  Replacing Text 130
Chapter 5 Quiz..132

6 Communicating with Other Users   135

Internal Communication 135
  Terminal-to-Terminal Communication 136
  Sending Reminders to Yourself 138
  Using the Basic Mail Facility...........................139
  Using the Extended Mail Facility 142
External Communication 146
  Calling Another System 146
  UNIX-to-UNIX Communication 151
    Sending Mail to Users on Another System 151
    Copying Files to Another System 154
    Executing Commands on Another System 156
Using the UNIX Bulletin Board 157
  Newsgroups 157
  Reading the Bulletin Board 159
  Writing to the Bulletin Board 160
  Setting Up to Use the Bulletin Board 161
Chapter 6 Quiz..162

7 Formatting UNIX Documents   165

Formatting Programs 165
The mm Macro Package 167
Formatting Paragraphs...168
  Forming a Block Paragraph 168
  Forming an Indented Paragraph 168
Formatting Display Text 169
  Forming an Indented Display 169
  Forming a Double-Indented Display 170
  Forming a Centered Display 171
  Forming a Blocked Display 171
Formatting Lists 172
  Forming a Bullet List 172
  Forming a Dash List 173
  Forming a Mark List 173
  Forming a Reference List 174
  Forming a Variable-Item List 175
  Forming an Auto-Number List 175
Other Formatting Features 178
  Justifying Text 178
  Skipping Lines 179
  Highlighting Text 179
  Changing Point Size 180
Chapter 7 Quiz..182

8 The X Window System   187

A Sample Session with X 189
  The Workspace...189
  The File Manager 190
  The Terminal Emulator 190
  Other Tools...191
  Ending the Session 191
X Terminology...192
  Managing the Display 192
  Performing Applications...................................193
  Managing the Windows 193

The OPEN LOOK File Manager 194
  A Tour of the Menu 194
  Selecting Items 195
  Opening Items....................................195
  Copying Items 196
  Moving Items 196
The OPEN LOOK Terminal Emulator 197
  Window Control 198
  Working with the Menu 198
The OPEN LOOK Window Manager 200
  The Workspace Menu 200
  Help Windows 201
  Scrolling Through a Window..................202
  Controlling Windows 203
More on X Clients 204
  Commands and Options 204
  Initialization 208
Chapter 8 Quiz.......................................209

9 The System Administrator   213

  What a System Administrator Does 214
  Logging In as System Administrator.................214
  The System Administrator's Directory 215
Working with Users...................................216
  Reaching Users 216
  Setting Up New User Accounts...................217
  Finding Out Who Is Logged In 221
Checking Disk Space 223
  Checking Space Used by Files 223
  Checking Free Disk Space...................224
Backing Up Files 225
  The Copy I/O Program 225
  Options for the cpio Command..................226
  Copying Files Out 226
  Copying Files In 228
  Passing Files 229
  Other Backup Programs 230
Setting Up Terminals 231

Basic Terminal Settings 231
Describing Full-Screen Features 234
Preparing for the X Environment 238
Shutting the System Down 239
The Shutdown Script 240
Chapter 9 Quiz 240

Appendix A Glossary   245

Appendix B Quick Reference   277

Appendix C The C and Korn Shells   301

Initialization Files 303
Retrieving Command Lines 308
Selecting Arguments on a Command Line 309
Changing a Command Line 313
Using Abbreviations 315

Answers to Quizzes   317

Introduction

This book introduces the features of UNIX that are most useful to a new user. You will learn how to begin working on UNIX System V immediately. However, this book covers only those features suitable for beginners; it contains no programming or highly technical information.

Chapter 1 introduces you to operating systems and UNIX and then shows you how to log in and start working right away. You'll learn about file administration in Chapter 2 and about command processing in Chapter 3. These three chapters provide you with a solid foundation for understanding how to use the UNIX system.

Chapter 4 demonstrates how to use many of the most common utility programs. These utilities let you perform many important tasks that you must use all the time, such as printing, searching, and sorting.

Chapter 5 offers a thorough introduction to text-editing with the built-in vi (visual interpreter) program. You'll learn how to adjust the screen display, insert and delete text, move text, search for text, and replace text. These skills will enable you to create and edit documents with confidence.

Chapter 6 shows you how to communicate with other users on your own UNIX system and on other systems using electronic mail and a UNIX network called uucp. With the skills you learn in this chapter, you will be able to send and receive messages to many other users and use a bulletin board.

Chapter 7 explains how to use the mm program to format text before printing your documents. After reviewing the tools provided by UNIX, you will learn how to format paragraphs, display text, and create lists. You will also learn how to justify text, skip lines, highlight text, and change point size.

Chapter 8 teaches you the basics of the x Window System. You will learn how to start X, how to work with files under the File Manager, how to execute programs and copy and move text in the Terimal Emulator, how to run a program under the Workspace Manager, and how to use the general purpose options and initialization file for X clients.

In each chapter, you will go through a number of simple step-by-step exercises to learn the basic information. A chapter summary and a quiz help to reinforce your understanding of the subject. No knowledge of mathematics or programming is required.

Conventions Used in This Book

As you use this book, you will notice that it includes several special elements to highlight important information.

- Actions that you take, whether it's pressing a key or selecting a menu, will appear in color.

- Characters that you see on-screen appear in computer font like this.

- Text that you should type in is printed in a bold, color, computer font like this.

- Keys that you press are shown as keycaps, like ⏎Enter and Esc.

- Many commands are activated by pressing two or more keys at the same time. These key presses or selections are separated by a minus sign (-) in the text. For example, "press Ctrl-W" means that you should hold down the Ctrl key while you press the W key. (You don't type the minus sign.)

Look for this icon for Quick Steps that give you
at-a-glance steps to quickly perform important tasks.

TIP: Helpful tips and shortcuts are included in TIP
boxes.

NOTE: Important information that should be noted is
included here.

These are potential pitfalls and problems
which you should avoid.

Acknowledgments

I want to thank Bill Gladstone and Matt Wagner of Waterside
Productions, along with Seta Frantz, Liz Keaffaber, and Ella
Davis of Alpha Books, for making this book possible.

Trademarks

All terms mentioned in this book that are known to be trade-
marks have been appropriately capitalized. Alpha Books cannot
attest to the accuracy of this information. Use of a term in this
book should not be regarded as affecting the validity of any
trademark or service mark.

In This Chapter

What Is an Operating System?

How UNIX Differs from DOS

Some Typical UNIX System Configurations

How to Log In

Logging In to the System

1. Connect your terminal to the system.
2. Type your login name, and press ⏎Enter.
3. Type your password, and press ⏎Enter.

Changing Your Password

1. Type *passwd*, and press ⏎Enter.
2. Type your current password, and press ⏎Enter.
3. Type a new password, and press ⏎Enter.
4. Type the new password again, and press ⏎Enter.

Logging Out of the System

1. Type Ctrl-D, and wait for the login: prompt.
2. On some systems, you can type *logout*.

Introduction to UNIX

This chapter introduces you to the UNIX operating system. It assumes that you have used a computer and that you have some knowledge of the Disk Operating System (DOS) used on IBM and IBM-compatible PCs.

What Is an Operating System?

An *operating system* is the software that allows a computer's hardware and software to work together. It consists of programs and routines that coordinate processes, translate data from input and output devices, regulate data storage in memory, and allocate tasks to different processors. It also provides programs and functions that help programmers develop new software.

An operating system provides a standardized method for starting a computing session, storing files, working with files, accessing peripheral devices, and ending a computing session.

You can concentrate on working rather than on learning how to perform basic tasks on a variety of different computers. From your point of view, the operating system remains secondary. The application program is always your primary concern. However, the operating system is always in the background, supporting the application program in many different ways with many essential services.

How Does UNIX Differ from DOS?

The main difference between UNIX and DOS is that DOS was originally designed for single-user systems, while UNIX was designed for systems with many users. Many other differences between the two systems derive from this fundamental difference.

Common Characteristics

UNIX and DOS both provide you with an assortment of commands to be entered for processing. A prompt appears on the screen, you type a command according to some predefined syntax, and then you press ⏎Enter or Return to initiate processing. After the task has been completed, the prompt reappears. Both operating systems offer graphical interfaces with screen icons and mouse control. For DOS, both the dosshell and Microsoft Windows are graphical user interfaces. The X Window System, or X, is the standard graphical user interface (GUI) for UNIX.

Note, however, that UNIX is a *multitasking* operating system, which means that you can run more than one program at a time; you can run three or four tasks simultaneously.

DOS was originally patterned after its predecessor for personal computers: CP/M (control program/monitor). Since its introduction in late 1981, however, DOS has been strongly influenced by UNIX. The inclusion of directories and subdirectories and the addition of new commands to support these structures are the most obvious influences of UNIX on the later versions of DOS.

Table 1.1 shows some of the important commands in these two operating systems. Note that several commands perform similar functions. In fact, some commands are identical (or nearly identical) in both operating systems.

UNIX Command	DOS Command	Function
ls	dir	Displays the contents of the current directory.
cd	cd	Changes directories (moves from one directory to another).
mkdir	md	Creates a new subdirectory under the current directory.
rmdir	rd	Deletes (or removes) an existing directory.
cat	type	Displays the contents of a file.
cp	copy	Copies a file (or a group of files).
mv	ren	Renames a file.
rm	del	Deletes a file (or group of files).
ln	–	Forms a link to a file.
chmod	–	Sets file permissions.
cal	–	Displays a calendar for a year or month.
lp	print	Queues a file for printing.
pstat	print	Displays the printing queue.
find	–	Lists file names that meet criteria.
grep	find	Lists lines in a file that meet criteria.
sort	sort	Sorts lines in a file.
dc	–	Starts the desk calculator.
bc	–	Starts the high-precision calculator.
vi	edit	Creates and edits text.
write	–	Sends a message to another terminal.
calendar	–	Sends a reminder to yourself.
mail	–	Sends electronic mail to another user.
cu	–	Calls another system.
uucp	–	Communicates with other system.
nroff	–	Formats text for printing (fixed width).
troff	–	Formats text for printing (variable width).
cpio	xcopy	Backs up and recovers files.

Table 1.1
Corresponding Commands

Text Processing and Formatting

In UNIX, extensive text-processing and text-formatting features are included with the operating system. UNIX provides vi (the visual interpreter) and nroff and troff (the text formatters for daisy-wheel printers, typesetters, and laser printers). This follows the tradition of mainframe operating systems.

In DOS, text-processing and text-formatting that approach the level of sophistication of vi and nroff and troff can be found only in application programs. For many years, DOS provided only a simple and extremely limited line editor called edlin. But the newest releases of DOS now provide full-screen editing (edit).

Programming Tools

UNIX also includes extensive programming tools with the operating system. UNIX provides a built-in programming language for the command processor (also called the *shell*), the C programming language, and a variety of debuggers, analyzers, compilers, and other tools.

DOS provides a debugger, along with QBasic. DOS allows automated operation through batch files, but batch files are less sophisticated than the programming structures offered in the shell scripts of the UNIX system.

System Administration

As a relatively large system with many users, each UNIX operating system requires a *system administrator*. The system administrator sets up new accounts for users, assigns passwords, installs terminals and printers, starts and stops the system, backs up files, provides system security, and helps new users. The software tools that aid the system administrator are, naturally, included with UNIX.

As a single-machine operating system, DOS can be maintained and administered much more easily. Generally, you are responsible only for less involved tasks, such as initializing the system and backing up files. Tools for performing these tasks are available within DOS, but more elegant and sophisticated programs are often available as separate third-party application programs.

UNIX and Standards

One of the strongest criticisms of UNIX throughout the years is that it has never been a single, unified product with total compatibility from one system to another, as DOS has been. The most significant differences have arisen from different versions developed by the three major standard-bearers:

- AT&T UNIX
- Microsoft XENIX
- Berkeley UNIX BSD

The Three Versions

AT&T's System V, the current commercial UNIX for medium-sized and large systems, is derived primarily from AT&T's earlier System III and Version 7, but includes some Berkeley features. System V, Release 3 introduced extensive new communications features, including an improved version of the uucp (UNIX-to UNIX copy and communication) program and a new Remote File Sharing (RFS) system.

In the late 1970s and early 1980s, Microsoft developed an offshoot of UNIX, called XENIX, which was specifically designed for personal computers. In the late 1980s, with the emergence of the Intel 80386 microprocessor, personal computers now rival the processing power of minicomputers. Because there is no longer a need for a separate UNIX-derived product, AT&T and Microsoft have merged UNIX and XENIX into a product called System V/386, Release 3.2.

The University of California began diverging from AT&T's UNIX in the late 1970s, offering a UNIX system that appeals to scientific research centers, universities, and engineering firms. The most recent release is called BSD (Berkeley standard delivery) 4.3. AT&T merged the AT&T and Berkeley versions in System V, Release IV. Now, AT&T UNIX, XENIX, and Berkeley UNIX are finally united as a single product called UNIX.

For a brief chronology of the three main versions of UNIX, see Figure 1.1.

Figure 1.1

The versions of UNIX.

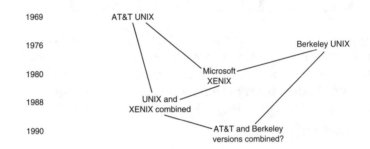

Other Standards

In the area of hardware, a consortium called X/Open has defined a Common Applications Environment (CAE) for computers that run UNIX. Some of the companies actively complying with CAE are Hewlett-Packard, NCR, Unisys, Siemens, Bull, Olivetti, and ICL.

Meanwhile, the Institute of Electrical and Electronic Engineers (IEEE) has also been pressing for a standard for UNIX design called Posix (portable operating system environment standard). Because companies have proliferated so many variations of UNIX, Posix may offer all companies that produce versions of UNIX a means of reaching agreement.

Ever since the introduction of the Macintosh, with its icon-driven graphical user interface, most computer manufacturers have accepted the concept of bit-mapped graphic displays. Such a display is required for both icon-based user interfaces and desktop publishing. To unify the efforts to produce graphic displays for UNIX, some companies have been supporting a standard called the X Window System, or X. Their intention is that all bit-mapped displays should adhere to a single standard, just as all character coding now conforms to the standard ASCII.

Until 1993, Sun Microsystems and AT&T had a user interface called Open Look, which is based on the X Window and Posix standards. DEC, Hewlett-Packard, IBM, and others have formed an Open Software Foundation (OSF), which has responded with a rival user interface of its own, called Motif. However, in 1993, all vendors joined together to develop a common desktop environment (CDE).

If you want to run the X Window System, you have to have a powerful terminal with a bit-mapped display and mouse control. You also have to make sure that your system administrator has given you authorization and has made the necessary modifications to your working environment.

Getting Started

Now let's consider the basic steps required for you to begin using the UNIX operating system:

- Preliminary setup
- Logging into the system
- Changing your password
- Entering commands
- Logging out of the system

Preliminary Setup

Before you can log in, you need a *login name* and a *password* to access the UNIX operating system. The system administrator sets these up for you. Your password helps maintain the security of your computer system. Each time you log into the system, you must enter your login name; then the system prompts you for a password. Only after you enter the correct password can you use the system.

Your login name may be your first name, your last name, or a combination of the two. For example, if your name is John G. Rogers, then your login name might be one of the following:

```
john

jrogers

jgr

rogers

johnr
```

At first, the system administrator determines your password for you, and tells you what it is. You can change your password to whatever you like. Your password can be up to fourteen characters long. One difference between DOS and UNIX is that UNIX distinguishes between upper- and lowercase letters. For the protection of the system, it's best to choose a longer password, especially if it includes uppercase letters, numbers, and special characters. With all of these characters, you can invent a password that is easy to remember, yet is difficult for intruders to guess. Following are a few examples:

```
Don't_4GET-it!

Easy.2.recall

It's-too-late

Laurel&Hardy
```

Most UNIX users communicate with the system through a terminal (or a computer in *terminal mode*). If you are using a terminal, your terminal must use communication settings that agree with the settings of the host computer. If your terminal is set incorrectly, one of the following might occur when you attempt to log in:

- The screen will be blank.

- Each character will appear twice.

- Random characters (called "garbage") will appear on the screen.

To correct any of these problems, you may have to run the stty (set terminal) program. Check with your system administrator if you need help using this command.

Logging into the System

After you have a login name, a password, and a correctly set terminal, you can log into your UNIX system. To do so, you must use the following basic steps.

1. Connect your terminal to the system by doing one of the following:

   Turn on your terminal.

   Press a key (or a combination of keys).

   Dial a telephone number through your modem.

The system will respond with the following prompt:

```
login:_
```

2. Type your login name, and press ⏎Enter.

The system will respond by prompting for your password:

```
login: larry

Password: _
```

3. Type your password, and press ⏎Enter.

   Your password will not appear on the screen.

   Information, such as the following, will appear on your screen.

```
Last login: Wed May 3  03:28:17   on tty07
UNIX System V, Release 4.2
$ _
```

The dollar sign ($) prompt tells you that the UNIX system is ready to accept a command.

> **NOTE:** The symbol that actually appears on your screen may be a dollar sign ($), a percent sign (%), or a pound sign (#). This symbol is called the UNIX *shell prompt*. It corresponds to the DOS prompt `C:\>`.

If you are authorized to use the X Window System, if your system administrator has made the necessary modifications to your initialization files, and if your terminal is powerful enough, you will see a completely different display when you log in. You will probably see a File Manager window, a mailbox window, and a term-window, as shown in Figure 1.2. You can move the mouse pointer to one of the windows and click on the window to activate it. Within the xterm-window, which is used to emulate an ordinary terminal, you will see a shell prompt in the form of a dollar sign ($), as described above. You can move the mouse pointer to the xterm-window and click to activate it. As soon as you activate the xterm-window, you can enter commands at the shell prompt, just as you can when you log in on an ordinary terminal.

The X Window System is described in more detail in Chapter 8.

Figure 1.2
An X Windows screen.

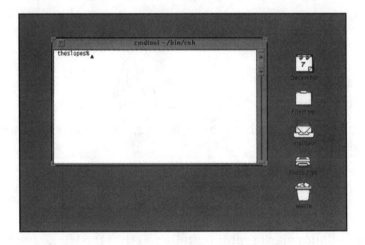

Entering Commands

You can type any UNIX command at the shell prompt, and the system will display the result on the screen. Simply type the name of the command, and press ⏎Enter. Following are a few examples.

To display the date and time, type `date` and press ⏎Enter. This causes UNIX to display the date and time, as in the following example:

```
Thu May 4  08:53:29 PST 1994
$ _
```

Note that after the system displays this information, the shell prompt returns.

To find out which users are currently logged in, type `who` and press ⏎Enter. UNIX displays information such as:

```
pat          tty02      May 4     08:51
lee          tty03      May 4     08:23
marie        tty05      May 4     08:04
larry        tty07      May 4     08:53
anne         tty08      May 4     08:19
paul         tty09      May 3     19.28
frog         tty11      May 4     07:47
terry        tty12      May 4     08:39
```

The `who` display provides the following information:

- The login name of each user logged in
- The name of the user's terminal (tty*nn*)
- The date and time when the user logged in

and then returns you to the shell prompt.

When you type a non-UNIX command, such as `sho`, and press ⏎Enter, UNIX displays the following:

```
sh:  sho:    not found
```

Because no such UNIX command exists, an error message appears.

Changing Your Password

When you first start working on a UNIX system, the system administrator usually assigns you a simple password so that you can initially log onto the system. One of the first things you should do after you first log in is to change your password so that it is more difficult for outsiders to guess. On some systems, you are required to change your password periodically. The command for making this change is called passwd (note the two missing letters). Use this command as follows:

Changing Your Password

1. Type *passwd* and
   press ⏎Enter.

2. Type your current
   password, and
   press ⏎Enter.

   ```
   $ passwd
   Changing password for
   larry
   Old password: -_
   New password:
   Retype your new password:

   _
   $ _
   ```

3. Enter a new password,
   and press ⏎Enter.

4. Enter your new password
   again, and press ⏎Enter.

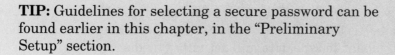

TIP: Guidelines for selecting a secure password can be found earlier in this chapter, in the "Preliminary Setup" section.

Entering a Command Line

Earlier in this chapter, you used the who command to list all users currently logged onto the system. If you occasionally work on more than one terminal in a UNIX system, you might need to use a variation of the who command. This who command includes an *argument* that modifies the action of the command:

```
$ who am i
larry      tty0?      May 4     08:53
$ _
```

Note that UNIX lists the names of the user on the terminal at which the command was typed; it also notes the communication line (tty07) being used.

Most UNIX commands allow you to add arguments that modify the output. Some commands have long lists of arguments too numerous to remember. Commands and arguments and shortcuts for remembering them are discussed at length in the "Some Utility Programs" section of Chapter 4.

When you are entering a command line, the key combinations that let you erase a single character or erase the entire command line can be helpful. To erase a single character, press one of the following:

- # (the pound sign) or ⇧Shift-3
- Ctrl-H
- ⬅Backspace (a separate key on some keyboards)

Experiment with these combinations to find out which work on your keyboard. Following is an example of how to use the # symbol as the erase key. Let's assume you made a mistake when you meant to type date and actually typed *daet*:

```
$ daet
```

Press # once to erase the t:

```
$ dae
```

Press # again to erase the e:

```
$ da
```

Type *te* to correct, and press ⏎Enter:

```
$ date
Thu May 4 08:53:29 PST 1991
$ -_
```

To cancel the command or erase the entire line, press the @ (the "at" sign) key before you press ⏎Enter. Following is an example of how to use this key (referred to as the *kill* key). Let's assume you made a mistake when you meant to type who am I and actually typed *sho am i*.

Re-Entering a Command Line

1. Press @ to erase the entire command line.

```
$ sho am i
```

2. Retype the command line, and press ⏎Enter.

```
$ who am i
larry      tty07      May 4
08:53
$ _
```

The kill key (@) probably won't erase the command line from the screen. Instead, the cursor will probably move down to the next line without displaying a new shell prompt. That is where you retype the command line.

If you enter a command and nothing happens (generates no output and no shell prompt appears), the process might have *hung up* (failed) in the system. If this ever happens, merely press ⌷Del⌷ to restore the shell prompt. For example, if you enter the date command and nothing happens, press ⌷Del⌷. The shell prompt immediately returns to the screen.

Logging Out of the System

At the end of a session, you have to log out of the system. If you merely turn off your terminal and walk away, UNIX assumes you are still logged in. If you are paying for time on the system, you will be billed for the extra time—even though you aren't really using the system.

Don't be billed for time you aren't using. Always log off when you are done.

The most common way to log off is to press ⌷Ctrl⌷-⌷D⌷. After you've done this, the login prompt (login:) returns to the screen. For example, if you press ⌷Ctrl⌷-⌷D⌷ at the shell prompt ($), UNIX does not display the key combination; it merely clears the screen and displays the following:

```
login: _
```

Be sure your screen displays the login prompt before you turn off your terminal. Otherwise, you are still logged onto the system.

NOTE: On some systems, you may be able to log out by typing *logout* at the shell prompt. After you press ⌷⏎Enter⌷, UNIX displays the usual login: prompt. This lets you know that you are now disconnected from the system.

Chapter 1 Quiz

1. Select the statement that best describes the purpose of an operating system:

   A. To handle file management

   B. To manage the operation of the disk drives

   C. To provide a shell prompt at each user's terminal

   D. To provide a common environment for programmers and users

2. Identify one feature from the following list that is common to both UNIX and DOS:

   A. Commands for creating and deleting directories

   B. Commands for text processing and editing

   C. Commands to facilitate software development

   D. Commands to carry out all aspects of system administration

3. True or false: Personal computers connected in a local area network can form a UNIX system.

4. Which of the following organizations did *not* develop one of the major variations of UNIX?

   A. AT&T

   B. IBM

   C. University of California, Berkeley

   D. Microsoft Corporation

5. Which of the following is *not* required to log in and start using UNIX?

   A. A login name

   B. A password

   C. Knowledge of system administration

   D. A terminal that has been set up to communicate with the host computer

6. Which of the following passwords represents a good, sensible choice?

   A. abc

   B. dan

   C. 2B,or.not-2B?

   D. password

7. Which of the following commands would you use to change your password?

   A. date

   B. who

   C. who am i

   D. passwd

8. The key that you press to delete the character most recently typed on the command line is called the

   A. Del

   B. Erase key

   C. Kill key

   D. Enter

9. The key that you press to delete the entire command line is called the

   A. Kill key

   B. Erase key

   C. Del

   D. Enter

10. What combination of keys do you press to log out of the system?

   A. QUIT

   B. OUT

   C. EXIT

   D. Ctrl-D

In This Chapter

Overview of the File System

Handling Directories

Handling Files

File Permissions

Overview of the File System

- The file system includes structured directories starting at the root.
- Files with file names that reside in the directories are also included in the file system.
- Three types of files are included: directory file, ordinary file, and special file.

Handling Directories

- Use ls (list) to display the contents of a directory.
- Use cd (change directory) to change to a different directory.
- Use mkdir (make directory) to create a new directory.
- Use rmdir (remove directory) to delete a directory.

Handling Files

- Use cp (copy) to copy a file.
- Use cat (concatenate) to display the contents of a file.
- Use mv (move) to move or rename a file.
- Use rm (remove) to delete a file or a set of files.
- Use ln (link) to link files.
- Use the wild-card characters ?, *, and [...] to match file names.

File Permissions

- Use ls -1 (list with long option) to display file permissions.
- Use chmod (change mode) to change file permissions.

The File System

In the UNIX system (as in DOS), text, data, and programs are stored as *files*. Files, in turn, are stored in directories. Files, directories, and the information UNIX uses to keep track of them comprise the *file system*.

An Overview of the File System

The UNIX system, like DOS, has a file system that is organized in a hierarchical structure. At the top of the hierarchy is the *root directory* (or *root*). Under the root directory are the major directories. By convention, each UNIX system includes at least five major directories, which have standard names. If you've been using DOS, this is one of the first things you must get used to, because DOS directories don't use standard names.

The names and contents of the five standard UNIX directories are summarized in Table 2.1.

Table 2.1
Major UNIX Directories

Name	Contents
/home	Where the user home directory is located
/bin	Binary or executables directory
/tmp	Temporary files
/dev	Device directory
/etc	System administration files
/var	Where accounting and spooling files are located
/export	Files available to other systems in network

The root directory is identified by a slash (/). (Note that below the root directory, a slash indicates another level lower in the file system hierarchy.) Each user has a directory under /usr. Your *home directory* is /usr/*your directory name.*

NOTE: Where DOS uses backslashes (\), UNIX uses slashes (/).

The five major directories are identified by the following names (see Figure 2.1):

```
/usr
/bin
/tmp
/dev
/etc
```

Figure 2.1
The major directories.

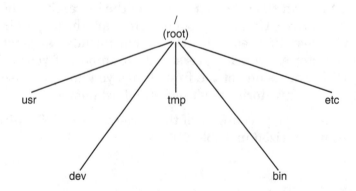

Naming Files

A file in directory /home called alice is identified by the notation /home/alice. A directory under /usr called mail is identified by the notation /usr/mail. A file in /usr/mail called alice has a *full pathname* called /usr/mail/alice. The lineage of a file through the various directories above it is called a *path*. The complete name of any file that traces its location in the file system from the root directory is referred to as a full pathname. As with DOS, one period (.) in a pathname represents the current directory, and two periods (..) represent the parent directory (the directory directly above the current directory). For example, if the current directory is /etc, the pathname to /etc/passwd/alice can also be written ./passwd/alice.

A UNIX file name can contain as few as one and as many as 32 characters, excluding slashes (/), question marks (?), asterisks (*), quotation marks (' or "), brackets ([or]), braces ({ or }), or control characters. Unlike a DOS file name, a UNIX file name can include one or more periods in any position in the file name. Another difference is that UNIX distinguishes between upper-case and lowercase letters in file names. That is, the names REPORT, Report, and report indicate three different file names in UNIX.

Here are some examples of valid UNIX file names:

```
news.report
o1.week.TEST
interest.rates
fp
ABC-123
```

As these examples show, UNIX provides more flexibility than DOS for naming files. Periods, if used, can be placed anywhere in the file name. You are not restricted to a three-character extension following a period, as you are in DOS. (Note the comparison of file names in Figure 2.2.)

Figure 2.2

A comparison of DOS and UNIX file names.

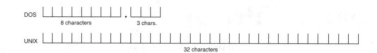

Types of Files

In the UNIX system, as in DOS, directories are actually files. However, UNIX *devices* are also represented as files; in this regard, UNIX differs considerably from DOS. DOS has a few fixed device names, such as COM1 (first serial port), LPT1 (first parallel port), and so on, which are directly related to specific hardware devices. However, UNIX lets you access all devices through file names. Your system can have as many file names as necessary, and it usually stores the names in a subdirectory of the major directory /dev.

The three types of UNIX files are summarized in Table 2.2.

Table 2.2

Types of Files

Type	Description
Directory file	A file that contains the names of other files (including other directories).
Ordinary file	A file that contains text, data, or programs.
Special file	A file that represents a particular hardware device.

Handling Directories

A file system is similar to a filing cabinet: A directory is like a drawer in that filing cabinet, and each "drawer" contains individual file folders. The tools described in this section allow you to look at directories, change directories, and create and delete directories.

Looking at Directories ls

The ls (list) command displays the contents of a directory; thus, the UNIX ls command is similar to the DOS dir command. When you use ls without any options, it displays the file names in the current directory, as in this example:

```
$ ls
answers
bates.file
call_FILES
ddd-125
zero+one
$ _
```

This simple directory listing doesn't distinguish between ordinary files and directories. It also doesn't display any information about individual files. To access this additional information, add an option to request a long listing by adding -l (hyphen el) to the basic ls command, as follows:

```
$ ls -l
total 10
drwx—x—  2   paul   258   Jul 18   15:42   answers
-rwxr-x—  1   paul    92   Feb 20   09:14   bates.file
drwx—x—  1   paul   126   Nov 31   08:57   call_FILES
-rw-r——   3   paul   415   Aug  3   13?09   ddd-125
-rw-r——   1   paul   361   May 11   10:38   zero+one
$ _
```

NOTE: If you want to use an option with a command, always insert a space between the command name and the option (or options).

This display includes seven major columns of information. Figure 2.3 illustrates the meaning of each of these columns.

Figure 2.3

Information in a long listing.

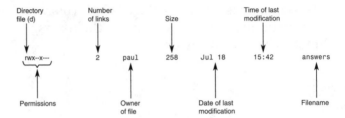

Let's review the information shown in Figure 2.3. The first column of the display contains ten characters. The first character indicates whether the file is an ordinary file (-) or a directory (d). The remaining nine characters indicate file permissions (discussed in the "File Permissions" section of this chapter).

The number in the second column is the number of *links* in the file system to this file (discussed under "Linking Files" later in this chapter). The name in the third column is the *owner* of the file (the user who originally created in the file). The number in the fourth column is the size of the file in characters (or bytes).

The fifth and sixth columns give the date and time when the file was last modified. Finally, the seventh column gives the name of the file itself.

Changing Directories   cd

The UNIX command for changing directories has the same name as the DOS command: cd. When you first log into UNIX, you are located in your home directory. You can change to one of your own subdirectories and work in it at any time. If you have permission, you can also move to other users' directories and work there.

A common use of the cd command is to change from the current directory to the parent directory. To do this, use the command:

```
$ cd ..
$ _
```

The parent directory is now your *working* (current) directory. In DOS, the PROMPT $P command displays the name of your current directory; in UNIX, the pwd (print working directory) command displays the pathname. This example uses pwd before and after changing directories (see Figure 2.4):

```
$ pwd
/usr/allen
$ cd letters
$ pwd
/usr/allen/letters
$ _
```

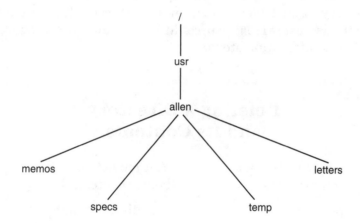

Figure 2.4
Changing directories.

Creating a Directory   mkdir

The UNIX mkdir (make directory) command works exactly like the DOS md (or mkdir) command. When you need a new directory, move to the directory under which you want it created, and use the command mkdir *dirname*, as in this example:

```
$ cd letters
$ mkdir plans
$ _
```

The commands in this example create a new subdirectory (called plans) under letters.

UNIX directories, like DOS directories, help you organize your work. Instead of accumulating all your files in one large directory, you can group your files by project or subject matter in different directories.

Deleting a Directory   rmdir

If you no longer need a directory, you can remove it from the file system with the rmdir command, which works like the DOS rd (or rmdir) command. You can delete a directory only when you are located in the directory's parent and only when the directory to be deleted contains no files. For example, suppose you want to delete a directory named /usr/allen/letters/storage. If your current directory is /usr/allen, you could carry out the procedure by using these individual steps.

Deleting a Directory and Its Contents

1. Type: **$cd /letters /storage**

   You move to the directory being deleted.

2. Type: **$ pwd**
   /usr/allen
   /letters/storage

   The directory name is checked.

3. Type: **$rm -i ***
   old.letter: **?y**
   old.memo: **?y**
   old.study: **?y**

   All files are deleted.

4. Type: **$ cd ..**

   You move to the parent directory.

5. Type: **$ rmdir storage**

   The directory $ _ deletes.

Handling Files

Most of the work you do with a computer involves manipulating files. Some of the more common operations you perform are creating new files, examining files, deleting old files, and moving files around.

Copying Files   cp

The copy command in UNIX is called cp. To use this command, type cp, the name of the original file, and then the name of the target (new) file. For example, the command:

```
$ cp old.file new.file
$ _
```

makes a copy of old.file called new.file.

> **TIP:** This example illustrates a common ordering of UNIX commands: *command previous next*. We'll talk more about this ordering later. You'll notice this in other commands later in the book.

You can use cp to copy one or more files from the current directory to another, as shown in the example:

```
$ cp memo letter report ../papers
$ _
```

This example copies the files memo, letter, and report from the current directory to another directory called papers under the same parent directory. This is shown in Figure 2.5. (Note that the files retain their names in the new directory.)

Figure 2.5

Copying files to another directory.

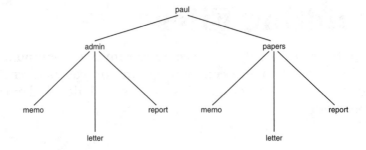

If you are copying a single file from one directory to another, you can give the file a new name in the other directory. This example copies the file old.file to the directory papers and renames it new.file:

```
$ cp old.file ../papers/new.file
$ _
```

Examining Files   cat

The UNIX cat (concatenate) command, like the DOS type command, displays the contents of a file on the screen. Here is an example of its usage:

```
$ cat memo
This is a reminder
about Thursday's
meeting at 3:00.
$ _
```

If you misspell the name of the file, or if no such file exists, the only output UNIX generates is an error message, as in this example. (Note that you can use cat as a fast way to find out whether or not a file exists.)

```
$ cat memmo
cat: cannot open memmo
$ _
```

Thus, file memmo does not exist in the current directory.

The other major function of this command—concatena-tion—is discussed in Chapter 4.

Renaming and
Moving Files   mv

The UNIX mv (move) command works somewhat like the DOS rename command to give a file a new name. To rename a file (or directory), the safest procedure is to check to see that the target name doesn't already exist, and only then make the change, as shown here:

```
$ cat new.file
cat: cannot open new.file
$ mv old.file new.file
$ _
```

You use the cat command to make sure that new.file isn't already the name of a file. If it isn't (UNIX returns an error message), then you can proceed to change the name of old.file to new.file, without having to worry about overwriting an existing file.

CAUTION

The preceding example illustrates one of the characteristics of the UNIX system: It doesn't include the safeguards and conveniences that many application programs include. When you use mv, UNIX doesn't offer a prompt to protect you, such as:

```
A file with that name already exists. Do you want to
overwrite the file? (Y/N).
```

With UNIX, you usually have to provide your own safeguards.

As its name implies, the other major function of mv is to move files from the current directory to another. In this example, you will be moving files ltr.101, ltr.102, and ltr.103 from the current directory (admin) to directory letters (see Figure 2.6):

```
$ mv ltr.101 ltr.102 ltr.103 ../letters
$ _
```

Figure 2.6

Moving files to another directory.

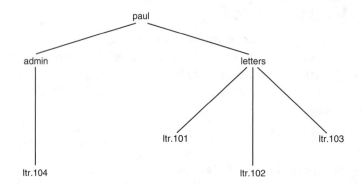

In the preceding example, letters is another subdirectory whose parent is the same directory as that of the current directory. You could use the ls command to confirm the move, as follows:

```
$ ls ../letters
ltr.101
ltr.102
ltr.103
$ _
```

When you move a single file, you can also rename it, as shown in this example:

```
$ mv ltr.104  ../letters/conference
$ _
```

In the preceding example, you are changing the name of ltr.104 to conference while moving it to the directory letters. Again, you could use ls to confirm the move and name change.

Deleting Files   rm

The rm (remove) command lets you delete files, either one at a time or in groups. Here is an example of the basic command:

```
$ rm memo test
$ _
```

When you use the basic form of the rm command, the files are deleted immediately; UNIX doesn't prompt you for confirmation of the action. If you prefer the extra safety of having to confirm each deletion before it is actually made, include the -i (interactive) option to the rm command. Here is the same example with the interactive option added:

```
$ rm -i memo test
memo: ?y
test: ?n
$ _
```

When you request confirmation in this way, UNIX displays each file name one at a time with a question mark. At each line, type either y to confirm the deletion or n to prevent the file from being deleted.

Linking Files   ln

A group of users on the same UNIX system can *share* a file while working on a joint project. Sharing the file allows any of the users to update the file at any time. One user can modify the file at 1:17; then another user can modify it at 2:03. If a third user displays the file at 2:34, the third user sees the changes made by the previous two users.

UNIX makes file-sharing possible by providing *links* to any existing file. Each link to the file is simply another name by which the file is known to another user in another directory. Although only one file exists on the system, each link makes the file accessible to another user on the system.

Consider the following situation: Lisa and Paul are both working on a project that requires the use of file `results`, which is located in Lisa's `letters` directory. Paul wants to access file `results` from his own directory, named `support`. He can obtain access to `results` by executing the `ln` (link) command from his directory `support`, like this:

```
$ cd support
$ ln /usr/lisa/letters/results progress
$ _
```

After executing these commands, Paul now has access to the file `results` from his own directory `support`. Notice that Paul has renamed the file as `progress` (but he could have retained the name `results`). The link between files and directories is illustrated in Figure 2.7.

After working on the file, Paul can always remove the link by using the `rm` command, as follows:

```
$ pwd
/usr/paul/support
$ rm progress
$ _
```

Figure 2.7

A link to a file called results.

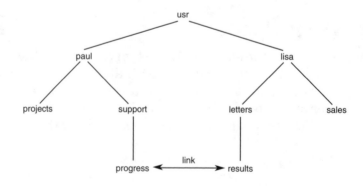

With this command, Paul removes his own link to the file, but not the original file in Lisa's directory.

Matching Characters

When you are working with UNIX files, you can use *wild-card* characters to help select file names. Two of the wild-card characters used in UNIX—the questions mark (?) and the asterisk (*)—are also used in DOS. As in DOS, the question mark is used to match a single character, and the asterisk is used to match any number of characters. In UNIX, however, you can also enumerate specific characters to be matched between a pair of brackets. These three wild-card selectors are summarized in Table 2.3.

Symbol	Meaning
?	Match any single character in the position of the symbol.
*	Match any number of characters in the position of the symbol.
[xxx]	Match the specific characters typed between the brackets.

Table 2.3
Wild-Card Symbols

Let's assume you have three files named memo.1, memo.2, and memo.3. You can use this command to copy them to a directory called MEMOS:

```
$ cp memo.? ../MEMOS
$ _
```

To delete these files from the current directory, you can use the command:

```
$ rm memo.?
$ _
```

If you had three files called test.c, algorithm.c, and abstract.c, you could move them to directory c_progs with the command:

```
$ mv *.c ../c_progs
$ _
```

In UNIX, a third type of wild-card notation lets you narrow the match to a set of specified characters. For example, suppose your directory contains these nine files:

```
test.1     test.2     test.3
test.4     test.5     test.6
test.7     test.8     test.9
```

To delete only the three files in the middle column, you could include their suffix numbers within brackets, as follows:

```
$ rm test.[258]
$ _
```

This command is equivalent to the following expanded command:

```
$ rm test.2 test.5 test.8
$ _
```

For consecutive numbers (or letters), such as those in the file names in the middle row, you can use a hyphen in the brackets to indicate a range, as shown in the following command:

```
$ rm test.[4-6]
$ _
```

This command is equivalent to the following expanded command:

```
$ rm test.4 test.5 test.6
$ _
```

File Permissions

A system administrator for a UNIX system can maintain a measure of security among its users through a system of file permissions, which determine who may or may not read or use a given file. All files (including all directories) are assigned permissions by the system administrator, which apply to the individual users, to any *group* to which the user belongs, and to all other users on the system. We'll begin with a discussion of how to read the symbolic representation of permissions, and then consider how to change permissions for a file.

Reading Permissions   ls -l

Earlier in this chapter, you saw the display created by the "long listing" option of the ls command:

```
$ ls -l
total 10
drwx—x—   2   paul   258   Jul 18   15:42   answers
-rwrx-x—   1   paul    92   Feb 20   09:14   bates.file
drwx—x—   1   paul   126   Nov 31   08:57   call)FILES
-rw-r——    3   paul   415   Aug  3   13:09   ddd-125
-rw-r——    1   paul   361   May 11   10:38   zero+one
$ _
```

The first column of the long listing includes ten characters. The first character, as noted earlier, denotes the type of file:

-	Ordinary file
d	Directory

The next nine characters give a symbolic representation of the permissions currently in effect for the file. These nine characters are actually three columns of three characters each, even though they are not separated by spaces. The first column represents permissions for the user, the second represents permissions for the user's working group (if the user belongs to a group), and the third represents permissions for all other users on the system. Let's look at the files permission column of the ls-l display and add spaces to make it easier to read. The listing would now look like this:

Type	Owner	Group	Others	Name
d	rwx	- - x	- - -	answers
-	rwx	r - x	- - -	bates.file
d	rwx	- - x	- - -	call_FILES
-	rw-	r - -	- - -	ddd-125
-	rw-	r - -	- - -	zero+one

Each of the three permission groups contain three characters. These represent permission to read (r), permission to write (w), permission to execute (x), and permission denied (-). The meanings of the permissions differ somewhat for files and directories, as shown in Table 2.4.

Table 2.4
Explanation of Permissions

Permission	Meaning for a File	Meaning for a Directory
Read	Look at the contents	View the list of file names.
Write	Change the contents	Add files to and remove files from the directory.
Execute	Use the file name as a UNIX command	Change to the directory, search the directory, and copy files from it.

Let's single out one of the lines from the preceding ls -l display and read the permissions from left to right:

-    rwx   r-x   —   bates.file

After the first hyphen, which indicates that this is an ordinary file, the nine permissions symbols are as follows:

The **owner** of bates.file can: r read the file
                                       w write to (change) the file
                                       x execute the file

| Other members of the owner's working **group** can: | r read the file
- not write to the file
x execute the file |
| All other users are denied access to the file: | - no reading
- no writing
- no executing |

Changing Permissions   chmod

You can use the chmod (change [access] mode) command to change permissions for any files that you have created. If you are the owner of a file, the chmod command lets you use the + symbol on the command line to add new permissions and use the - symbol to remove existing permissions. The command also lets you use the = symbol to assign permissions absolutely, which means that you replace all existing permissions with a completely new set of permissions.

You can use ten different symbols to change permissions on a chmod command line. These symbols are summarized in Table 2.5. Each change requires you to choose one of the symbols from the first column, one from the second column, and at least one from the third column.

Users Affected	Action Requested	Permission
u owner (user	+ add permission	r to read
g group	- remove permission	w to write
o all others	= absolute permission	x to execute
a all users (default		

Table 2.5
Symbols for chmod

For example, to allow the other members of your working group (g) to write to bates.file, you would execute this command:

```
$ chmod g+w bates.file
$ _
```

To change permissions for more than one class of users, you can include additional change requests on one command line. Simply separate each change from the others with a comma, with no space before or after the comma. For example, to add write permission to members of your working group, and also add read and write permissions to all other users, execute the command:

```
$ chmod g+w,o+rw bates.file
$ _
```

To display the result of this command very clearly, you could use ls -l (specifying one file) before and after you execute chmod. Then you can see the permissions displayed before and after the change. This is how it would look:

```
$ ls -l bates.file
-rwxr-x—  1   paul     92   Feb 20   09:14 bates.file
$ chmod g+w,o+rw bates.file
$ ls -l bates.file
-rwxrgxrw- 1   paul     92   Feb 20   09:14 bates.file
$ _
```

To revoke permissions currently in effect, use a minus sign instead of a plus sign. The following example shows you how to revoke the permissions that were granted in the preceding example:

```
$ ls -l bates.file
-rwxrwxrw- 1   paul     92   Feb 20   09:14 bates.file
$ chmod g-w,o-rw bates.file
$ ls -l bates.file
-rwxr-x—  1   paul     92   Feb 20   09:14 bates.file
$ _
```

An alternate approach to granting or revoking permissions is to use the equal sign (=) to clear all current permissions and set new ones. For example, suppose you decide to revoke all permissions for bates.file, but you want to reset permission to read and write for yourself and permission to read for your group. You can accomplish this by using the following series of commands:

```
$ ls -l bates.file
-rwxr-x—  1   paul      92   Feb 20    09:14   bates.file
$ chmod u=rw,g=r,o= bates.file
$ ls -l bates.file
-rw-r——  1   paul      92   Feb 20    09:14   bates.file
```

CAUTION

A word of caution about the chmod command: Be careful when you use this command. You can lock yourself out of your own files if you make a mistake with chmod. For example, the command:

```
$ chmod u=,g=,o= filename
```

makes a file inaccessible to *all* users, including yourself.

Chapter 2 Quiz

Match each command listed on the left with one of the tasks described on the right:

1. cat file.101

    A. Display the names of all files in the current directory (with out any other information).

2. rm memo.101

    B. Display the names of all files in the current directory (along with permissions, size, and date and time of last change).

3. cd ../NOTES

    C. Change to directory NOTES.

4. ls -l

    D. Create a new directory called NOTES.

5. cp memo.101 memo.102

    E. Delete directory NOTES (assuming that it is already empty).

6. `ls`   F. Display the contents of `file.101`.

7. `mkdir NOTES`   G. Make a copy of `memo.101` called `memo.102`.

8. `ln ../memo.101 memo.101`   H. Add write permission for other users for file `memo.101`.

9. `chmod o+w memo.101`   I. Delete file `memo.101`.

10. `rmdir NOTES`   J. Add a link to file `memo.101`.

11. `mv memo.101 memo.102`   K. Move file `memo.101` to directory `NOTES`.

12. `mv memo.101 ../NOTES`   L. Change the name of file `memo.101` to `memo.102`.

Using the partial diagram of the file system shown in Figure 2.8, write a command line to accomplish each of the following tasks:

13. Lisa: Copy files `memo.1`, `memo.2`, `memo.3`, and `memo.4` from the directory `sales` to the directory `MEMOS`. (Assume you are now in `sales`.)

14. Paul: Change from the directory `projects` to the directory `paul`.

15. Lisa: Move files `personnel.G`, `materials.G`, and `expenses.G` from the directory `letters` to the directory `sales`. (Assume that these are the only files in the directory `letters` that end with the suffix `.G`.)

Figure 2.8

A sample file system.

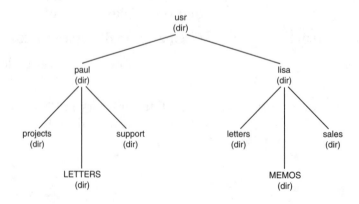

16. Paul: Display the permissions of all files in directory support. (Assume you are now in support.)

17. Lisa: Add a link in your current working directory (let-ters) to a file called expedite in Paul's directory LETTERS, using the same name for the file.

18. Paul: In your home directory, create a new subdirectory called news.

19. Lisa: Make the following changes to permissions for file meeting in the directory sales: grant permission to ex-ecute to yourself; grant permission to **write** to members of your working group; revoke permission to **read**, **write**, and **execute** to all other users. (Assume you are now in directory sales.)

20. Paul: Delete the following files from directory LETTERS: interest.K, interest.N. and interest.R. (Assume that you have 26 files that end with the suffix .K in this directory.)

In This Chapter

How to Type a Command at the Shell Prompt

Redirection

Connecting Processes

How to Run a Command in the Background

Shell Scripts

Initialization Files

Shell Programs

- **Bourne shell**   The original command processor.
- **C shell**   Command processor developed at Berkeley.
- **Korn shell**   The new standard command processor.

Parts of a Command Line

- The shell prompt is where you enter a command line.
- A command line consists of a command name, along with optional arguments (options and file names).
- Entering a command line results in a process in memory.

Redirection

- Use the left symbol (<) to redirect input from the keyboard to a file.
- Use the right symbol (>) to redirect output from the monitor to a file.

Connecting Processes

- Use the vertical bar (¦) to connect two processes with a pipe, by which the output of one process becomes the input of another.
- Use the notation ¦ tee to form a tee, by which you create a pipe with screen display.

Background Processes

- Use the ampersand (&) at the end of a command line to request background processing.
- Use the ps (process status) command to check the status of all active processes, foreground and background.

3

Processing Commands

When you have a job to do in UNIX, you use a command. Every command that you enter is executed by the UNIX command processor, called the *shell*. The resulting operation is called a *process*. This chapter shows you how the UNIX shell executes commands and how you can use various shell features to modify UNIX commands.

The Different Shell Programs

The original command processor, which was developed at AT&T by Stephen R. Bourne in the early 1970s, is known as the *Bourne shell*. This is the official shell that is distributed with UNIX systems. The Bourne shell is the fastest UNIX command processor available.

Another command processor, developed by William Joy and others at the University of California in the mid-1980s, is known as the *C shell*. This program, which borrows many concepts from the C language, offers greater versatility than the Bourne shell; its main drawback is its slower execution. Although not considered to be part of System V, the C shell is nearly always available as an alternate command processor. In fact, as soon as you request a login account, the first thing the system administrator usually asks you is which shell you prefer. (For detailed information about the C shell, see Appendix C.)

A third command processor, developed by David Korn in the early 1980s, is called the *Korn shell*. This program combines many of the best features of the two earlier command processors, and it is gaining in popularity.

Most of the features described in this chapter are supported by all the different command processors. One difference between the Bourne and C shells is that the default shell prompt uses different symbols:

Bourne Shell	**C Shell**	**Korn Shell**
$ _	% _	$ _

Any features unique to the C shell or the Korn shell are noted in the appendix.

Commands and Command Lines

The Shell Prompt

After you log in, the command processor, or shell, displays a prompt on the screen:

$ _

This *shell prompt*, which is similar to the DOS prompt C>, tells you that the shell is ready to accept input in the form of a *command line*. A command line includes the name of a command, any command options that you want to add, and the name(s) of any file(s) to be processed. Every command line must include the name of a command; command options and file names may or may not be required.

Entering a Command Line

As you learned in Chapter 2, a command like ls (list the contents of a directory) can be entered without a single option or file name, as shown here:

```
$ ls
answers
bates.file
call_FILES
ddd-125
zero+one
$ _
```

However, you can also enter an ls command line that includes an option, like -1 (long listing):

```
$ ls -l
total 10
drwx—x—  2   paul    258   Jul 18   15:42   answers
-rwxr-x—  1   paul     92   Feb 20   09:14   bates.file
drwx—x—  1   paul    126   Nov 31   08:57   call_FILES
-rw-r——   3   paul    415   Aug  3   13:09   ddd-125
-rw-r——   1   paul    361   May 11   10:38   zero+one
$ _
```

A third variation executed from a different directory, includes a directory name:

```
$ ls /usr/roger/misc
answers
bates.file
call_FILES
ddd-125
zero+one
$ _
```

Finally, a fourth variation, also executed from a different directory, includes both the option and the directory name:

```
$ ls -l /usr/roger/misc
total 10
drwx—x—    2    paul    258    Jul 18    15:42    answers
-rwxr-x—    1    paul     92    Feb 20    09:14    bates.file
drwx—x—    1    paul    126    Nov 31    08:57    call_FILES
-rw-r——    3    paul    415    Aug  3    13:09    ddd-125
-rw-r——    1    paul    361    May 11    10:38    zero+one
$ _
```

Command Arguments

The -l option and the file name are referred to collectively as *arguments*. Arguments on a command line modify the way the command works. The -l option is one of 22 options supported by the ls command. A few of the other options include -t (sort entries by the time of their last modification), - (sort entries by the time of their last access), -s (sort entries by their size), and -r (list entries in reverse order).

Each command line, which always includes a command name and may or may not include command arguments, can be described by the following generic representation. (Note that the brackets indicate optional items on the command line. Do not type the brackets as part of the command line.)

```
$ name [options] [files]
```

in which

> *name* is the command name

> *options* represents one or more command options

> *files* represents one or more file names (including directory names)

As shown, options precede file names on a command line. If you must use more than one file name, list the names in order (from first to last or from *source* to *target*).

Commands and Processes

New users are often perplexed by the distinction between a command and a process. Here is a brief clarification: A command names a program file, which is stored in a directory on disk. A process is a sequence of actions that take place in memory after a command has been executed. A command is static; a process is active. A command represents potential action; a process is the realization of that potential.

Redirection of Input and Output

In the preceding section, each example of the ls command shows the basic elements of processes; *input* (the command line), *processing* of the input, and *output* (the listing of file names). The output is the result of the processing. These actions are illustrated in Figure 3.1.

Figure 3.1

Standard input and output.

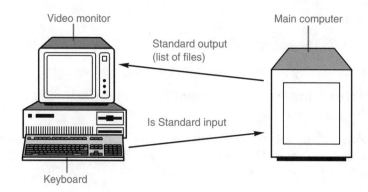

You ordinarily enter input from your keyboard and display output on your video screen. To the UNIX system, your keyboard is the *standard input* and your video screen is the *standard output*. However, many commands let you *redirect* the input or output. On the one hand, you can have the shell receive input from a file instead of the keyboard. On the other hand, you can have the shell send output to a printer instead of the screen.

The symbols used to request redirection are the less than sign (<) and the greater than sign (>):

<   Redirects input from the file (including a device) named on the right.

>   Redirects output to the file (including a device) named on the right.

You can think of these symbols as arrows pointing in the direction of the flow of text during processing.

Redirection of Input

In Chapter 6, you will learn about the `mail` command, which allows you to send a message to another user via electronic mail. Ordinarily, you type your message from the keyboard after you enter the `mail` command. However, with the aid of redirection, you can also send a message that you have already stored in a file. For example, suppose you have the this message stored in a file called `meeting`:

```
$ cat meeting

I need the notes you took at last month's
meeting. Can you send me a copy some time
later this week?
$ _
```

To send this message to John via electronic mail, you would enter the command line:

```
$ mail john < meeting
```

The redirection symbol (<) tells the shell to receive its input from file meeting rather than from the keyboard. The shell locates file meeting, reads the message, and forwards it to the user named John. This is illustrated in Figure 3.2.

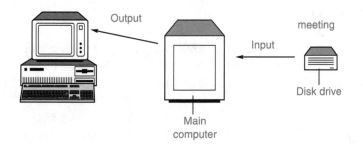

Input redirected from keyboard to a file called meeting

Figure 3.2
Redirection of input.

Redirection of Output

Earlier in this chapter, you saw four variations of the ls command used to display the contents of a directory. In each instance, the list was displayed on the screen. However, by using redirection, you could send the list to a file instead. For important information, storing the output in a file gives you a permanent record rather than merely a fleeting screen display. Here is an example of a command line that illustrates redirection of the output of a process (illustrated in Figure 3.3):

```
$ ls -l > file.list
$ _
```

Figure 3.3

Redirection of output.

Output redirected from video monitor to a file called file.lst

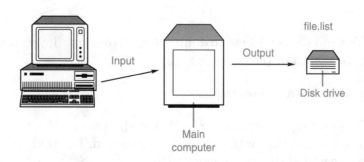

If you want to collect a series of lists in a single file, you can use a variation of the redirection symbol to *append* a new list to an existing file. For example, suppose you want to store lists of the contents of three subdirectories (first, second, and third) in a file named dirs.123, which is stored in the parent directory. To do so, execute this sequence:

Input

Output

file.list

Disk drive

Main
computer

This time, you don't see the list displayed. To see the list, you can use a command, such as cat, to display file.list on the screen, as shown here:

```
$ cat file.list
total 12
drwx — x —   2   paul   258   Jul 18   15:42   answers
- rwxr - x —   1   paul   92    Feb 20   09:14   bates.file
drwx — x —   1   paul   126   Nov 31   08:57   call_FILES
- rw - r — —   3   paul   415   Aug  3   13:09   ddd - 125
- rw - r — —   1   paul   0     Sep 12   11:24   file.list
- rw - r — —   1   paul   361   May 11   10:38   zero+one
$ _
```

If you want to collect a series of lists in a single file, you can use a variation of the redirection symbol to *append* a new list to an existing file. For example, suppose you want to store lists of the contents of three subdirectories (first, second, and third) in a file named dirs.123, which is stored in the parent directory. To do so, execute this sequence:

```
$ ls -l first > ../dirs.123
$ ls -l second >> ../dirs.123
$ ls -l third >> ../dirs.123
$ _
```

The ordinary symbol (>) is used for the first directory; then the symbol for appending text (>>) is used for the second and third directories. Consequently, dirs.123 contains all three lists in consecutive order.

If the target file doesn't exist, either symbol (> or >>) creates a new file. If the target file already exists, the ordinary symbol (>) will cause the file to be overwritten, while the append symbol (>>) will merely append the new text to the existing text.

To dispose of the output of a command, rather than save it, you can redirect it to a file called /dev/null. This special device file is the UNIX system's version of a wastebasket—any output sent there merely disappears and never reaches your screen. For example, to discard older articles from Usenet (Chapter 6), you can use the command:

```
$ readnews -p -n all > /dev/null
$ _
```

Connecting Processes

You can make your commands more efficient by connecting processes directly, rather than redirecting the output of one process to a file and then redirecting the input of another process from that file.

Using Pipes

Another way to control the flow of processing is to have the shell connect two processes with a *pipe*. When you use a pipe, the output of one process becomes the input of another. The pipe eliminates the need for intermediary files that temporarily hold the results of one process until you use them in another process. (These files eventually have to be deleted when you finish your operation.)

The symbol for a pipe is a vertical bar (¦), which you enter between the command names on the command line. For example, suppose that you want to print three files called ch.1, ch.2, and ch.3. Rather than print each one separately with the lp command, you can concatenate and print the files with a single command line, as follows:

```
$ cat ch.1 ch.2 ch.3 ¦ lp
request id is epson-143 (1 file)
$ _
```

As the sample system message indicates, the lp command handled only one file because the three files were concatenated by cat before they reached lp. This example of a pipe is illustrated in Figure 3.4.

Figure 3.4

An example of a pipe.

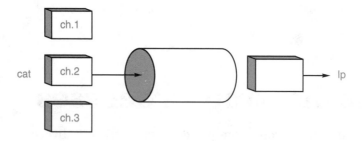

Using Tees

The tee command, which is used in conjunction with a pipe, allows you to write text to a file while simultaneously displaying it on your video screen. This is a remarkably handy command, because it combines the advantages of viewing text and storing it in a file. In the following example, you display the contents of a directory and write the list to a file called dir.files:

```
$ ls -l ¦ tee dir.list
total 10
drwx—x—  2  paul  258  Jul 18  15:42  answers
-rwxr-x—  1  paul   92  Feb 20  09:14  bates.file
drwx—x—  1  paul  126  Nov 31  08:57  call_FILES
```

```
-r-r — — —   3    paul    415    Aug  3    13:09    ddd-125
-rw-r — —    1    paul    361    May 11    10:38    zero+one
$ _
```

With this command line, which is illustrated in Figure 3.5, you get an immediate display and also a file that you can refer back to at your leisure.

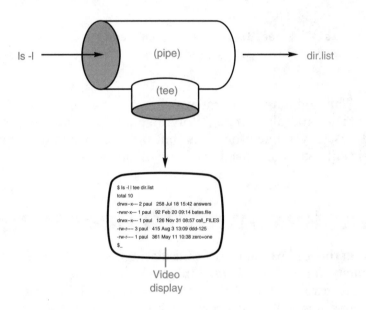

Figure 3.5
An example of a tee.

After you've executed the preceding tee command, you can retrieve the listing at any time. Simply display the contents of dir.list, as follows:

```
$ cat dir.list
total 10
drwx — x —    2    paul    258    Jul 18    15:42    answers
-rwxr-x —     1    paul     92    Feb 20    09:14    bates.file
drwx — x —    1    paul    126    Nov 31    08:57    call_FILES
-rw-r — —     3    paul    415    Aug  3    13:09    ddd-125
-rw-r — —     1    paul    361    May 11    10:38    zero+one
$ _
```

Since the `tee` command sends output to the video screen, you can request additional processing for this output. For example, referring to the preceding example, suppose all you wanted to display on the screen was the entry for the file that included ddd in its name. To do so, you could pipe the preceding output to the grep command (a text-searching command that is described in detail in the next chapter). The new command line would look like this:

```
$ ls -l ¦ tee dir.files ¦ grep  ddd
-rw-r——  3  paul    415  Aug 3   13:09   ddd-125
$ _
```

This command generates a complete listing of your files in `dir.files` and also immediately displays the entry for the file `ddd-125`. (If you had other files that included ddd in their names, their entries would also have been displayed.)

Background Processing

One of the features of UNIX that distinguishes it from DOS is its capacity for *multitasking*. Multitasking makes it possible for each user to have more than one process active in the system at any one moment. With multitasking, you could, for example, initiate the formatting of a large file, and then immediately begin editing another file. Formatting would take place as a *background process*, while editing would proceed as a *foreground process*. Background processing relinquishes the screen immediately, while foreground processing requires user interaction and doesn't allow you to start another process.

Requesting a Background Process &

The symbol used to request background processing is the ampersand (&), which you type at the end of the command line. Here is an example of its usage, using commands from later chapters:

```
$ nroff -cm ch. 5 ¦ lp &
289
$ vi ch.6
```

In this example, you begin formatting ch.5 with the nroff command, and then immediately begin editing ch.6 without waiting for the preceding process to complete. The shell initiates the formatting process, the *kernel* assigns a process number (289), and then it returns control of the screen to you. If you ever need to terminate the background process, you must refer to it by this number. (See "Terminating a Background Process" later in this chapter.)

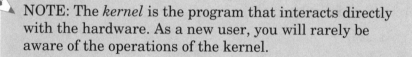

NOTE: The *kernel* is the program that interacts directly with the hardware. As a new user, you will rarely be aware of the operations of the kernel.

When you perform background processing, you have to be careful that the background process and the foreground process don't interfere with each other. Any screen output from the background process could disrupt the screen in the middle of your work with the foreground process. In the preceding example, when nroff processing is completed and the text is piped to lp, the lp command displays a message on the screen, such as:

```
request id is epson-132 (1 file)
```

This message writes over your current screen display, but it does not change anything in the foreground file. Merely clear the message and resume work in vi, the UNIX text editor. (The command to clear a message like this is Ctrl-L.)

Messages like this are relatively harmless, but you don't want the actual output from the background process displayed on the screen. To avoid this, merely redirect the output from all background processes that would ordinarily send output to the screen. Because the output of lp is sent to a printer, this example requires no redirection.

Checking on Background Processes   ps

Sometimes, you will need to check on a background process to determine its current status. Is it still running? Has it completed? Or did it run into problems? The ps (process status) command generates a one-line entry for each of your processes that is currently active. This display shows the active processes in the preceding example:

```
$ ps
PID     TTY     TIME     COMMAND
289     05      0:03     nroff ch.5
291     05      0:04     sort list
052     05      0:29     -sh
301     05      0:01     -ps
$ _
```

These four columns display the following information: the process identifier (PID), your current terminal number (TTY), the length of time each process has been active, in minutes and seconds (TIME), and the name of the command (COMMAND). The process number of the background formatting job (289) appears at the top of the list, indicating that it has started. In the COMMAND column, note that the shell (-sh) and the process status command (-ps) are listed with your other processes. If you use the ps command, but don't find your background process listed in the display, the process may be already completed.

Terminating a Background Process   kill

If you ever need to terminate a background process, you can use the kill command to do the job. This command requires one argument—the process identifier (PID), which is first displayed when you start a background process and later when you use the ps command. The following command terminates the formatting job in the preceding example:

```
$ kill 289
$ _
```

Unfortunately, the kill command doesn't report any results. The only way to determine whether or not your request has been successful is to run ps again, as follows:

```
$ ps
PID     TTY     TIME    COMMAND
289     05      0:07    nroff ch.5
291     05      0:08    vi ch.6
052     05      0:33    -sh
301     05      0:01    -ps
$ _
```

If ps indicates that your process is still active, as it does in this display, then you must use a more effective version of the command. You can run kill again with the -9 option, which specifies that kill cannot be ignored by the target process. Use this command as follows:

```
$ kill -9 289
$ _
```

The -9 option is more powerful, but also riskier. If the process identifier in this instance is either 0 or 52 (the process number of your shell), you will automatically log yourself out.

Executing Commands from Files

If you are used to working with DOS, then you are probably familiar with the concept of a batch file: you store a sequence of commands in a file; then you execute the file as if it were a command to cause the entire sequence to be carried out. You can do something very similar in UNIX with a *shell program* (also referred to as a *shell script* or *shell file*). The main difference is that a shell script lets you use much more sophisticated constructions than a batch file. However, this chapter will introduce only the simpler techniques.

Obtaining Directory Information

Suppose you'd like to set up an executable file that would do the following three things:

- Display the date and time
- Display the name of the current directory
- Display the contents of the current directory

You also want to run this sequence each time you enter a new directory. To do so, you need only to enter three lines into a file and then make the file executable. You can create the file and enter the command lines by using the cat command, as follows:

```
$ cat > dir.look
date
pwd
ls -l
Ctrl - D
$ _
```

In DOS, you have to give each batch file a certain extension to its name (BAT). In UNIX, you can use any legal file name, but you have to remember to make the file executable. In the following example, you do this by using the command:

```
$ chmod u+x dir.look
$ _
```

Now the three-line shell script is ready to use. Just move to a directory with cd and type dir.look. The result will look something like this:

```
$ cd ../admin
$ dir.look
Wed  Oct 19  11:03:52   PST   1990
/usr/larry/admin
total 10
drwx—x—   2   paul   258   Jul 18   15:42   answers
-rwxr-x—   1   paul    92   Feb 20   09:14   bates.file
drwx—x—   1   paul   126   Nov 31   08:57   call_FILES
-rw-r——    3   paul   415   Aug  3   13:09   ddd-125
-rw-r——    1   paul   361   May 11   10:38   zero+one
$ _
```

In this example, the three commands are all very simple, and the shell script doesn't really save a lot of time. But you can probably begin to see the potential of a shell script. Suppose you have commands that are very long and complex. If you store them in a shell script, you won't have to type them every time you need to use them.

Adding Another Function

Let's make the preceding shell script more versatile by including the cd command with the three other commands. This presents a problem because you want to be able to use this script in any directory. If you include a directory name in the script, then you can use the script only for that one directory—not a very useful script!

The solution is to use a variable name in the script. The variables used to identify the arguments on a UNIX command line are called *positional parameters*. The notation for this type of variable includes a dollar sign ($) and a number. By convention, $0 identifies the command name, $1 identifies the first argument, $2 identifies the second, and so on. Here is an example:

```
$ ls      -1      ../admin

$0        $1      $2
```

The cd command requires only one argument (the directory name). So the identification is even simpler, as in the following:

```
$ cd      ../admin

$0        $1
```

Using this type of variable in the preceding shell script will let you change to any directory whose name you specify when you execute the script. All you need to do is include the following line at the beginning of the shell script:

```
cd $1
```

Let's create such a script with the cat command and make the file executable with the chmod command (Ctrl-D terminates input):

```
$ cat > new.dir
cd $1
date
pwd
ls -1
Ctrl-D
$ chmod u+x new.dir
$ _
```

This four-line shell script now includes the cd command. In essence, you have just created a new command called new.dir that accepts as an argument the name of any directory to which you have access. Here is an example that uses this new command:

```
$ pwd
/usr/paul
$ new.dir /usr/larry/admin
Wed Oct 20 11:12:24 PST 1993
/usr/larry/admin
total 10
drwx—x—   2   paul   258   Jul 18   15:42   answers
-rwxr-x—   1   paul    92   Feb 20   09:14   bates.file
drwx--x—   1   paul   126   Nov 31   08:57   call_FILES
-rw-r——    3   paul   415   Aug  3   13;09   ddd-125
-rw-r——    1   paul   361   May 11   10:38   zero+one
$ _
```

The Initialization Files

DOS executes a special batch file called AUTOEXEC.BAT every time you boot your computer. UNIX uses an analogous file when it starts each command processor. In the Bourne shell, this file is called .profile; the C shell uses a pair of files called .login and .cshrc. The rest of this chapter primarily discusses the initialization file for the Bourne shell. For more information about the C shell, please see Appendix C.

NOTE: For the system as a whole, the startup file is called /etc/rc.

Using the Shell Start-Up File   profile

Each time you log into UNIX, the settings in the .profile file are used to create your working *environment*. (The C shell calls its start-up file .login and also uses an additional file named .cshrc, which contains settings unique to the C shell.) Here is an example of a simple .profile file in which you assign values to four shell variables:

```
$ cat .profile
HOME=/usr/ray
PATH=/bin:/usr/bin:$HOME/bin
MAIL=/usr/spool/mail/'basename $HOME'
TERM=tv950
export HOME PATH MAIL TERM
$ _
```

TIP: You can use basename with a full pathname to extract the last directory name in the string. For example, 'basename/usr/ray' means ray.

The four shell variables are summarized in Table 3.1 and described in greater detail in the paragraphs that follow.

Table 3.1
*The Basic Shell
Variables*

Variable	Description
HOME	**Home Directory** The name of the directory that becomes your current directory when you log in.
PATH	**Command Search Path** A list of the directories in which UNIX will search for commands that you enter.
MAIL	**Mail File** The name of the file to which your incoming mail is sent.
TERM	**Terminal Type** The type of video display terminal you are using.

Home Directory   The HOME variable provides the name of your login directory. If you execute the cd command without an argument, the value of HOME is displayed by default. In the preceding .profile example, the following two commands are equivalent:

```
cd
```

and

```
$cd/usr/ray
```

Note that the HOME variable (preceded by a dollar sign) is referred to in subsequent .profile entries. In each instance, you can substitute for $HOME the value assigned above (/usr/ray, in this example).

Command Search Path   This identifies the directories that contain executable commands. The directories assigned to the PATH variable must be separated by colons (:). In the preceding example, the following directories contain command files available to this user:

```
/bin
/usr/bin
/usr/ray/bin
```

Mail File   The file named here holds your incoming electronic mail messages. In the preceding example, the file identified is /usr/spool/mail/ray.

Terminal Type   The terminal type assigned here must be named in one of the following, depending on which is used on your system:

```
/etc/termcap
/etc/terminfo/*/*
```

Note that /etc/termcap is a single file, but the /etc/terminfo directory contains a collection of files. A terminal type is necessary only if you plan to use programs like the vi editor, which uses the entire screen.

> **NOTE:** Notice the fifth line in the preceding sample
> `.profile` file. The `export` command causes the four
> environmental variables to be *exported*, which means
> that these settings apply to every command that you
> execute.

Changing the Environment from the Command Line

It is generally best to set environmental variables in your start-up file; however, you also can set any of them from the command line. The procedure for setting these variables in the Bourne shell differs from that used in the C shell. In the Bourne shell, you must first assign the value and then export the value. In the C shell, you can perform both of these steps with a single command, called `setenv`. The following example changes the terminal type to `VT100`:

Bourne Shell	**C Shell**

```$ TERM=vt100```
 ```$ export TERM```
 ```$ _```
	```% setenv TERM vt100```
	 ```% _```

The `setenv` command of the C shell is equivalent to the two Bourne shell commands. (For more information about the C shell, refer to Appendix C.)

Chapter 3 Quiz

1. What is the name of the official System V shell program?

   A. The Bourne shell

   B. The Korn shell

   C. The C shell

   D. The Clam shell

2. Which of the following is required on every command line?

   A. At least one command option

   B. At least one file name

   C. A command name

   D. At least one user's name

3. After you enter a command line, what is activated in the host computer's memory?

   A. A command

   B. A process

   C. An activity

   D. A function

4. Which of the following command lines would you use to redirect input from the file named TEST?

   A. *command* > TEST

   B. *command* >> TEST

   C. *command* TEST ¦ command

   D. *command* < TEST

5. Which of the following command lines would you use to redirect output to the file named TEST?

   A. *command* > TEST

   B. *command* >> TEST

   C. *command* TEST ¦ command

   D. *command* < TEST

6. Which of the following command lines would you use to redirect output to the file named TEST and append data to the file?

   A. *command* > TEST

   B. *command* >> TEST

   C. *command* TEST ¦ command

D. *command* TEST ¦ tee TEST

7. Which of the following command lines would you use to redirect output of a command to a file and also display the output on the screen?

   A. *command > file*

   B. *command >> file*

   C. *command file ¦ command*

   D. *command file ¦ tee file*

8. Which command line would you use to run a command in the background?

   A. *command **

   B. *command &*

   C. *command @*

   D. *command #*

9. Which command would you use to find out which commands are running in the background?

   A. date

   B. who

   C. ls

   D. ps

10. Which command would you use to terminate a background process?

    A. stop

    B. cease

    C. kill

    D. desist

11. True or false: It's possible to place a sequence of UNIX commands in a file, make the file executable, and then execute the commands by entering the name of the file on a command line?

12. What is the name of the variable that indicates the first argument on a command line?

    A. `$first`

    B. `$FIRST`

    C. `$one`

    D. `$1`

13. What is the name of the Bourne shell's start-up file?

    A. `.profile`

    B. `begins`

    C. `sfile`

    D. `start`

In This Chapter

Displaying a Calendar

Displaying Text on the Screen

Printing

Finding Files

Searching for Text in a File

Sorting Lines in a File

Performing Calculations

Displaying a Calendar

- Use the `cal` command to display a calendar for one month or a full year.

Displaying Text on the Screen

- Use the `cat` command to display the contents of a file on the screen or to concatenate two files.
- You can also use `cat` with redirection to enter text into a file.
- Use the `pg` or `more` command to display a large file one screen at a time.

Printing

- Use the `lp` (lineprinter) command to queue a file for printing.
- The `lp` command has a number of options, including `-m` (mail), `-c` (copy), and `-d` (directed output).
- Use the `lpstat` (lp status) to display the current printing queue.

Finding Files

- Use the `find` command to search for files and execute commands, using the files found as arguments.
- You can search for files by file name, type, user, group, size, links, or time of last change, modification, or access.
- Once files have been selected, you can display, execute, or make backup copies.

Searching for Text in a File

- Use the `grep` command to search for text in a file or a set of files.
- You can use regular expressions, formed with special characters, to help make a selection.

4

Some Utility Programs

This chapter describes the most commonly used utility programs of the UNIX systems.

Displaying a Calendar cal

The `cal` (calendar) command lets you display a calendar for any year from 1 A.D. to 9999 A.D. For example, to display the calendar for 1994, type the following command:

```
$ cal 1994
```

1994

	Jan							Feb							Mar					
S	M	Tu	W	Th	F	S	S	M	Tu	W	Th	F	S	S	M	Tu	W	Th	F	S
						1			1	2	3	4	5			1	2	3	4	5
2	3	4	5	6	7	8	6	7	8	9	10	11	12	6	7	8	9	10	11	12
9	10	11	12	13	14	15	13	14	15	16	17	18	19	13	14	15	16	17	18	19
16	17	18	19	20	21	22	20	21	22	23	24	25	26	20	21	22	23	24	25	26
23	24	25	26	27	28	29	27	28						27	28	29	30	31		
30	31																			

```
         Apr                    May                    Jun
  S  M Tu  W Th  F  S     S  M Tu  W Th  F  S     S  M Tu  W Th  F  S
                 1  2     1  2  3  4  5  6  7              1  2  3  4
  3  4  5  6  7  8  9     8  9 10 11 12 13 14     5  6  7  8  9 10 11
 10 11 12 13 14 15 16    15 16 17 18 19 20 21    12 13 14 15 16 17 18
 17 18 19 20 21 22 23    22 23 24 25 26 27 28    19 20 21 22 23 24 25
 24 25 26 27 28 29 30    29 30 31               26 27 28 29 30

         Jul                    Aug                    Sep
  S  M Tu  W Th  F  S     S  M Tu  W Th  F  S     S  M Tu  W Th  F  S
                 1  2        1  2  3  4  5  6              1  2  3
  3  4  5  6  7  8  9     7  8  9 10 11 12 13     4  5  6  7  8  9 10
 10 11 12 13 14 15 16    14 15 16 17 18 19 20    11 12 13 14 15 16 17
 17 18 19 20 21 22 23    21 22 23 24 25 26 27    18 19 20 21 22 23 24
 24 25 26 27 28 29 30    28 29 30 31            25 26 27 28 29 30
 31

         Oct                    Nov                    Dec
  S  M Tu  W Th  F  S     S  M Tu  W Th  F  S     S  M Tu  W Th  F  S
                    1        1  2  3  4  5              1  2  3
  2  3  4  5  6  7  8     6  7  8  9 10 11 12     4  5  6  7  8  9 10
  9 10 11 12 13 14 15    13 14 15 16 17 18 19    11 12 13 14 15 16 17
 16 17 18 19 20 21 22    20 21 22 23 24 25 26    18 19 20 21 22 23 24
 23 24 25 26 27 28 29    27 28 29 30            25 26 27 28 29 30 31
 30 31
```

You can also display the calendar for a single month: Simply enter a number from 1 to 12 before you type the year. For example, here is the calendar for July 1994:

```
$ cal 7 1994
```

```
     July 1994
  S  M Tu  W Th  F  S
                 1  2
  3  4  5  6  7  8  9
 10 11 12 13 14 15 16
 17 18 19 20 21 22 23
 24 25 26 27 28 29 30
 31
```

Displaying Text on the Screen   cat

Chapter 2 introduced you to the cat (concatenate) command. As its name implies, one of the functions of this command is to concatenate (join) files. For example, to concatenate two files, intro.1991 and sales.1991, into a new file called report.1991, you could use the following command (see Figure 4.1):

```
$ cat intro.1991 sales.1991 > report.1991
```

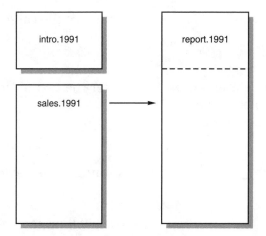

Figure 4.1
Concatenating two files.

TIP: When you use cat in this way, be sure the new file (which will hold the combined result) is not one of the original files being concatenated. Otherwise, you will lose text.

Entering Text Manually

If you want to enter the text yourself, rather than use text from existing files, you can omit the names of the source files entirely. Simply type the cat command, redirect input to a target file, and type what you want in the file. When you finish, press ⌈Ctrl⌉-⌈D⌉ to end the file. After you press ⌈Ctrl⌉-⌈D⌉, UNIX redisplays the shell prompt. Here is a short example:

Creating a File with cat

1. `$ cat > sample`   Creates a file called sample.

2. This brief statement is an example of creating a small file with cat.   Enter the text of the file.

3. Press ⌈Ctrl⌉-⌈D⌉.   Nothing is displayed.

4. Type: `$ _`   The shell prompt reappears.

You can also use cat (without redirection) to display the text you have just entered:

```
$ cat sample
This brief statement is
an example of creating
a small file with cat.
$ _
```

Displaying Large Files   pg

If you want to display text stored in a large file, you may not want to use cat because there will be too much text for your screen. One solution is to use the pg command instead. The pg (page) command works like cat but pauses each time a full screen of text has been displayed. Then, you can respond to the prompt at the bottom of the screen (:) by pressing ⏎Enter. Here is an example:

```
$ pg chapter.5
.
(a screenful of text)
.
: _
```

Some systems also use the more command. If this command is available on your system, you have a wider selection of options at the bottom of each page. (It also supplies information about the size of the file by displaying the percentage of the file that you've already read.) Press ? for help. Here is an example:

```
$ more chapter.5
.
(a screenful of text)
.
—More— (4%)
```

When the display pauses and the prompt appears, you can choose one of the following options:

- Type h for help information.
- Press ⏎Enter to display one more line.
- Press the Spacebar to display the next screen.
- Begin a search by entering a slash (/) and the text you want to find. (For example, /select displays the text that contains the word select.)

- Press ⌜Esc⌝ to leave the more command and return to the shell prompt. How the pg and more commands display discrete screenfuls of text is depicted graphically in Figure 4.2.

Figure 4.2
Paging text.

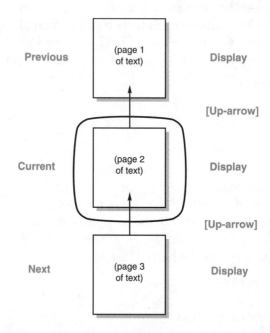

Previous   (page 1 of text)   Display

[Up-arrow]

Current   (page 2 of text)   Display

[Up-arrow]

Next   (page 3 of text)   Display

NOTE: The more and pg commands, like vi, require terminal definitions.

Printing   lp

To print text, use the lp (lineprinter) command. This command, which can route text to any printer in your system, places your request in a *queue* and completes the printing job when the printer you specify is available. If you enter the command in its simplest form, printing is performed on the default printer. Here is an example:

```
$ lp chapter.5
request id is epson-128 (1 file)
$ _
```

This prints the file chapter.5 on the Epson printer specified as the default.

> **NOTE:** Printing jobs lined up to be carried out form a queue (from the French word for line).

The lp command responds to your request with a one-line message that identifies your printing job and tells you how many files have been queued for printing. The identifier includes the name of the printer to which your job will be directed and a sequence number. If necessary, you can cancel the printing job by referring to the identifier, as shown in the following example:

```
$ cancel epson-128
$ _
```

You can also queue several files for printing at the same time, as shown in this example:

```
$ lp chapter.1 chapter.2 chapter.3
request id is epson-136 (3 files)
$ _
```

Printing Options

Because all printing jobs must be queued, your request may be delayed while other jobs are being processed. If the printers on a system are very busy, you may have to wait a long time for your printing job to be executed. The lp command includes two options that can make the waiting period a little easier to tolerate.

The -m (mail) option tells lp to send you a message by electronic mail when your printing job has been completed. The command line would look like this:

```
$ lp -m chapter.5
request id is epson-143 (1 file)
$ _
```

To ensure that the information in your file is backed up, the -c (copy) option tells lp to make a copy of your file (or files). Then, if your original file(s) should be misplaced during processing, lp can retrieve the backup copy (or copies). You would enter this command:

```
$ lp -c chapter.5
request id is epson-147 (1 file)
$ _
```

Requesting a Specific Printer

In all the examples shown so far, the job has been sent to the default printer (epson). However, if your system uses more than one printer, you always have the option of requesting a specific printer. Furthermore, if your system has many printers and they have been grouped into classes (such as dot-matrix printers and laser printers), you can request a particular class. To request either a specific printer or a class of printers, include the -d option on the lp command line, as shown in the examples that follow.

To illustrate this feature, let's assume that your system has a printer named nec. (Note that these names will vary from one system to another.) If you want to have a job printed on that particular printer, you can use a command line like the following:

```
$ lp -dnec chapter.6
request id is nec-23 (1 file)
$ _
```

The names for classes of printers also vary greatly. Suppose the printers on your system are grouped into three classes with the following names: matrix (dot-matrix printers), daisy (daisy-wheel printers), and laser (laser printers). If you want to be certain that one of your jobs is sent to a laser printer, you can request class laser with a command like this:

```
$ lp -dlaser chapter.7
request id is lw3-52 (1 file)
$ _
```

The message from the printer spooler tells you that your job is queued for lw3 (Apple LaserWriter number 3). Figure 4.3 shows an example of a system that uses nine printers grouped into three classes.

matrix	daisy	Laser
mt	nec	lw1
oki	diablo	lw2
epson	qume	lw3

Figure 4.3
An example of printer classes.

This example system calls its three classes matrix, daisy, and laser, and lists three printers under each class. Using the -d option described above, you could direct printing to any of these three classes or to any of these nine individual printers.

Displaying the Printing Queue   lpstat

As noted earlier in this section, printing jobs are queued for all users on the system. To display the print queue after you've requested printing, you can use the lpstat (lineprinter status) command. Here is an example of running this command:

```
$ lpstat
total 28
epson-143    paul    789    May 3    10:09 on epson
epson-147    paul    632    May 3    10:12
nec-23       paul    236    May 3    10:17 l
w3-52        paul    189    May 3    10:19
$ _
```

The display is similar to the display for ls-l, with six columns of information. The first column gives the name that lp assigns to your file in directory /usr/spool/lpd, the directory in which the print queue is usually stored.

The lpstat display shows the identifier (printer name and sequence number), your login name, the size of the file in characters, and the date and time of your printing request. The job the system is currently printing is shown on the far right (for example, on epson).

Finding Files   find

The find command lets you search for files and execute a specific action. You can search by file name, type, owner, group, permission, or date of last modification. The action you take can include displaying on the screen, printing, copying, moving, or deleting. The general command line for the find command is shown in Figure 4.4.

Figure 4.4
The find command line.

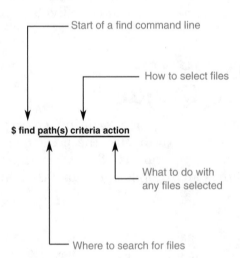

The simplest form of the `find` command displays the names of the files you are looking for. It's a good idea to begin every `find` search with this form of the command. For example, suppose you want to find out how many files in directory `/usr` are called `test.file`. To do so, you use the `-name` option to search by file name and the `-print` option to display the names on your screen. The command line and output will look something like the following:

```
$ find /usr -name test.file -print
/usr/alfred/control/test.file
/usr/charles/procedures/test.file
/usr/dean/new/test.file
/usr/evelyn/future/test.file
 $ _
```

Figure 4.5 gives you a graphical look at the preceding command line.

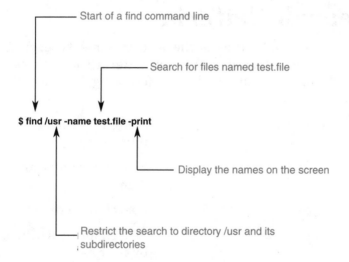

Start of a find command line

Search for files named test.file

$ find /usr -name test.file -print

Display the names on the screen

Restrict the search to directory /usr and its subdirectories

Figure 4.5
A Specific `find` *command line.*

NOTE: In UNIX, the word *print* often doesn't refer to printing on a system printer; instead it refers to displaying text on the screen. When UNIX was being developed in the early 1970s, video display terminals were not yet widely used. TeleType machines were used as terminals, and text was displayed to the user by printing it on rolls of paper. On a video screen, text is *displayed*, not *printed*, but some of the older UNIX terminology still remains.

The first two items on the command line (the name of the command and the pathname) are self-explanatory. However, the third and fourth items (criteria and action) require further discussion.

Search Criteria

You can search for files on the basis of name, type, or numerical information. Some of the search criteria that you can specify include names and types. The following list describes these options:

`-name file`	Search for file(s) named `file`.
`-type f`	Search for an ordinary `file`.
`-type d`	Search for a directory.
`-user name`	Search for files owned by user `name`.
`-group name`	Search for files owned by members of group `name`.
`-newer file`	Search for files modified more recently than file `file`.

The following example uses a few of these search criteria. This command line searches all directories for any ordinary files owned by Evan that have been modified more recently than a file called /usr/paul/entry:

```
$ find / -type f -user evan -newer /usr/paul/entry -
print
/usr/evan/test/features
/usr/evan/test/test.mode
/usr/evan/new/memo.201
...
$ _
```

Some of the search criteria that you can specify include numbers. The following list describes these options:

-size +n	Search for files with more than n blocks.
-size n	Search for files with exactly n blocks.
-size -n	Search for files with fewer than n blocks.
-links +n	Search for files with more than n links.
-links n	Search for files with exactly n links.
-links -n	Search for files with fewer than n links.
-ctime +n	Search for files changed more than n days ago.
-mtime +n	Search for files modified exactly n days ago.
-atime --n	Search for files accessed fewer than n days ago.

The following example uses some of these search criteria. This command line searches for all files in /usr that are larger than 10 blocks and that were accessed more than 90 days ago.

> **NOTE:** A *block* is a larger unit of measure in a computer system. In UNIX, a block is typically 512; 1,024; or 2,048 characters (bytes).

```
$ find /usr -size +10 -atime +90 -print
/usr/alice/memos/memo.302
/usr/carl/news/entry.89
/usr/dale/test/test.493
...
$ _
```

Action Statements

The action statements that you can use with find, including -print, are listed below. Two of the statements relate to the cpio command, which is used for copying files to backup devices.

-print	Display the full pathname of each file found.
-exec *command*	Execute *command* on each file found (unconditional).
-ok *command*	Execute *command* on each file found (with confirmation).
-depth	Used only before -cpio; copy the files in a directory, and then copy the directory itself.
-cpio *device*	Copy each file to *device* in cpio format.

> **TIP:** A *directory* is a file. If the command can be applied to a directory, it will be.

The -exec and -ok statements require further explanation. If a command uses a file name as an argument, you must type {}\; after the name of the command. The empty braces serve as a place-holder for the names of any files to be processed. The following command line uses the -ok statement:

```
$ find / -name core -atime +7 -ok rm {}\;
< rm ... /usr/paul/plans/core > ? y
< rm ... /usr/quinn/arch/core > ? y
< rm ... /usr/stan/memos/core > ? y
...
$ _
```

This command searches all directories for files called core that haven't been accessed in more than seven days. For each file found, the system prompts you for confirmation. If you answer yes, the system deletes the file.

Searching for Text in a File grep

Just as find allows you to search for files in the file system, another command, called grep, allows you to search for text in a file or in a group of files. The simplest form of a grep command line includes the name of the command, the test you are looking for, and the name of a file. The output of grep consists of only those lines in the file that contain the text. For example, suppose you want to display all lines in the file sample that contain the word is, assuming sample reads as follows:

```
$ cat sample
This brief statement is
an example of creating
a small file with cat.
$ _
```

Then enter a grep command line to conduct the search and display the lines that contain is:

```
$ grep is sample
This brief statement is
$ _
```

Suppose you want to display the name of all files that include the letters ddd. Use a pipe between ls and grep to display the matching names, as follows:

```
$ ls -l ¦ grep ddd
-rw-r----- 3 paul     415  Aug 3  13:09  ddd-125
-rwx------ 5 paul     705  Aug 4  16:15  1-ddd-txt
$ _
```

In this example, grep doesn't require a file name because ls supplies the text through the pipe. Programs, like grep, that process data are called *filters*.

Searching More Than One File

Suppose you have a series of parts lists with names like parts.Bell, parts.Hall, and parts.Smith. For the sake of simplicity, this example includes only these three files, but you could specify many more. Let's begin by looking at the contents of these parts lists.

```
$ cat parts.Bell
Bolt, hex              00891-00      0.25
Bolt, square           00784-00      0.18
Nut, hex               00643-00      0.08
Nut, square            00675-00      0.06
$ _


$ cat parts.Hall
Plate, rectangular     00632-00      2.15
Bar, square            00578-00      2.50
Rod, round             00601-00      2.35
$ _
```

```
$ cat parts.Smith
Screw, small               00329-00        0.02
Washer, round              00274-00        0.03
Washer, round              00407-00        0.05
$ _
```

You can search all of these files with grep. Real parts lists, of course, would be much longer and more complex; however, these small files will clearly show you how to use this important command. Let's use grep to answer various questions: For example, does Bell supply bolts?

To determine the answer, check file parts.Bell for the word Bolt:

```
$ grep Bolt parts.Bell
Bolt, hex                  00891-00        0.25
Bolt, square               00784-00        0.18
$ _
```

Answer: Yes, Bell supplies bolts.

Let's try another example: Does Hall supply washers? Use the following command to check file parts.Hall for the word Washer:

```
$ grep Washer parts.Hall
$ _
```

Because the command generates no output, the answer is no.

Does Smith supply small screws? To determine this, check parts.Smith for Screw, small:

```
$ grep 'Screw, small' parts.Smith
Screw, small               00329-00        0.02
$ _
```

Answer: Yes, Smith supplies screws.

> **NOTE:** The quotation marks around Screw, small were necessary in this example because you were searching for two words separated by a space.

Let's try one more example: Who supplies washers? To check all three files for the word Washer, you can use the following single command:

```
$ grep Washer parts.*
parts.Smith:Washer          00274-00          0.03
parts.Smith:Washer          00407-00          0.05
$ _
```

Answer: Smith.

The wild-card symbol * allows you to search all three files (parts.Bell, parts.Hall, and parts.Smith) with a single grep command. Note that when you search more than one file, grep precedes each line of output with the name of the file that contains the line.

Using Regular Expressions

You can use wild cards and other *metacharacters* in searches to match a greater variety of words and expressions. When you use these characters in search strings, you form *regular expressions*. For example, if you want to form an expression that matches either Washer or washer, you could use the following regular expression in your search:

```
[Ww]asher
```

The following list summarizes the metacharacters available in UNIX:

^	Beginning of line
.	Any single character
[ ]	Specific characters
$	End of line
*	Any number of characters
\	Escape character

> **NOTE:** If you want to search for one of these charac-
> ters, precede it with the escape character (\). For ex-
> ample, to search for a dollar sign in a file, you would
> have to type \$ in the search string.

There are many ways you can use regular expressions to
search for text. In the following examples, we'll focus on numbers
in the parts.Bell, parts.Hall, and parts.Smith files.

Suppose you want to determine if any items cost exactly
$2.50? To do so, you would check all files for the characters 2\.50
(note that to search for a period—which UNIX assumes is a
metacharacter—you must precede it with the escape character
(\)):

```
$ grep 2\.50 parts.*
parts.Hall: Bar, square      00578-00        2.50
$ _
```

The answer to your query is: Hall's square bar costs exactly
$2.50.

Let's try another example: Do any items cost less than
$0.10? You can use the following command to check all files for
any amounts less than $0.10.

```
$ grep 0\.0[0-9] parts.*
parts.Bell:Nut, hex          00643-00        0.08
parts.Bell:Nut, square       00675-00        0.06
parts.Smith:Screw, small     00329-00        0.02
parts.Smith:Washer             00274-00        0.03
parts.Smith:Washer             00407-00        0.05
$ _
```

Both of the preceding examples illustrate the use of the
backslash to escape the decimal point. Without the backslash,
UNIX would read the period as a metacharacter. (Note also that
the fields were not aligned in the output display.)

Sorting Lines in Files   sort

The sort command allows you to sort (reorder) the lines in a file. If all the text in a file is alphabetic, the lines are arranged in alphabetic order after a sort. Here is an example. Begin with the following file:

```
$ cat flowers
roses
petunias
orchids
daisies
begonias
$ _
```

In the simplest form of a sort command line, you enter only the name of the command and a file name, as shown here:

```
$ sort flowers
begonias
daisies
orchids
petunias
roses
$ _
```

Selecting Fields

You can achieve more sophisticated results with the sort command by choosing a file arranged in columns and then selecting individual items to sort. For example, take another look at parts.Hall:

```
$ cat parts.Hall
plate, rectangular        00632-00        2.15
Bar, square               00578-00        2.50
Rod, round                00601-00        2.35
```

From the point of view of the sort command, blank spaces on a line represent a *field separator*, and therefore each line in this file contains four *fields*. If you give each field a name, you can display the file as shown in Figure 4.6.

Part name	Shape	Part no.	Price
Plate,	rectangular	00632-00	2.15
Bar,	square	00578-00	2.50
Rod,	round	00601-00	2.35
Field 1	**Field 2**	**Field 3**	**Field 4**

Figure 4.6

Fields in a parts file.

Suppose you want to sort the lines by shape. Using notation that is unique to the sort command, you would enter the following command:

```
$ sort +1 -2 parts.Hall
Plate, rectangular     00632-00       2.15
Rod, round             00601-00       2.35
Bar, square            00578-00       2.50
$ _
```

In this command line, the notation +1 -2 means, "Begin sorting after field 1; stop sorting after field 2." In other words, sort only field 2. This is illustrated in Figure 4.7; the vertical lines indicate where sorting begins and ends.

Begin after field 1		Stop sorting after field 2 (exclude field 3 and 4 from the sort)	
Field 1	**Field 2**	**Field 3.**	**Field 4**
Plate,	rectangular	00632-00	2.15
Bar,	square	00578-00	2.50
Rod,	round	00601-00	2.35

Figure 4.7

Sorting field 2 only.

Using Sort Options

Next, let's assume you want to sort the lines by part number. Using the field notation from the preceding example, you would include the -n (numeric) and -r (reverse order) options to produce the following command:

```
$ sort -nr +2 -3 parts.Hall
Plate, rectangular          00632-00          2.15
Rod, round                  00601-00          2.35
Bar, square                 00578-00          2.50
$ _
```

In the preceding command line, the two options -n and -r are said to be *bundled* (combined after a single minus sign). The notation -nr means, "Sort as numeric information in reverse order." The notation +2 -3 means, "Begin sorting after field 2; stop sorting after field 3." In other words, sort only field 3. This is illustrated in Figure 4.8; the vertical lines indicate where sorting begins and ends.

Figure 4.8
Sorting field 3 only.

Begin sorting after field 2 (that is, start after field 3)		Stop after field 3	
Field 1	Field 2	Field 3.	Field 4
Bar,	square	00632-00	2.50
Rod,	round	00601-00	2.35
Plate	rectangular	00578-00	2.15

The sort command also includes a number of other options, including options for ignoring leading blanks, sorting months of the year, folding uppercase letters onto lowercase, sorting in dictionary order (disregarding case), ignoring nonprinting characters, discarding identical lines, merging sorted files, and setting your own field separator. These options are listed in the Quick Reference section at the end of this book.

Sorting More Than One File

You can also sort more than one file at a time. The following command sorts all three parts files by price, highest price first:

```
$ sort -nr +3 parts.*
Bar, square              00578-00         2.50
Rod, round               00601-00         2.35
Plate, rectangular       00632-00         2.15
Bolt, hex                00891-00         0.25
Bolt, square             00784-00         0.18
Nut, hex                 00643-00         0.08
Nut, square              00675-00         0.06
Washer, round            00407-00         0.05
Washer, round            00274-00         0.03
Screw, small             00329-00         0.02
$ _
```

Sending the Output to a File

Let's conclude this section on sorting by discussing one more important feature: sending the output of a sort to a file (instead of displaying it on the screen). Let's repeat an earlier example in this section with a slight modification that redirects the output. The following procedure sorts the file parts.Hall and sends the recorded output to a file called shape.Hall:

```
$ sort +1 -2 parts.Hall > shape.Hall
$ _
```

Display the output file as follows:

```
$ cat shape.Hall
Plate, rectangular          00632-00          2.15
Rod, round                  00601-00          2.35
Bar, square                 00578-00          2.50
$ _
```

Notice that the sorted output is now in another file, ready to be processed in some other way if necessary.

Performing Calculations

Two UNIX utilities allow you to perform calculations on the screen of your terminal.

Using the Desk Calculator   dc

The dc command gives you the convenience of having a simple desk calculator on your screen. The following session illustrates how dc works:

Using the dc Calculator

1. Type: $ **dc**	Begins a session.
2. Type: **6**	Enters 6.
3 Type: **7**	Enters 7.

4. Type: +	Performs addition.
5. Type: **p**	Displays the result: 13.
6. Type: **3+p**	Adds 3 and displays the result: 16.
7. Type: **9*p**	Multiplies by 9 and dis plays the result: 144.
8. Type: **12/p**	Divides by 12 and displays the result: 12.
9. Type: **9-p**	Subtracts 9 and displays the result: 3.
10. Type: **q**	Ends the session (quits).
11. Type: $ _	Shell prompt appears.

Other features of dc include scaling, number bases, subscripts, functions, and logical control. For a complete list of desk calculator commands, see the Quick Reference section at the end of this book.

Using the High-Precision Calculator   bc

The bc command brings you a much more sophisticated calculator with unlimited precision, variables, and a range of 0–99 places after the decimal point. The following session illustrates some of the things you can do with bc:

$ **bc**	Begin a session.
17 + 36	Add two numbers.
53	
23 - 41	Subtract one number from another.
-18	
12 * 13	Multiply two numbers.
156	
96 / 12	Divide one number by another.
8 sqrt (64)	Take the square root of a number.
8	
scale = 6	Request six places after the decimal point.
r = sqrt(17)	Assign a value to the variable r.
r	Display the value of r (to six places).
4.123105	
define f(x,y) {	Define a function called f
auto z	
z = x-y	that subtracts y from x
return(z) }	and returns the difference as the value of function f.

`a = sqrt(47)`	Assign the square root of 47 to variable a.
`b = sqrt(19)`	Assign the square root of 19 to variable b.
`f(a,b)`	Compute the difference with function f.
`2.496756`	
`quit`	End the session.
`$ _`	

The bc calculator also allows conversion of numbers from one base to another, arrays, and comments. In addition, the -l (library) option lets bc use a mathematical library that includes sine (s), arctangent (a), exponential (e), natural logarithm (l), and Bessel (j(n,x)) functions. The following command line invokes the math library:

```
$ bc -l
```

If you often use long functions that are difficult to type repeatedly, you can enter them into a file and then retrieve the file when you begin a session. For example, suppose you store a set of functions in a file called math.bc. When you begin a new session, you can invoke these functions by entering the following command line:

```
$ bc math.bc
```

Chapter 4 Quiz

Match each command listed on the left with one of the functions described on the right:

1. find A. Display a calendar.

2. cat B. Combine two files to form a third.

3. cal C. Print two files on a system printer.

4. bc   D. Display all lines in a file that contain a specific word.

5. lp   E. Display the names of all files in your working directory that you last modified on a specific date.

6. sort   F. Arrange all line entries in a file.

7. grep   G. Calculate the square root of a number to 20 decimal places.

Write a command line to perform each of the following functions:

8. Display a calendar for October 1562.

9. Create a small file called test.doc with the following contents:

   This is a very,
   very small file.

10. Print files memo.101 and memo.102 with notification by electronic mail.

11. Locate any files in directory /usr owned by user Penny that were last accessed more than 30 days ago.

12. Display all lines in files parts.Bell, parts.Hall, and parts.Smith that have part numbers between 00601-00 and 00700-00.

13. Create a new file called parts.price that contains one large parts list combined from files parts.Bell, parts.Hall, and parts.Smith sorted by price.

14. Create a new file called parts.partno that contains one large parts list combined from files parts.Bell, parts.Hall, and parts.Smith sorted by part number.

15. Compute the value of the square root of 500 to five decimal places.

In This Chapter

Beginning and Ending an Editing Session

Moving the Cursor

Adjusting the Screen Display

Entering Text

Deleting and Moving Text

Finding and Replacing Text

Beginning and Ending an Editing Session

1. Type `vi`, followed by the name of the file to be edited, and press `⏎Enter`.
2. Press `a` to get into text entry mode.
3. Enter text.
4. Press `Esc` to leave text entry mode.
5. Type `:w` to write the text to the file.
6. Type `:q` to leave vi and return to the shell prompt.

Moving the Cursor

- Use any of the arrow keys to move the cursor one space.
- Type `.` to repeat or undo keystrokes.
- Type `^` or `$` to move to the beginning or end of the current line, respectively.
- Type `b` or `w` to move backward or forward one word.
- Type `(` or `)` to move backward or forward one sentence.
- Type `{` or `}` to move backward or forward one paragraph.
- Type `H`, `M`, or `L` to move to the high, middle, or low line of the screen.
- Type `nG` to move the cursor to line *n*.

Entering Text

- Type `i`, `a`, or `o` to insert text before or append text after the cursor position, or open a new line below the current line to enter text.
- Type `I`, `A`, or `O` to insert text before or append text after the current line, or open a new line above the current line to enter text.

Editing with vi

This chapter introduces the UNIX text editor known as *vi* (visual interpreter). The original text editor for UNIX was a primitive line editor called ed. In the late 1970s, William Joy and others at the University of California developed an enhanced version of ed called ex. One of the key features of ex is its visual interpreter, vi (prounounced "VEE-eye"), which is similar to many of the word processors that people use today.

Beginning and Ending an Editing Session

This section shows you how to start the vi editor, enter text, repeat and undo keystrokes, save your text in a file, and leave the vi editor. It assumes the following two conditions have been met:

- Your terminal has been identified to the UNIX system and is ready to perform full-screen editing.

- You have selected the subdirectory in which you want to work.

1. Start the editor:

   At the shell prompt, enter the vi command, followed by the name of a file:

   ```
   $ vi first.doc
   ```

Your screen will soon clear and then display the following:

```
_
~
~
~
~
~
~
~
~
~
~
~
~
"first.doc" [New file]
```

2. Select a text-entry mode:

   Type a (but don't press Enter) to select the *append* text-entry mode. The a won't appear on the screen. Now, you can begin entering text.

3. Enter your text. For example, type the following paragraph; be sure to press ⏎Enter at the end of each line and to insert two spaces after each period:

   ```
   The UNIX text editor is called vi
   (pronounced by spelling the word).
   The vi editor is actually the visual
   interpreter of the ex editor.  When
   you use vi, you will find that the
   two editors become intertwined
   during an editing session.
   ```

Note that the text appears on the screen as you type it, replacing the tildes on the left side one at a time.

4. Return to the vi command mode:

   To leave text entry mode, press Esc (the Escape key).

   Again, the screen won't change or display a prompt, but nevertheless, you will return to vi command mode, from which you can enter editing commands.

5. Write (save) the text to a file, and exit vi:

   To write the text to a file named first.doc, type :w and press ↵Enter.

   After the :w appears at the bottom of the screen, vi displays the following message:

   ```
   "first.doc" [New file] 8 lines, 241 characters
   ```

   To leave vi and return to the shell prompt, type :q and press ; the shell prompt will appear on the screen:

   ```
   $ _
   ```

The preceding steps illustrated one complete editing session from beginning to end. You have just used the editor to create a small text file.

Comments on the Session

The preceding steps are typical for any vi editing session. You begin by entering the vi command from the shell prompt (Step 1). Then you request text-entry mode (Step 2), enter the text (Step 3), and return to command mode (Step 4). Finally, you end the session (Step 5).

NOTE: vi is actually the visual mode of an editor called ex.

The write and quit commands (Step 5) are actually ex editor commands. A colon (:) always starts ex command mode. In Step 5, you entered ex command mode twice: first, to write (:w) and then, to quit (:q). You can either use these commands separately, as you did in Step 5, or you can enter them simultaneously (:wq).

TIP: To write text to a file only if it has been modified and then exit, use either :x or ZZ.

Command Mode and Text-Entry Mode

When you first begin a session with vi, you're in command mode. Command mode is used to tell vi what you want to do. So far, you've learned different commands to write the file and quit. To enter text, you need to be in text-entry mode. To get there from command mode, type a command such as a for append, i for insert, or o for open. (You'll learn about insert and open a little later.) To get back to command mode, just press the Esc. In vi, you can go between command mode and text-entry mode as many times as you need.

Moving the Cursor

One of the most basic operations in using an editor is moving the cursor from one location to another. Many of the editing functions of vi work in conjunction with cursor position and cursor motion. Since vi doesn't require the mouse to move the cursor, use the keyboard to control the position of the cursor.

Moving One Position at a Time

If your keyboard has a cursor motion pad with a set of four arrow keys, as shown in Figure 5.1 (left), you can use these to move the cursor. If your keyboard doesn't have these keys, you can use either of two alternative sets of cursor motion keys, as shown in Figure 5.1 (middle and right).

NOTE: On many keyboards, the numeric keypad also serves as a cursor movement pad.

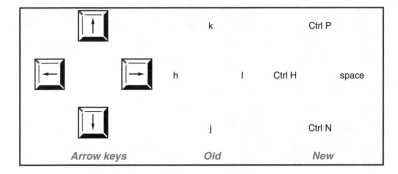

Figure 5.1
Cursor motion keys.

TIP: Remember, case doesn't make any difference when you're using the Ctrl key. Ctrl -P is the same as Ctrl -p.

Remember that cursor movement commands are vi commands. Therefore, you must be in vi command mode to use them. If you aren't sure which mode you're in, press Esc. If you hear a beep, then you are already in command mode.

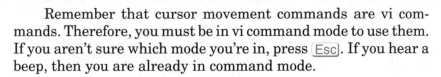

TIP: Any time you are using vi, you can press Esc to return to command mode.

To practice moving the cursor, begin another session, and try the commands you just learned. Then, select the set that you prefer working with. The following command retrieves the file you created in the preceding section:

```
$ vi first.doc
```

After you've experimented with the basic cursor motion keys, add two more paragraphs to the file (remember to press ⏎Enter between paragraphs and after each line):

```
When you first begin a session with vi,
you are in vi command mode. To enter
text, press a (or another text-entry
command) to enter text-entry mode.
Once you've entered the desired text,
press Esc to return to vi command mode.

When you're ready to save the text, type
:w and press Enter to write the text
to a file. Then type :q and press Enter
to leave vi and return to the shell prompt.
The colon (:) begins ex command mode, and
the Enter key returns you to vi command
mode.
```

In case you need a reminder, here are the steps for entering these two paragraphs:

- While you're in command mode, move the cursor to the end of the file.

- Type a to append text in text-entry mode. Press ⏎Enter to insert a blank line; and then begin typing the text.

- After you type the last line, press Esc to return to vi command mode.

- Type :w and press ⏎Enter to write the text to the file first.doc (but don't quit vi yet).

After you complete these steps, the editor displays the following message at the bottom of the screen:

```
'first.doc' 23 lines, 732 characters
```

Repeating and Undoing Keystrokes

Before we continue discussing cursor motion commands, try the following short exercise, which shows you how to repeat and undo keystrokes. Here are the steps:

1. Enter two lines of text.

   With the cursor still positioned at the bottom of the file, press ⏎Enter, and type two more lines of text:

   ```
   These two lines show what you can

   do with the repeat and undo keys.
   ```

   Then press Esc to get into command mode.

   The lower part of the screen should look like this:

   ```
   The colon (:) begins ex command mode, and
   the Enter key returns you to vi command mode.

   These two lines show what you can
   do with the repeat and undo keys.


   _
   ~
   ~
   ```

2. Repeat your keystrokes.

   To repeat these two lines, press the period . key (but not ⏎Enter).

The screen now looks like this:

```
The colon (:) begins ex command mode, and
the Enter key returns you to vi command
mode.

These two lines show what you can
do with the repeat and undo keys.

These two lines show what you can
do with the repeat and undo keys.


  _
  ~
  ~
```

3. Undo the keystrokes:

   To undo the repeat command (.) of Step 2, press u (but not ⏎Enter).

   The copy of the paragraph will disappear, and the screen will look like this again:

```
The colon (:) begins ex command mode, and
the Enter key returns you to vi command mode.

These two lines show what you can
do with the repeat and undo keys.

  _
  ~
```

   To restore the copy, press u again.

   To undo the copy again, press u once more.

4. Abandon the extra two lines:

   To leave vi without saving the extra lines, type :q! (with an exclamation point) and press ⏎Enter.

   The shell prompt returns to the screen:

```
$ _
```

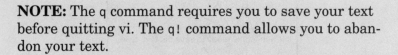

NOTE: The q command requires you to save your text before quitting vi. The q! command allows you to abandon your text.

The repeat command (Step 2) allows you to duplicate a sequence of keystrokes. The undo command (Step 3), which is usually used to undo a deletion, lets you reverse the preceding change to your text. Note that when you use the undo command more than once, it reverses itself. These two commands are introduced here because they are so handy in everyday editing.

Moving to the End of the Line

The keys that move the cursor to the beginning of the current line (^) or to the end of the line ($) are the same two characters that are used throughout UNIX in searching for text. You can try these keys now, as shown in Figure 5.2.

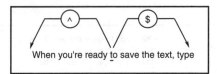

Figure 5.2
Cursor motion to end of line.

If your cursor is currently on the t in "to," then typing ^ while in command mode moves your cursor to the beginning of the line. Similarly, typing $ moves your cursor to the end of the line.

Practice using these keys a few times before you continue with the next section.

Moving a Word at a Time

Now let's examine the commands that move the cursor a word at a time. These commands are illustrated in Figure 5.3.

Figure 5.3
Cursor motion by word.

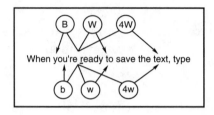

Use b or B to move one word back; use w or W to move one word forward. The b and B (as well as the w and W) commands are equivalent except that the capitalized versions ignore punctuation, such as apostrophes ('). You can also use a multiplier, such as the 4 in 4w, to move a specific number of words at one time.

Moving a Sentence at a Time

You can use left and right parentheses in vi command mode to move the cursor a sentence at a time. The left parenthesis moves back to the beginning of the current sentence; the right parenthesis moves forward to the beginning of the next sentence, as shown in Figure 5.4.

Figure 5.4
Cursor motion by sentence.

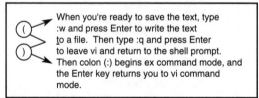

NOTE: If the cursor is already at the beginning of a sentence, the (command moves the cursor to the beginning of the preceding sentence.

Moving a Paragraph at a Time

The left and right braces ({}) function like the left and right parentheses in vi command mode, but they move the cursor a paragraph at a time instead of a sentence at a time. The left brace moves back to the beginning of the current paragraph; the right brace moves forward to the beginning of the next paragraph, as shown in Figure 5.5. (The beginning of a paragraph is usually the blank line that precedes it.)

When you first begin a session with vi, you are in command mode. To enter text, press a (or one of six other letters) to enter text entry mode.

Once you've entered the desired text, press Esc to return to vi command mode.

When you're ready to save the text, type :w and press Enter to write the text to a file. Then type :q and press Enter to leave vi and return to the shell prompt. The colon (:) begins ex command mode, and the Enter key returns you to vi command mode.

Figure 5.5
Cursor motion by paragraph.

TIP: You can use multipliers with the (,), {, and } commands.

Moving Around the Screen

Three capital letters (H, M, and L) allow you to move to one of three locations on the current screen display:

H (high)	Top of screen
M (middle)	Middle of screen
L (low)	Bottom of screen

Practice using these commands now.

Moving to a Specific Line Number

Another capital letter, G (Go to...), moves the cursor to any line of text, even if that line is not currently displayed on the screen. Simply type a line number in front of the G command, as shown in the following examples:

3G   Move to line 3

7G   Move to line 7

G   Move to the last line

A related command (Ctrl-G) displays the line number at which the cursor is located. Whenever you press Ctrl-G, a message such as the following appears on the screen:

```
'first.doc' [Modified] line 12 of 23 —52%—
```

Now is a good time to practice these commands.

Adjusting the Screen Display

This section describes different ways you can adjust the screen display, such as paging, scrolling, repositioning the current line, and clearing system messages.

Paging

Paging is displaying an entirely new screenful of text. The vi editor has one command for paging back (Ctrl-B) and one command for paging forward (Ctrl-F), as shown in Figure 5.6.

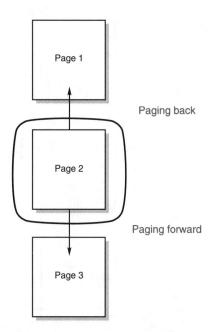

Figure 5.6
Paging commands.

Paging back

Paging forward

TIP: To remember the key combination to page forward, think of *F* in *forward* (Ctrl-F). Similarly, to remember how to page back, think of *B* in *back* (Ctrl-B).

Scrolling

Scrolling, which is similar to paging, is moving the display half a screen at a time. vi provides one command for scrolling up (Ctrl-U) and one for scrolling down (Ctrl-D), as shown in Figure 5.7.

Figure 5.7
Scrolling commands.

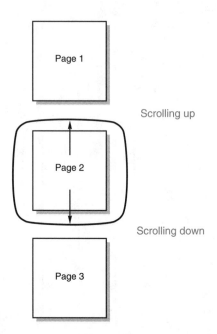

Scrolling up

Scrolling down

TIP: To remember the key combination to scroll half a screen up, think of *U* in *up* (⟨Ctrl⟩-⟨U⟩). Similarly, to remember how to scroll down, think of *D* in *down* (⟨Ctrl⟩-⟨D⟩).

Controlling the Screen Display

There might be times when you want to slide the screen display up or down. The z (zero screen) command allows you to perform these operations. By pressing a key after the z command, you can control the placement of the current line of the screen:

z ⟨⏎Enter⟩   Place the current line at the top of the screen.

z ⟨.⟩   Place the current line in the middle of the screen.

z ⊡   Place the current line at the
bottom of the screen.

> **TIP:** Unlike most UNIX commands, which are mne-
> monically related to their actions, the names of these
> keys are completely arbitrary and meaningless. There
> is no easy way to remember these three commands.

The commands described in this subsection are illustrated
in Figure 5.8.

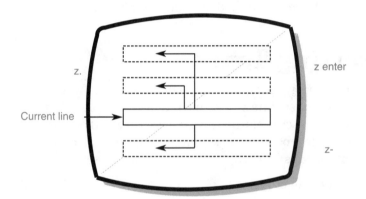

Figure 5.8
*The Zero screen
command.*

Clearing System Messages

Sometimes, the system writes messages on your screen while you
are working. At other times, vi itself might write extraneous
characters on the screen. In either case, you can use the following
command to clear messages from your screen and redisplay any
lines that might have been overwritten:

    Ctrl-L Clear message from your screen

Entering New Text

After you've created a file, you often have to return to the file and
add new text to it. vi provides several commands through which

you can select text-entry mode and add the new text, depending on where the new text will be placed in relation to the existing text:

- If you want the new text to go in front of the existing text, you can *insert* the new text.

- If you want the new text to follow the existing text, you can *append* the new text.

- If you want the new text to be placed on a new line above or below the existing text, you can *open* a new line.

In this section, you will try each of these commands in the previously created sample document `first.doc`.

Inserting Text   i

After you position the cursor somewhere on a line, you can use the i command to insert new text in front of the cursor. As you insert the new text, the cursor and the existing text will be pushed to the right to make room. Try the following exercise in the first paragraph of `first.doc`.

1. Position the cursor.

   Move the cursor to the i in `intertwined` on line 6:

   ```
   The UNIX text editor is called vi
   (pronounced by spelling the word).
   The vi editor is actually the visual
   interpreter of the ex editor. When
   you use vi, you will find that the
   two editors become intertwined
   during an editing session.
   ```

   Be sure you are in vi command mode.

2. Insert a word in front of `intertwined`:

   Type i to request insertion when you get into text-entry mode.

Type `completely` (with a space following), and press Esc to return to vi command mode.

If you want to insert text at the beginning of the current line, you can either move the cursor and use `i` or you can leave the cursor where it is and use `I` (capitalized). Repeat the preceding Steps 1 and 2, but use the `I` command to insert `fifty-` at the beginning of line 6 (that is, change `two` to `fifty-two`). After you've made this change, the paragraph should look like this:

```
The UNIX text editor is called vi
(pronounced by spelling the word).
The vi editor is actually the visual
interpreter of the ex editor. When
you use vi, you will find that the
fifty-two editors become completely intertwined
during an editing session.
```

Appending Text   a

You used the `a` command in the first session of this chapter. You can use `a` any time you want to append new text after existing text. The new text will be inserted after the current cursor position. The cursor will remain in its present location, while existing text after the new text will be pushed to the right. Let's use this command in the first paragraph of `first.doc`.

1. Position the cursor:

   Move the cursor to the second l in `will` on line 5:

```
The UNIX text editor is called vi
(pronounced by spelling the word).
The vi editor is actually the visual
interpreter of the ex editor. When
you use vi, you will find that the
fifty-two editors become completely intertwined
during an editing session.
```

   Be sure you are in vi command mode.

2. Append a word after `will`:

Press `a` to request append text-entry mode.

Type `always` (with a space in front) and press `Esc` to return to vi command mode.

If you want to append text to the end of the current line, you can either move the cursor and use a or you can leave the cursor where it is and use A (capitalized). Repeat the preceding Steps 1 and 2, but use the A command to append `one hundred` to the end of line 5 (that is, change `fifty-two` to `one hundred fifty-two`). After you've made this change, the paragraph should look like this:

```
The UNIX text editor is called vi
(pronounced by spelling the word).
The vi editor is actually the visual
interpreter of the ex editor. When
you use vi, you will always find that the one hundred_
fifty-two editors become completely intertwined during
an editing session.
```

Opening a New Line   o

You have just learned the commands for inserting and appending text, all of which insert text into the current line. Another pair of commands allow you to insert text above or below the current line. Well begin with the `0` command, which opens a new line above the current line. Let's practice using this command in the first paragraph of `first.doc`.

1. Position the cursor.

Move the cursor to the `e` in `editor` on line 1 (or anywhere on line 1):

```
The UNIX text editor is called vi
(pronounced by spelling the word).
The vi editor is actually the visual
interpreter of the ex editor. When
you use vi, you will find that
```

```
the one hundred
fifty-two editors become completely intertwined
during an editing session.
```

Be sure you are in vi command mode.

2. Open a line above the first line.

Type capital O to open a line above.

Type The **UNIX Text Editors**, press ⏎Enter to leave a blank line, and press Esc to return to vi command mode.

If you want to open a line *below* the current line, you can use o (uncapitalized). Repeat the preceding Steps 1 and 2 (without pressing ⏎Enter), but use the o command to open a new line that says short for the visual interpreter below the first line of the first paragraph. After you've made this change, the display should look like this:

```
The UNIX Text Editors

The UNIX text editor is called vi
(short for the visual interpreter)_
(pronounced by spelling the word).
The vi editor is actually the visual
interpreter of the ex editor. When
you use vi, you will always find that the one hundred
fifty-two editors become completely intertwined
during an editing session.
```

This time, use :wq (or :x) to save the text. A display similar to the following will appear:

```
'first.doc' 26 lines, 831 characters
$ _
```

Figure 5.9 summarizes the commands for entering and exiting the different modes.

Figure 5.9
Editing modes.

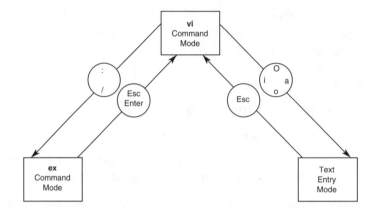

Deleting Text

You probably delete text about as often as you insert new text. The commands for deleting text, like those for moving the cursor, have many variations. You can delete characters, words, lines, sentences, and paragraphs, as well as parts of words, lines, sentences, and paragraphs. The command to delete is d; the letter designators for words, lines, sentences, and paragraphs are the same as those used for cursor motion.

Deleting Characters   x

The command to delete a character doesn't follow the pattern of the other commands for deleting text. To delete a single character, move the cursor to the character and type x. To delete several characters, move the cursor to the first character, and type a number in front of x. For example, to delete five characters, use **5x**.

Deleting Words   dw

To delete a word, move the cursor to the first letter of the word and type **dw** from vi command mode. (If the word contains punctuation, you must use **dW**.) To delete several words, use *n***dw** (or *n***dW**). To practice these commands, let's delete some of the words that you inserted in the preceding section.

1. Retrieve the document:

   At the shell prompt, enter the following:

   $ `vi first.doc`

   The text will appear on the screen.

2. Move the cursor into position:

   Move the cursor to the first `f` in `fifty-two`:

   ```
   The UNIX Text Editors

   The UNIX text editor is called vi
   (short for the visual interpreter)
   (pronounced by spelling the word).
   The vi editor is actually the visual
   interpreter of the ex editor. When
   you use vi, you will always find that the one hundred
   fifty-two editors become completely intertwined
   during an editing session.
   ```

   Be sure you are in vi command mode.

3. Delete a few words:

   Type `dw` to delete `fifty-`.

   Advance the cursor to the `c` in `completely` on the same line, and delete it with `dw`.

   Use the same method to delete `always` on the preceding line.

4. Delete several words:

   Move the cursor to the `o` in `one hundred`.

   Type `2dw` to delete `one hundred`.

   After these changes, the display should look like this:

   ```
   The UNIX Text Editors

   The UNIX text editor is called vi
   ```

```
(short for the visual interpreter)
(pronounced by spelling the word).
The vi editor is actually the visual
interpreter of the ex editor. When
you use vi, you will find that the _
two editors become intertwined
during an editing session.
```

Deleting Lines   dd

To delete one line, move the cursor to any position in the line and
type dd. To delete more than one line, precede the command with
a number (*ndd*). Here are some examples:

1. Move the cursor into position:

   Move the cursor to the v in visual, which is about the
   middle of the second line of the paragraph:

   ```
   The UNIX Text Editors

   The UNIX text editor is called vi
   (short for visual interpreter)
   (pronounced by spelling the word).
   The vi editor is actually the visual
   interpreter of the ex editor. When
   you use vi, you will find that the
   two editors become intertwined
   during an editing session.
   ```

   Be sure you are in vi command mode.

2. Delete one line:

   Type dd to delete the entire line.

   The line will vanish, and the cursor will end up on the
   next line.

3. Delete several lines:

   Type 3dd to delete the next three lines.

   Then, type u to restore these lines.

After these changes, the display should look like this:

```
The UNIX Text Editors

The UNIX text editor is called vi
(pronounced by spelling the word).
The vi editor is actually the visual
interpreter of the ex editor. When
you use vi, you will find that the
two editors become intertwined
during an editing session.
```

You can also delete text from the cursor to either the beginning of a line (d^) or the end of the line (d$).

Deleting Sentences   d)

For deleting a sentence, we'll move to the second paragraph. To delete a sentence, move the cursor to the beginning of the sentence and **type d)**. Here's an example:

1. Move the cursor into position:

   Move the cursor to the T in To enter on the second line:

   ```
   When you first begin a session with vi,
   you are in vi command mode. To enter
   text, press a (or one of six other
   letters) to enter text-entry mode.
   Once you've entered the desired text,
   press Esc to return to vi command mode.
   ```

   Be sure you are in vi command mode.

2. Delete a sentence:

   Type **d)** to delete the second sentence.

   Type **u** to restore the sentence.

3. Delete two sentences:

   Type **2d)** to delete the second and third sentences.

   Type **u** to restore the sentences.

Because you restored the deleted text in each instance, the display will be unchanged at this point. To delete part of a sentence, move the cursor to the appropriate location in the sentence and type one of the following:

d(Delete from the cursor to the beginning of the sentence.

d)   Delete from the cursor to the end of the sentence.

Deleting Paragraphs   d}

To delete a paragraph, move the cursor to the beginning of the paragraph and type d}. Here's an example:

1. Move the cursor into position:

    Move the cursor to the blank line above When you on the first line.

    ```
    ―
    When you first begin a session with vi,
    you are in vi command mode. To enter
    text, press a (or one of six other
    letters) to enter text entry mode.
    Once you've entered the desired text,
    press Esc to return to vi command mode.
    ```

    Be sure you are in vi command mode.

2. Delete a paragraph:

    Type d} to delete the second paragraph.

    After examining the display, type u to restore the paragraph.

3. Delete two paragraphs:

    Type 2d} to delete the second and third paragraphs.

    Type u to restore the paragraphs.

Because you restored the deleted text in each instance, the display will be unchanged at this point. To delete part of a paragraph, move the cursor to the appropriate position in the paragraph and type one of the following:

d{	Delete from the cursor to the beginning of the paragraph.
d}	Delete from the cursor to the end of the paragraph.

Moving Text

Moving text is similar to deleting text. The key concept is that deleted text isn't completely gone: it's placed in temporary storage. To move text from location A to location B, simply follow these four general steps:

1. Move the cursor to location A.

2. Delete the text with one of the delete commands you just learned in the preceding section.

3. Move the cursor to location B.

4. Insert the text with a put command (p), which you will learn about in this section.

Because we have already discussed deletion of characters, words, lines, sentences, and paragraphs in some detail, we won't repeat those instructions in this section. Instead, we'll concentrate on moving sentences and summarize the rest.

Moving Sentences   d) and p

To demonstrate the process of moving text, let's select a sentence in the second paragraph and move it to another location. The following exercise expands on the four general steps outlined previously:

1. Move the cursor to the current location:

   Move the cursor to the T in To enter on the second line of the second paragraph:

   ```
   When you first begin a session with vi,
   you are in vi command mode. To enter
   text, press a (or one of six other
   letters) to enter text entry mode.
   Once you've entered the desired text,
   press Esc to return to vi command mode.
   ```

   Be sure you are in vi command mode.

2. Delete a sentence from its current location:

   Type d) to delete the second sentence.

   The paragraph should look like this:

   ```
   When you first begin a session with vi,
   you are in vi command mode.
   @
   @
   Once you've entered the desired text,
   press Esc to return to vi command mode.
   ```

3. Move the cursor to the target location:

   Move the cursor to the T in Then on the third line of the third paragraph.

   The paragraph should now look like this:

   ```
   When you're ready to save the text, type
   :w and press Enter to write the text
   to a file. Then type :q and press Enter
   to leave vi and return to the shell prompt.
   The colon (:) begins ex command mode, and
   the Escape key returns you to vi command mode.
   ```

4. Insert (put) the sentence at the new location:

With the cursor on the T, type uppercase P to insert the sentence at this location.

The screen display should now look like this:

```
When you're ready to save the text, type
:w and press Enter to write the text
to a file. To enter
text, press a (or one of six other
letters) to enter text entry mode. Then type :q and ...
to leave vi and return to the shell prompt.
The colon (:) begins ex command mode, and
the Escape key returns you to vi command
mode.
```

You have now moved a sentence from one location to another. Repeat the preceding Steps 1 through 4 to move the sentence back to its original location. (When you are ready to restore the sentence, type lowercase p in Step 4 rather than uppercase P.) As you can see from this example, successfully moving text depends on getting the cursor in the proper position and using the right put command. You can use either of the following two put commands:

P   Insert the text in front of the cursor (or above the current line).

p   Append the text after the cursor (or below the current line).

Moving Other Units of Text

You can transpose two adjacent characters by placing the cursor on the first one and typing xp. For example, suppose you typed hte instead of the. Move the cursor to the h and type xp. The x command deletes the h, and the p command puts the deleted character after the cursor (which now is located under the t).

You can move words from one location to another by deleting them from their original location, with commands such as dw, 5dw, 5dW, and then inserting them at the target location with P or p. Delete lines with commands such as dd, 3dd, d^, d$. Delete paragraphs with d{}, d}, d4}, and so on.

> **NOTE:** You can use either d5w or 5dw to delete five words. You have this choice for most vi commands.

Finding and Replacing Text

This section demonstrates the vi commands that let you find and replace text. The commands are quite straightforward, so you should be able to learn them quickly.

Searching for Text

To search for text from the current location toward the end of the file, type a slash (/), followed by the text, and press ⏎Enter. The cursor will move to the first occurrence of the text. If you want to search for the next occurrence, type n (next). Here is an example of a simple search:

1. Move the cursor into position:

   If you have just opened the file, the cursor will automatically be on the first line.

   If you've been working with the file, move the cursor to the first line with the 1G command.

2. Begin the search for a word:

   Type /**you** and press ⏎Enter.

   The cursor will move to the y in the first you in line 7:

   ```
   The UNIX Text Editors

   The UNIX text editor is called vi
   (pronounced by spelling the word).
   The vi editor is actually the visual
   interpreter of the ex editor. When
   you use vi, you will find that the
   two editors become intertwined
   during an editing session.
   ```

3. Continue the search:

   Type **n** (next) to continue the search.

   The cursor will move to the y in the second you in line 7:

   ```
   The UNIX Text Editors

   The UNIX text editor is called vi
   (pronounced by spelling the word).
   The vi editor is actually the visual
   interpreter of the ex editor. When
   you use vi, you will find that the
   two editors become intertwined
   during an editing session.
   ```

4. Continue the search again:

   Press **n** again.

   Press **n** six more times to continue the search.

   The cursor always moves to the next occurrence of you in this document. To reverse the direction of the search, press N (upper-case) rather than n. If you don't want the cursor to stop at words such as you're, your, youth, and so on, type a space after the u when you begin the search.

To search in the other direction (toward the beginning of the file), initiate the search with a question mark (?) rather than a slash (/).

Replacing Text

One of the most useful features of a text-editing program like vi is the ability to search for each instance of a word or expression and replace it with another. This feature allows you to correct multiple spelling errors or change terminology in a file.

The s (substitute) command begins with a colon (:), which signals the change to ex command mode. Follow the colon with the beginning and ending line numbers (separated by a comma) you want to search, the s command, the text you are searching for, and then the text you want to substitute. The following breakdown explains the command in general terms:

`:start,stops/s_text/r_text/g`

in which

:	Indicates that this is an ex command.
start	Is the starting line number of the search.
stop	Is the ending line number of the search.
s	Is the substitute command.
s_text	Is the search string (the text you are looking for).

*r*_text	Is the replacement string (the text to be substituted for the search string).
g	(global) indicates that all occurrences of the search string on a given line are to be replaced, not just the first occurrence.

The following example changes each occurrence of vi to vee-eye:

1. Change vi to vee-eye throughout the file:

   Type the following command:

   ```
   :1,$s/vi/vee-eye/g
   ```

   Press ⏎Enter to make the substitutions.

2. Change vee-eye back to vi again:

   Type the following command:

   ```
   :1,$s/vee-eye/vi/g
   ```

   Press ⏎Enter to make the substitutions.

You can restrict the search by selecting specific starting and ending line numbers. A line number can be a number, a search string, or a symbol such as . (current line) and $ (last line). Here are a few examples:

3,.	Search from line 3 to the current line.
.,/step/	Search from the current line to the first line that contains the word step.
-5,$	Search from five lines above the current line to the end of the file.

Chapter 5 Quiz

Match each command listed at the left with one of the functions
described at the right:

1. }   A. Move cursor to beginning of line

2. (B. Move cursor to end of line

3. ^   C. Move cursor to previous word

4. H   D. Move cursor to next word

5. 18G   E. Move cursor to previous sentence

6. w   F. Move cursor to next sentence

7. $ G. Move cursor to previous paragraph

8. M   H. Move cursor to next paragraph

9. b   I. Move cursor to top of screen

10. {   J. Move cursor to middle of screen

11. L   K. Move cursor to bottom of screen

12.)   L. Move cursor to line 18

Match each command listed at the left with one of the
functions described at the right:

13. [Ctrl]-[D]   A. Page back

14. [Ctrl]-[L]   B. Page forward

15. z .   C. Scroll up

16. [Ctrl]-[B]   D. Scroll down

17. [Ctrl]-[U]   E. Move current line to middle of screen

18. [Ctrl]-[F]   F. Clear the screen

Match each command listed at the left with one of the functions described at the right:

19. o   A. Insert new text at beginning of line

20. :w   B. Insert new text in front of cursor

21. i   C. Append new text at end of line

22. a   D. Append new text after cursor

23. o   E. Open new line above current line

24. I   F. Open new line below current line

25. :q   G. Return to vi command mode

26. A   H. Write text to file

27. :q!   I. Abandon text without saving

28. Esc   J. Leave vi and return to shell prompt

Write a command to accomplish each of the following:

29. Delete five lines, including the current line and the next four.

30. Delete text from the current location to the end of the line.

31. Delete text from the current location to the beginning of the sentence.

32. Delete five paragraphs.

33. Delete five characters.

34. Search for the word select.

35. Insert text deleted at another location after the cursor (that is, move the text to the current location).

36. Replace select with choose throughout the current file (every occurrence found).

In This Chapter

Internal Communication

External Communication

Using the UNIX Bulletin Board

Internal Communication

- Use the write or talk command to communicate with another user on your system.
- Use the calendar command to send yourself a reminder.
- Use mail or mailx to send electronic mail to another user on your system.

External Communication

- Use the cu command to call another system.
- Use uucp (UNIX-to-UNIX copy) to copy files to or from another system, send and receive intersystem electronic mail, or execute commands on another system.

Using the UNIX Bulletin Board

- UNIX networks, such as uucp, carry an informal bulletin board called Usenet.
- Use the readnews command to read notices on the bulletin board.
- Use the postnews command to post your own notices on the bulletin board.
- Use the .newsrc file to select your own newsgroups for perusal.

6

Communicating with Other Users

This chapter describes different methods for sending and receiving messages both within your own UNIX system and to other UNIX systems.

Internal Communication

UNIX provides three different facilities for exchanging information between users on the same system: terminal-to-terminal communication, automatic reminder service, and electronic mail. The following sections discuss these features in detail.

Terminal-to-Terminal Communication
write and talk

The simplest way to reach another user on your UNIX system is to send a direct terminal-to-terminal message with the write command. For example, to reach Janice immediately, you can send her a message like this:

```
$ write janice
Do you still have that report on last-
 month's sales? -o
  Ctrl-D
$ _
```

NOTE: When you press Ctrl-D, the system does not display a character on your screen.

If Janice is accepting messages, the following appears on her screen immediately:

```
Message from paul (tty05) [Thu Apr 17 09:32:21]...
Do you still have that report on last-
 month's sales? -o
<EOT>
```

If Janice is at her terminal when this message arrives, she can respond with another write command back to Paul:

```
$ write paul
Yes. Do you need it right away? -o
  Ctrl-D

$ _
```

TIP: To indicate that you have completed a message (or a dialogue), you can establish a simple protocol. You can use `-o` at the end of each message for *over* and `-oo` at the conclusion of a dialogue for *over and out*.

A message sent with the `write` command appears right on the recipient's screen, often overwriting other displays. If you are engaged in an important task and don't want to be interrupted by `write` messages, you use the `mesg` command to prevent these messages from being displayed on your screen. Merely add the `n` (no) option, as follows:

```
$ mesg n
$ _
```

After you finish your task, you can accept all messages again by issuing another `mesg` command with the `y` (yes) option, as follows:

```
$ mesg y
$ _
```

Another command that works like `write`, but offers more flexibility, is called `talk`. Like `write`, `talk` requires that both users be logged on at the same time. (You can also block incoming `talk` messages with the `mesg` command.) The difference is that, with `talk`, your screen is divided into two halves, with your messages displayed in the upper half and the other party's messages displayed in the lower half.

If Paul wanted to talk with Janice, the session between them would look something like this:

```
$ talk janice
[No connection yet]
```

If Janice is accepting messages, the following appears on her screen:

```
$
Message from paul
talk: connection requested by paul
talk respond with: talk paul
```

Janice can respond with a reciprocal `talk` command:

```
$ talk paul
```

Once Janice responds, Paul's screen display will be horizontally split, with the following line in the middle of the screen:

```
------[Talking to janice on tt12]------
```

As mentioned, Paul can type outgoing messages above the line and read incoming messages below the line.

A similar display also appears on Janice's screen.

```
------[Talking to paul on tt09]------
```

If Janice is not receiving messages, Paul's screen display shows

```
[Your party would not respond]
```

Sending Reminders to Yourself   calendar

The `calendar` command (not to be confused with the `cal` command) provides you with an electronic reminder service. Since a system utility searches each user's home directory for a file named `calendar` every day (or every other day), all you have to do is create a file with this name and enter your reminders into it. Consider the following example:

```
$ cat calendar
Jun 12    Thursday at 10:00    Department meeting
Jun 16    Monday at 12:00      Deadline for report
Jun 17    Tuesday at 8:00      Monthly PCUG meeting
Jun 20    Friday at 6:00       Farewell party for Steve
$ _
```

The calendar command will search this file for you, extract each line that contains either today's or tomorrow's date, and mail any pertinent lines to you. If you prefer, you can also use other formats for the date, such as June 12 or 6/12. However, whatever format you choose, each line must contain a date. You don't need to wait for the system to check this file; you can also request your own check by executing the calendar command, as follows:

```
$ calendar
Jun 16        Monday at 12:00     Deadline for report
Jun 17        Tuesday at 8:00     Monthly PCUG meeting
$ _
```

Using the Basic Mail Facility   mail

You can use the mail command to send electronic mail to any user on your system. You construct a mail command much the way you construct a write command, as shown in the following example:

```
$ mail henry
I hope you have the proposal ready. We need it
by Wednesday afternoon at 3:00.
Ctrl-D
$ _
```

The mail command also allows you to address a group of users simultaneously, as follows:

```
$ mail anton beverly charles dana
We need to get together sometime on Monday to discuss
the forecast for the second quarter. Let me know what
time will be best for you.
Ctrl-D
$ _
```

These messages will not reach their recipients as quickly as a `write` message. Each recipient may not become aware of the message until the next time he or she logs in, as explained in the following paragraph.

Any time another user sends electronic mail to you, the message will be stored in a file with your login name in directory `/usr/mail`. (For example, if your login name is `steve`, your mail will be in `/usr/mail/steve`.) The next time you log in, you will see the message:

```
You have mail
```

To see what you have received, type the `mail` command without any arguments. The most recent message will appear on the screen, followed by a question mark (?). You can then take action by typing one of the mnemonic codes in Table 6.1. (Note that these often vary from one site to another.)

Table 6.1
Mail options.

Code	Action
* (or ?)	List all the mail commands.
p	Redisplay the current message (print).
d	Delete the current message.
m *user*	Forward the current message to *user*.
s	Save the current message (with header) in file `mbox`.
s *file*	Save the current message (with header) in *file*.
w	Save the current message (without header) in file `mbox`.
w *file*	Save the current message (without header) in *file*.
⏎Enter	Display the next message.
! *command*	Execute *command* without leaving mail.
q	Quit mail (retain only unexamined messages in mailbox).
x	Exit mail (retain all messages in mailbox).

Each time you take an action other than exiting mail (q or x), the mail command displays another message. The following sample session examines several messages:

```
$ mail
From judy Fri Feb 18 10:15:36    1994
We're still working on the sales figures.
Can you wait another week?
? s sales.judy
From will Thu Feb 17 16:08:49 1994
I need the sales figures for the Monday
morning meeting. Can you help me?
? m judy
From peter Thu Feb 17 13:27:42 1994
Can you play tennis this Saturday morning?
We're going to play doubles at 10:00.
? q
$ mail peter
yes! I'll be there at 9:30 to warm up.
Ctrl-D
$ _
```

In this sequence, you saved the first message in a file called sales.judy. Next, you forwarded the second message to Judy. Then, you quit mail and returned to the shell prompt, from which you mailed a response to the third message. Because you used the q command to leave mail, the three messages you previously examined will be gone the next time you check your mail.

If you want to reverse the order in which your messages are displayed, so that the first one received is also the first one displayed, you can use the -r (reverse order) option, as follows:

```
$ mail -r
From peter Thu Feb 19 13:27:42 1994
```

```
Can you play tennis this Saturday morning?
Were going to play doubles at 10:00.
? _
```

The -f option of mail lets you display mail in a file that you choose. Ordinarily, your mail is stored in /usr/mail/*name* (in which *name* is your login name). If you don't specify a name after the command, UNIX uses the default name mbox. The following two examples show how to use this option:

```
$ mail -f          Read mail in file
                   /usr/mail/name/mbox
$ mail -f sales    Read mail in file
                   /usr/mail/name/sales
```

Using the Extended Mail Facility   mailx

The mailx command, which is actually the Berkeley mail command, is an enhanced version of mail that contains many more features. If it is available on your system, you can use mailx instead of mail. One difference you will notice right away is that mailx displays a Subject prompt that lets you give your message a title before you actually type. Here is an example of sending mail with mailx:

```
$ mailx anton beverly charles dana
Subject: Meeting on Forecast
We need to get together sometime on Monday to discuss
the forecast for the second quarter. Let me know what
time will be best for you.
Ctrl-D
$ _
```

Another enhancement of mailx lets you interrupt text entry in the middle of your message, execute a command, and then resume typing your message. For example, suppose you are in the middle of your message and you suddenly remember that you omitted James and Elaine from the list of addressees. You can *escape* from the message with a command such as the following:

```
$ mailx anton beverly charles dana
Subject: Meeting on Forecast
We need to get together sometime on Monday to discuss
the forecast for the second
~t james elaine
```

Every escape command begins with a tilde (~) and includes at least one other character (t in the preceding example). Some of the other escape commands available in mailx are listed in Table 6.2.

Table 6.2
Escape Commands

Command	Action
~?	List all escape commands.
~s *subject*	Enter a subject title called *subject*.
~t *user(s)*	Add *user(s)* to the To list.
~c *user(s)*	Add *user(s)* to the Copy list.
~h	Display To, Subject, and Copy prompts.
~r *file*	Read text into your message from another *file*.
~w *file*	Write your message to another *file*.
~v	Use vi to edit your message.
~p	Display (print) the current message.
~f *message(s)*	Read in other *message(s)*.
~m *message(s)*	Read in other *message(s)* (indented to the first tab stop).
~! *command*	Run a UNIX *command* and return to mailx.
~¦ *command*	Pipe the message through *command* (UNIX command).
~q	Quit mailx (save current message in file dead.letter).
~x	Exit mailx (discard current message).

To find out whether you have received any messages from other users, enter the `mailx` command without any options. The `mailx` command then summarizes the mail you have received by displaying a *header* (a one-line synopsis) for each message. Each header is assigned a sequence number and is labeled with a one-letter code near the left margin:

N   New

R   Read

U   Unread

The `mailx` command also displays the size of the message in lines and characters (for example, 3/96), an optional subject, a pointer to the current message, and a question mark prompt, as shown in the following example:

```
$ mailx
'/usr/mail/jeff': 5 messages 2 new 3 unread
  U   1  james  Tue  Apr 16  09:36  3/96  Goals meeting
  U   2  paul   Tue  Apr 16  09:51  4/104 Clock times
  U   3  nancy  Tue  Apr 16  11:23  2/72
  N   4  ralph  Tue  Apr 16  11:42  5/167 VCR type
 >N   5  kelly  Tue  Apr 16  12:05  3/89  PTV changes
  ? _
```

At the ? prompt, you can use any of the commands in Table 6.3. The full command names are shown here, but the first letter is all you have to enter. In the following table, *list* is always optional (as indicated by the brackets [ ]). By default, it represents the current message. However, you can define *list* so that it becomes a list of messages specified by number, sender, type, or subject.

Commands	Action
?	List all commands with explanations.
list	List all commands without explanations.
headers [*list*]	Display designated headers.
z	Display the next page of headers.
z-	Display the last page of headers.
from [*list*]	Display header(s).
top [*list*]	Display only the first five lines of message(s).
next [*message #*]	Display the next message.
type [*list*]	Display message(s) (same as print).
preserve [*list*]	Preserve message(s) in mbox (same as hold).
save [*list*] *file*	Save message(s) (append) to *file*.
delete [*list*]	Delete message(s).
undelete [*list*]	Undelete deleted message(s).
edit [*list*]	Edit message(s).
Reply [*list*]	Reply to sender only.
reply [*list*]	Reply to sender and to other recipients.
cd [*directory*]	Change to directory (home if name omitted).
¦ command	Execute UNIX command and return to mailx.
quit	Quit (save only unread messages in mbox).
exit	Exit (save all messages in mbox).

Table 6.3
Mailx Commands

The -f option of mailx, like its counterpart in mail, lets you display mail in a file that you choose. Ordinarily, your mail is stored in /usr/mail/*name* (in which *name* is your login name). If you don't specify a name after the command, UNIX uses the default name mbox. The following two examples show you how to use this option:

```
$ mailx-f            Read mail in file
                     /usr/mail/name/mbox
$ mailx -f sales     Read mail in file
                     /usr/mail/name/sales
```

External Communication

UNIX offers several ways to communicate with users on other UNIX systems, including the cu (call up) and uucp (UNIX-to-UNIX copy) commands. The following sections describe these commands in detail.

Calling Another System   cu

The cu (call up) command allows you to communicate with another UNIX (or non-UNIX) system by dialing a telephone number. With this simple command, you can access any machine with a phone number and a serial port. If you have the proper permissions, you can also communicate with another UNIX system and log into it as if you were a local user. A technician or a programmer could use this command to log into a UNIX system remotely and conduct diagnostic or other tests. The cu command can also be used to test connections when you set up uucp for your UNIX system.

For example, suppose the number for another system is (408) 555-2000, and suppose both systems have been set up to communicate at a rate of 2,400 bits per second. Then you could use a command, such as the following, to call the other system. Assuming that the other system is also a UNIX system and that you have established a login account on that system, you can then proceed to log in, as shown in the following sequence:

```
$ cu -s2400 4085552000

Connected
login: paul
Password:
% _
```

NOTE: Specify the data rate (or speed) with the -s option. The telephone number doesn't require an option letter.

For the sake of simplicity, let's assume that the other system presents a C shell prompt. After you're connected, you can execute some commands on your own system and some on the other system. If you remember that the C shell prompt (%) represents the other system, we can eliminate some of the confusion in the discussion that follows.

If another system—called gemini—belongs to your uucp network, you may be able to call the system with a simpler command line than in the preceding example:

```
$ cu gemini

Connected
login: paul
Password:
gemini% _
```

If the serial line or modem on the other system is busy, then you may not get a connection right away, and the sequence will look like this:

```
$ cu gemini

Connect failed: No Device Available

$ _
```

If you use the wrong name, or a name that is not listed in the appropriate uucp file, the sequence may look like this:

```
$ cu lemony

Connect failed: Requested device/system name not
known.

$ _
```

A certain file contains the names of the systems on the uucp network that you can access. Before System V, Release 3, this file was called /usr/lib/uucp/L.sys; since System V, Release 3, its name has been changed to /usr/lib/uucp/Systems. To display a list of these systems, use the uuname command, as follows:

```
$ uuname
gemini
saturn
jupiter
neptune
venus
$ _
```

After you've made a connection and logged in, you can use several commands to interact with that system. For example, to send a file called report to the other system (UNIX or non-UNIX), you could use a command such as the following:

```
% ~> report
18 lines/1324 characters
% _
```

If both are UNIX systems and if you have the necessary permissions, you can use the following command to send a file (in this case report):

```
% ~%put report

... {system message}
% _
```

If both are UNIX systems and if directory permissions give you the authority, you can copy a file (sale) from the other system to your working directory. Here is the command:

```
% ~%take sale

...{system message}
% _
```

To run a command on your own system (as though you weren't connected to another system), precede the command by ~!. For example, to display today's date, you could use the following command:

```
% ~!date
Tue Mar 1 09:38:12 PST 1994
% _
```

Although you will see the output of the date on your screen, the other system will never even be aware that you entered the command.

To run a command on your own system, but send the output to the other system (rather than to your terminal), precede the command with ~$. For example, suppose you would like to send a file to a non-UNIX system. First, make sure the other system is prepared to receive a file; then, enter a command such as the following:

```
% ~$ put sales.1994
% _
```

This sends the text to the other system, not to your terminal. After the other system has received the file, you will regain access to that system. To change directories on your own system, use cd with the prefix ~%, not ~!, as shown here:

```
% ~%cd admin
% _
```

After you've finished exchanging files, you can log out and terminate the cu session with the ~. command, as follows:

```
% Ctrl-D
login: ~.
Disconnected
$ _
```

The Bourne shell prompt ($) is from your own system, and it indicates that the cu session is over. In some instances, the ~. command may log you out and disconnect the systems at the same time.

Sometimes, it can be useful to keep a record of your communication with another system by capturing the session in a file. You can do this by piping the entire session through the tee command. The following command line illustrates how you could begin the cu session:

```
$ cu -s2400 4085552000 ¦ tee capture.file

Connected login: paul
Password:

% _
```

Now, proceed through the session as described in this section, exchanging files as desired. After you end the session and return to your own system, you can display the contents of the capture file with a command like this:

```
$ pg capture.file
```

```
[Remote session]

$ _
```

UNIX-to-UNIX Communication   uucp

Strictly speaking, uucp (UNIX-to-UNIX copy) is just one UNIX command that is used for copying files. However, in everyday conversation, the term uucp is understood to include a suite of related commands (uucp, uux, and others), along with a network of UNIX systems and an inter-system mail facility. If uucp has been set up on your system, you can send mail to and receive mail from users on other systems, copy files to other systems, and execute commands on other systems.

Sending Mail to Users on Another System

The uucp network provides UNIX users with something similar to what commercial information services such as CompuServe and The Source provide personal computer users. One difference is that uucp is included with each UNIX system at no extra charge. For UNIX systems in the same building, uucp offers a means of sharing resources, such as laser printers, plotters, and high-speed tape drives.

After uucp has been set up on your system and on other systems, you can send mail to users on all of those systems as if they were on your own. For the simplest example, assume that your system is connected directly to another system called neptune and that you want to send a message to user bill. Then, you can send your message in the following way:

```
$ mail neptune!bill

The volleyball tournament will begin Saturday
afternoon at 1:00 in Green Oaks Park. Can you make it?

Terry
Ctrl-D
$ _
```

On the uucp network, the exclamation mark (!) functions like the slash (/) within your own system's file system. The exclamation mark (sometimes called *bang*) separates the name of one system from the name of another and separates the name of the destination system from the name of the user.

After the message has been forwarded to neptune, Bill has been notified. After Bill checks his mail, Bill will see something like the following:

```
From uucp Tue Apr 19 14:06 PDT 1994
>From terry Mon Apr 18 17:23 PDT 1994 remote from jupiter
Status: R
The volleyball tournament will begin Saturday
afternoon at 1:00 in Green Oaks park. Can you make it?
Terry
```

Now Bill can reply, using a command such as the following:

```
$ mail jupiter!terry
Yes. I'll bring Paula with me.
Ctrl-D
$ _
```

Naturally, sending electronic mail to a user on another system takes even longer (usually at least a day) than to a user on your own system. However, if the other system is far away, this can still be a fast way to communicate.

Next, suppose the user to whom you want to send a message is on a system that is not directly connected to yours. In that case, you will have to route your message through other systems. For example, Figure 6.1 shows a group of UNIX systems connected in a uucp network.

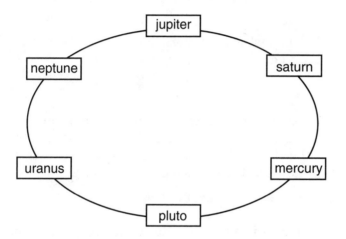

Figure 6.1
A Few UNIX systems on a network.

Bill can't send mail from his system (neptune) directly to Jeff on system mercury. Instead, he has to route it through jupiter and saturn, as shown in the following example:

```
$ mail jupiter!saturn!mercury!jeff
The volleyball tournament will begin Saturday
afternoon at 1:00 in Green Oaks Park. Can you make it?

Bill
Ctrl-D
$ _
```

People who work on UNIX systems every day and communicate through any kind of public forum often list their uucp addresses instead of their phone numbers for replies. It is not uncommon to see a listing such as the following at the end of a notice on an electronic bulletin board or following an article in a magazine:

```
J. R. Ewing
utvax!dallas!southfork!jre
```

NOTE: The last three letters in this example represent a login name.

This listing gives you the routing information you need to send a message to J.R. Ewing. If there are several alternate routes to the destination, these are listed between a pair of braces, as shown in the following address path:

```
{ucivax,trwb}!ucla-cs!lcc!hxn
```

This address is equivalent to the following two addresses, and you may select either address:

```
ucivax!ucla-cs!lcc!hxn
trwb!ucla-cs!lcc!hxn
```

Copying Files to Another System

Next, we'll discuss the second main function of the uucp network, which is copying files to other systems. In the interest of system security, one directory (called /usr/spool/uucppublic) has been designated as the place to send and receive files between systems. Therefore, the procedure for sending a file to someone on another system requires the following four steps:

1. If necessary, give other users read permission for the file.

2. Use the ordinary cp command to copy the file from your working directory to /usr/spool/uucppublic.

3. Use cd to move to /usr/spool/uucppublic.

4. Use uucp to copy the file to the other system.

In the following example, Terry on system jupiter sends a file named /usr/terry/admin/sales.1994 to Bill on system neptune. (For the sake of simplicity, assume that the two systems are directly connected on the uucp network.)

```
$ pwd
/usr/terry/admin
$ chmod o+r sales.1994
$ cp sales.1994 /usr/spool/uucppublic
$ cd /usr/spool/uucppublic
$ uucp sales.1994 neptune!/usr/spool/uucppublic/
sales.1994
$ _
```

The last command line can be abbreviated by substituting ~/ for /usr/spool/uucppublic, as follows:

```
$ uucp sales.1994 neptune!~/sales.1994
$ _
```

If you're using the C shell, you must escape each exclamation mark with a backslash (\), as shown on the following command line:

```
$ uucp sales.1994 neptune\!/usr/spool/uucppublic/
sales.1994
$ _
```

NOTE: The exclamation mark has another meaning in the C shell.

You can use the -m option of the uucp command to have UNIX mail you a message after the copy has been completed, as shown on this command line (Bourne shell):

```
$ uucp -m sales.1994 neptune!/usr/spool/uucppublic/
sales.1994
$ _
```

Once a copy of sales.1994 has been placed in /usr/spool/ uucppublic on system neptune, a message to this effect will be mailed to the sender.

The uucp command, like the cp command, supports the use of wild-card characters for selecting files. For example, suppose Terry wants to send three files called sales.1994, costs.1994, and summary.1994. The complete sequence for copying these files will be as follows:

```
$ pwd
/usr/terry/admin
$ cp *.1994 /usr/spool/uucppublic
$ cd /usr/spool uucppublic
$ uucp *.1994 neptune!~/
$ _
```

Executing Commands on Another System

The third major function of uucp is that it lets you execute commands on another system with the uux command. Suppose system neptune has a laser printer that is being shared by several other systems, including jupiter. In that case, a user on jupiter can route printing requests to the laser printer by executing a command like the following:

```
$ cat report ¦ uux - neptune!lp
$ _
```

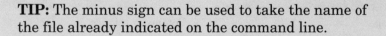

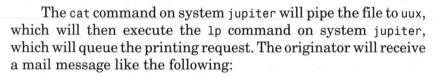

TIP: The minus sign can be used to take the name of the file already indicated on the command line.

The cat command on system jupiter will pipe the file to uux, which will then execute the lp command on system jupiter, which will queue the printing request. The originator will receive a mail message like the following:

```
From uucp Thu mar 17 10:42 PST 1994
>From uucp Thu Mar 17 11:15 PST 1994 remote from neptune
Status: R

uuxqt cmd (lp) status (exit 0, signal 0)
```

Using the UNIX Bulletin Board

Several networks, including uucp, ARPANET, Berknet, and X.25, provide an environment for an informal bulletin board called *Usenet* (Users Network). If Usenet has been set up at your installation, you can participate in the discussions on it. You can read notices posted by other users, and you can post your own notices for others to read.

Newsgroups

Notices are categorized into approximately 250 newsgroups, each of which contains messages concerning a limited special-interest subject. These newsgroups focus on various academic subjects, political issues, and recreational activities. The newsgroups have been placed in a set of seven major categories (see Table 6.4). Note that your installation may have added specialized newsgroups.

Table 6.4
Usenet Categories

Category	Description
comp	Computer science
misc	Miscellaneous
news	Net news and net users
rec	Recreational activities
sci	Natural sciences
soc	Social topics
talk	Discussion topics

To find out exactly which newsgroups are found at your site, you can display the contents of /usr/lib/news/newsgroups, using either the pg or more commands, as follows:

```
$ more /user/lib/news/newsgroups
ca.general        Of general interest to readers in
                  California only
ca.driving        California freeways and backroads
ca.earthquakes    What's shakin' in California
ca.environment    Environmental concerns in California
ca.news           USENET status and usage in California
ca.news.group     Existing or proposed newsgroups for
                  'ca' distribution
ca.politics       Political topics of interest to
                  California readers only
ca.test           Tests of 'ca' distribution articles
ca.unix           Unix discussion/help
ca.wanted         For Sale/Wanted postings throughout
                  California
junk              Articles that we have no newsgroup
                  for
comp.ai           Artificial intelligence discussions
comp.ai.digest    Artificial Intelligence discussions
                  (Moderated)
comp.ai.edu       Applications of Artificial
                  Intelligence to Education
...
$ _
```

Some newsgroups are for specific geographic areas (as in many groups in the preceding listing). There may be a category for your state, using the two-letter postal abbreviation as a prefix. For example, you may find the groups ca.driving, ca.wanted, and so on, in California-based systems. Other prefixes include usa (United States), can (Canada), na (North America), and so on.

One of the first things you need to do after you peruse the bulletin board is to select the newsgroups that interest you. (A list of newsgroups is called a *subscription list*, and the act of indicating a preference for a particular newsgroup is referred to as *subscribing* to that newsgroup.)

Reading the Bulletin Board

Checking the bulletin board is similar to checking your mail. You request a look at the notices for the day, the first notice appears, and you have a number of options you can select. To read the day's news, you can use one of three commands (readnews, vnews, or rn), depending on what is available at your installation. In this chapter, we'll assume that you are using readnews. You can use the following command from the shell prompt:

```
$ readnews
```

If you want to review your current subscription list, you can include the -s option, as follows:

```
$ readnews -s
```

To show only those articles that belong to newsgroups rec.games.chess and rec.pets, you can use a command line like the following:

```
$ readnews -n rec.games.chess rec.pets tb
```

The options that are available to you when you are perusing the day's articles are listed in Table 6.5.

Table 6.5
Bulletin Board Options

Option	Action
?	Help
N	Go to the next newsgroup
U	Unsubscribe from the current newsgroup
b	Back up one article in the current newsgroup
-	Return to the previous article
+	Skip the current article
e	Erase the current article
s *file*	Save the current article in *file*
r	Reply to the author of an article
f	Post a follow-up to an article
Del	Delete the rest of an article
x	Exit

Writing to the Bulletin Board

If you want to comment about an article that you've read, use the f option (follow-up) listed in Table 6.5. Then your comment will automatically be associated with the original article. On Usenet, as on most bulletin boards, commercial notices are not welcome.

If you want to comment about something not previously referred to in Usenet, use the postnews command in most instances (or Pnews if your system has rn). Here is how to begin:

```
$ postnews
Is this message in response to some other message: n
Subject: Bird-watching in eastern Missouri
Keywords: birds cardinals
Newsgroups (enter one at a time, end with a blank
line):
For a list of newsgroups, type ?
>rec.birds
>
Distribution (default=mo, ? for help) : mo
```

When the opening prompt asks you whether this is a follow-up, your answer should be no. (If the answer is yes, use the f option of readnews, not postnews.) If your reply is no, the next prompt asks you for the subject of your article. Enter a name that is as specific as possible.

Next, you will be prompted for pertinent newsgroups. If you aren't sure, type ? to display a list and make your selection. After this, you will be prompted for distribution to other users. Restrict the distribution to the smallest geographic area possible.

Finally, the editor will begin, and you can enter the text of your article. After you've saved your article, you will see a message such as the following:

```
Posting article ...
Article posted successfully.
A copy has been saved in /usr/paul/author_copy
```

You may also leave a signature at the end of each article posted with postnews (or Pnews). Simply place the desired information in your home directory in a file called .signature, and your posting program will automatically insert it for you. Here is an example of such a file:

```
$ cat .signature
Paul Fletcher (213) 555-1212
4243 Wilshire Boulevard
Beverly Hills, CA 90211
ucivax!ucla-cs!projects!paul
```

Setting Up to Use the Bulletin Board

Unless you specify otherwise, Usenet will give you a default subscription list, usually consisting of the general newsgroups. To select your own newsgroups, you can enter a customized subscription list in your home directory, using a file named .newsrc. (The file must have this name; no other name can be used.)

For example, suppose you want to subscribe to newsgroups `rec.arts.books`, `news.misc`, `comp.unix`, and `ca.general`. Create a file called `.newsrc` (or retrieve the file if it already exists), and enter these names on the options line. Separate individual names with commas, as illustrated here:

```
$ cat .newsrc
options -n rec.arts.books,news.misc,comp.unix,
 ca.general
$ _
```

If your list requires more than one line, begin each subsequent line with a blank space. Note that when you start readnews, the articles are displayed in the order you indicate in `.newsrc`.

When setting up your subscription list in `.newsrc`, you can use the `all` option to select all of a set of newsgroups or the `!` symbol to exclude all of a set. For example, to include everything related to UNIX, but exclude all `talk` news, you could set up the options line as follows:

```
$ cat .newsrc
options -n comp.unix.all,!talk.all
$ _
```

Chapter 6 Quiz

Match each command listed at the left with a function described at the right:

1. `mail`   A. Send a message directly from your terminal to another user's terminal (same system).

2. `uucp`   B. Prevent messages form being sent by other users to your terminal.

3. `mesg`   C. Send a reminder to yourself about an appointment.

4. `mailx`   D. Send a message to another user either on your own system or on another system.

5. `postnews` E. Send a message to another user via the extended electronic mail facility.

6. `write`   F. Call another UNIX system to check out the dial-in number.

7. `readnews` G. Send a copy of one of your files to a user on another system.

8. `cu`   H. Print a copy of one of your files on another system.

9. `calendar` I. Read today's articles on the Usenet bulletin board.

10. `uux`   J. Post an article of your own on the Usenet bulletin board.

Write a command (or a series of commands) to perform each of the following functions:

11. Send a message, which you have stored in a file called `hello`, directly to Sean (login name `sean`).

12. Prevent messages from being sent directly to your terminal.

13. Check on reminders that you have left for yourself.

14. Send a message, which you have already typed and stored in a file called `urgent`, to Linda, Mike, and Paula (login names `linda`, `mike`, and `paula`) via electronic mail.

15. Check for electronic mail that you've received from other users (extended facility).

16. After performing Exercise 15, you discover that Tanya (login name `tanya`) has mailed a message to you and four other users. Now, send a reply to Tanya and the other four.

17. Log into a neighboring UNIX system on the uucp network called `gemini`.

18. Log into `gemini`, and capture your remote session in a file in your working directory called `gemini.session`.

19. Send a message to Ken (login name `ken`) on neighboring UNIX system `minerva`.

20. Print a report called `sales.3Q` on a printer on the `minerva` system.

In This Chapter

Formatting Tools

Formatting Paragraphs

Formatting Display Text

Formatting Lists

Other Formatting Features

Formatting Tools

- Use the `nroff` command to format for fixed-width printers, such as daisy-wheel printers and line-printers.
- Use the `troff` command to format for variable-width printers, such as laser printers and typesetters.
- Use the `deroff` utility to remove formatting requests from a file.

Formatting Paragraphs

The following requests are used with the `mm` macro package:

- Use `.P0` to form a block paragraph.
- Use `.P1` to form an indented paragraph.

Formatting Lists

The following requests are used with the `mm` macro package:

- Use `.BL` to form a bullet list.
- Use `.DL` to form a dash list.
- Use `.ML` to form a mark list.
- Use `.RL` to form a reference list.
- Use `.VL` to form a variable-item list.
- Use `.AL` to form an auto-number list.

Formatting UNIX Documents

In Chapter 5, you learned how to create documents and enter text with the vi editor. You use a different program to format text. In UNIX, as in mainframe operating systems such as VM, editing and formatting are separate functions.

Formatting Programs

Formatting for UNIX began in the late 1960s with a text `runoff` program from the Massachusetts Institute of Technology (MIT) that was called `roff`. Joseph Ossanna developed an enhanced version of `roff` that was called the new `runoff` program, or `nroff`; then he developed a further enhancement for phototypesetters that was called the typesetter `runoff` program, or `troff`.

The `nroff` program (pronounced "EN-roff") works with line-printers and daisy-wheel printers, which produce typewriter-like characters having a fixed width. Although nroff includes most of the features of troff, it doesn't handle changes in point size and proportional spacing.

The troff program (pronounced "TEE-roff") works with typesetting equipment and laser printers, which produce characters having variable widths. This program includes every feature of nroff, plus those that produce font changes and proportional spacing.

Both of these programs, like VM's SCRIPT, employ embedded commands, or *requests*, that have short mnemonic names. Most of these requests begin with periods, like WordStar's dot commands, and many require following arguments.

Both nroff and troff allow you to build *macros* from the basic requests. Using this built-in macro feature, people have developed several macro packages derived from nroff and troff. Focusing on the formatting needs of ordinary users, these macro packages are designed to simplify the job of formatting a document. Three of the most prominent macro packages are:

ms   The mainstay of UNIX Version 7.

me   The macro package of choice for Berkeley versions of UNIX.

mm   The program selected for UNIX System V.

This chapter introduces text formatting with the mm macro package.

NOTE: A *macro* is a special command that includes other commands.

In addition to macro packages, other programs can also be used for formatting. Preprocessors handle specialized kinds of text for nroff and troff, including the following:

tbl   Formats tables for both programs.

negn   Formats mathematical expressions for nroff.

eqn   Formats mathematical expressions for troff.

Finally, the following two utilities handle miscellaneous tasks related to formatting:

checkeq Checks usage in material to be formatted by neqn or eqn.

deroff Removes formatting requests from a file, including all those for nroff, troff, tbl, neqn, and eqn.

The mm **Macro Package**

This chapter concentrates on the mm macro package. Formatting a document is accomplished in three general steps:

1. Enter the text with an editor such as vi.

2. Embed the formatting requests.

3. Process the formatted document, using a command line such as one of the following:

```
$ mm [option(s)] file(s)
$ nroff -cm [option(s)] file(s)
$ troff -cm [option(s)] file(s)
```

TIP: To preview a document on your screen, without printing it, you can use the following command:

```
$ mm file ¦ pg
```

The default printing characteristics for mm are as follows:

10 characters per inch (10 cpi, or pica)

6 lines per inch

3/4-inch offset for the left margin

60 characters per line (6 inches)

The following sections describe the individual formatting requests, including those used to take care of paragraphs, display text, lists, highlighting, spacing, and changes in point size. In each example, you will see the formatted document at the left and the printed result at the right.

Formatting Paragraphs

Paragraphs are the basic units in most documents. You have two formatting choices when you use mm, each selected with the .P request. You must precede every paragraph with a separate request. Both types of paragraphs are filled to the current margins.

Forming a Block Paragraph   .P 0

To produce a block paragraph, without indentation for the first line, place a .P 0 (dot P zero) request above the first line.

Original Document	**Printed Result**
| ```
.P 0
This is a block paragraph,
with all lines
left-justified. The first
line is unindented.
``` | ```
This is a block
paragraph,with all
lines left-justified.
The first line is
unindented.
``` |

Forming an Indented Paragraph   .P 1

To produce an indented paragraph, with the first line indented, place a .P 1 (dot P one) request above the first line.

Original Document	**Printed Result**

`.P 1`
`This is an indented`
`paragraph, which`
`begins with an`
`indented line. The`
`rest of the lines are`
`flush left.`
	`  This is an indented`
	`paragraph, which begins`
	`with an indented line.`
	`The rest of the lines`
	`are flush left.`

Formatting Display Text

You can display text on the printed page by setting it apart with various combinations of spacing, indentation, and centering. With mm, you have four formats to choose from, depending on what you want to display. You can also select between a *static* display and a *floating* display. Both types of display move text to the next page if it doesn't fit on the current page. The difference is that a floating display allows subsequent text to flow ahead of the display into the gap left on the preceding page. The basic commands for setting up displays are as follows:

.DS   Begin a static display

.DF   Begin a floating display

.DE   End either type of display

The examples that follow use the .DS request. However, you can substitute the .DF request on any line in which you see .DS.

Forming an Indented Display   .DS I

To indent display text five spaces, you can include the I (indent) argument with the .DS (or .DF) request, as shown on the following page:

Original Document	Printed Result

``
.P 1
Here is an example of a
quotation that is set apart
as display text:
.DS I
"I'm mad as hell and I'm
not going to take this
anymore."
.DE
.P 1
With these words, Howard
Beale concluded his
broadcast in Network.
``
	``
	    Here is an example of a
	    quotation that is set apart
	    as display text:
	
	        "I'm mad as hell and I'm not
	        going to take this anymore."
	
	    With these words, Howard
	    Beale concluded his broadcast
	    in Network.
	``

Forming a Double-Indented Display   .DS I F n

If you want the display text indented from both margins, include the I (indent) argument, the F (fill) argument, and a number *n* to indicate how many spaces you want to indent from the right margin. The following example requests an indentation of five spaces from the left margin, with text filled up to five spaces from the right margin:

Original Document	Printed Result

``
.P 1
Here is an example of a
quotation that is set apart
as display text:
.DS I F 5
"I'm mad as hell
and I'm not going
to take this any-
more."
``
	``
	    Here is an example of a
	    quotation that is set apart
	    as display text:
	
	        "I'm mad as hell
	        and I'm not going
	        to take this
	        anymore."
	``

```
.DE
.P 1
With these words, Howard
Beale concluded his
broadcast in "Network."
```

```
                With these words, Howard
                Beale concluded his broadcast
                in "Network."
```

Forming a Centered Display   .DS C

For a title or for verses of poetry, you may want to center your display text. Simply include the C (center) argument with your .DS (or .DF) request, as follows:

Original Document   **Printed Result**

```
.P1
He quoted from the
work named below:
.DS C
"Flying High"
by
Jerry Jett
.DE
.P 1
Then he went on to
discuss the importance
of air safety.
```

```
 He quoted from the work
 named below:


         "Flying High"
             by
          Jerry Jett


 Then he went on to
 discuss the importance of air
 safety.
```

Forming a Blocked Display   .DS CB

A variation of the centered display is the blocked display, in which the text is centered with left-justification. For this style, include the CB (center block) argument with your .DS (or .DF) request, as shown in this example:

Original Document	Printed Result
| ```
.P 1
He quoted from "The Fly" by
William Blake:
.DS CB
Am not I
A fly like thee?
Or art not thou
A man like me?
.DE
.P 1
Then he went on to quote
from Robert Burns and
other poets.
``` | ```
   He quoted from "The Fly"
by William Blake:

      Am not I
      A fly like thee?
      Or art not thou
      A man like me?


   Then he went on to quote
from Robert Burns and other
poets.
``` |

Formatting Lists

You can set up a list of items in any of several different styles with mm. Each item can begin with a bullet, a hyphen, a letter, a number, or a word. There is a different mm request for each type of list; however, you must precede each item with .LI (list item) and end every list with the .LE (list end) request. The examples that follow illustrate six different types of lists.

Forming a Bullet List   .BL

To precede each item in your list with a bullet, use the .BL (bullet list) request. Under nroff, the bullets are simulated (as plus signs); under troff, the bullets are real. Here is an example:

Original Document	Printed Result
| ```
.P 1
The steps to produce a
formatted document are
as follows:
.BL
``` | ```
   The steps to produce a
formatted document are as
follows:
``` |

```
.LI                              + Enter the text with vi
Enter the text with vi
.LI                              + Embed the formatting
Embed the formatting               requests
requests
.LI                              + Process the file with mm
Process the file with mm
.LE
```

Forming a Dash List   .DL

To precede each item in your list with a hyphen (not a dash) rather than a bullet, use the .DL (dash list) request, as follows:

Original Document   **Printed Result**

```
.P 1                               The steps to produce a
The steps to produce a             formatted document are as
formatted document are             follows:
as follows:
.DL
.LI                                   - Enter the text with vi
Enter the text with vi
.LI                                   - Embed the formatting
Embed the formatting                    requests
requests
.LI                                   - Process the file
                                        with mm
Process the file with mm
.LE
```

Forming a Mark List   .ML

If you want to select a character (or a sequence of characters) to precede each item, use the .ML (mark list) request, with the character(s) following the request. In the following example, we'll request an asterisk (*) in front of each item in the list:

Original Document	Printed Result
| ```
.P 1
The steps to produce a
formatted document are
as follows:
.ML*
.LI
Enter the text with vi
.LI
Embed the formatting
requests
.LI
Process the file with mm
.LE
``` | The steps to produce a formatted document are as follows:<br><br>* Enter the text with vi<br><br>* Embed the formatting requests<br><br>* Process the file with mm |

Forming a Reference List   .RL

If you want to list references by number (such as a list of sources for quotations), use the .RL (reference list) request. The results will be similar to the results in the preceding three examples, but the items will be automatically numbered (within brackets) in sequence:

Original Document	Printed Result
| ```
.P 1
The sources for quotations
cited in this book are
as follows
.RL
.LI
Arthur, Quinlan P., "New
Ways, New Winds"
.LI
Betters, Anne G., "Get
What You Want"
.LI
Childress, Layne R., "Why
Not Be a Winner?"
.LE
``` | The sources for quotations cited in this book are as follows:<br><br>[1] Arthur, Quinlan P., "New Ways, New Winds"<br>[2] Betters, Anne G., "Get What You Want"<br>[3] Childress, Layne R., "Why Not Be a Winner?" |

Forming a Variable-Item List .VL

If you want to list definitions or explanations with a different term at the beginning of each item, use the .VL (variable-item list) request. After the .VL request, you must provide a number that indicates how many columns you need between the current left margin and the starting column for each definition or explanation. Note that this number must be at least two more than the length of the longest term in the list. (The following example uses 10.) After each .LI request, you have to type the term for that item. This term is what varies from item to item (along with the definition or explanation that follows).

Original Document

```
.P 1
The preprocessors for mm,
nroff, and troff are as
follows:
.VL 10
.LI tbl
Formats tables for nroff
and troff
.LI negn
Formats equations for
nroff
.LI eqn
Formats equations for
troff
.LE
```

Printed Result

The preprocessors for mm, nroff, and troff are as follows:

tbl   Formats tables for nroff and troff

negn   Formats equations for nroff

eqn   Formats equations for troff

Forming an Auto-Number List .AL

In its simplest form, an *auto-number* list is similar to a reference list. Each item is numbered sequentially, beginning at 1. However, the .AL (auto-number list) request has additional options and is much more versatile. Following is an example of a simple .AL request without options:

Original Document	Printed Result
| ```
.P 1
The sources for quotations
cited in this book are
as follows:
.AL
.LI
Arthur, Quinlan P., "New
Ways, New Winds"
.LI
Betters, Anne G., "Get
What You Want"
.LI
Childress, Layne R., "Why
Not Be a Winner?"
.LE
``` | ```
   The sources for quotations
cited in this book are as
follows:

1. Arthur, Quinlan P., "New
   Ways, New Winds"

2. Betters, Anne G., "Get
   What You Want"

3. Childress, Layne R.,
   "Why Not Be a Winner?"
``` |

In the preceding example, the results are similar to the results for .VL. However, you can also request Roman numerals or letters rather than Arabic numbers. Type one of the following options after the .AL request to select the appropriate numbering scheme:

A	Uppercase LETTERS
a	Lowercase letters
I	Uppercase Roman NUMERALS
i	Lowercase Roman numerals

The following example selects uppercase letters:

Original Document	Printed Result
| ```
.P 1
The main topics to be
addressed tonight are
as follows:
.AL A
.LI
Making new contacts
``` | ```
   The main topics to be
addressed tonight are as
follows:

A. Making new contacts
``` |

```
.LI                          B. Cultivating new ideas
Cultivating new ideas
.LI                          C. Signing contracts
Signing contracts
.LE
```

By nesting .AL requests, you can construct an outline. Just use I for the first .AL request, A for the second, 1 for the third, and so on. The numbering for a given level remains in effect until the .LE request that ends the list. Here is an example of an outline:

Original Document   **Printed Result**

```
.AL I  [Start of Roman list]    I. Setup
.LI
Setup                              A. Introduce Dorothy
.AL A  [Start of "ABC" list]
.LI                                B. Introduce the
Introduce Dorothy                     others:
.LI
Introduce the others:                 1. Aunt and
.AL 1 [Start of "123" list]              uncle
.LI
Aunt and uncle                        2. Farm hands
.LI
Farm hands                            3. Mean
.LI                                      neighbor
Mean neighbor
.LI                                   4. County fair
County fair charlatan                    charlatan
.LE    [End of "123" list]
.LI                                C. Describe Dorothy's
Describe Dorothy's desire             desire to get away
to get away
.LI                                D. Cyclone sequence
Cyclone sequence ends Act I           ends Act I
.LE    [End of "ABC" list]
.LI                            II. Chase: the quest
for the
Chase: the quest for              wizard
the wizard
```

```
 . . .                              . . .
.LI                          III. Payoff: the return home
Payoff: the return home
 . . .                              . . .
.LE    [End of Roman list]
```

Other Formatting Features

This section discusses the mm requests for justifying text, skipping lines, highlighting text, and changing the point size of characters.

Justifying Text   .SA

By default, mm causes text to be printed flush left, but not flush right. To produce justification along the right margin, use the .SA 1 request. To turn off justification and return to the default, use the .SA 0 request. The following example uses both requests:

Original Document   **Printed Result**

```
.SA 1
.P 1
This paragraph will be              This   paragraph  will  be
printed flush left and         printed flush left and flush
flush right. Each line         right.  Each  line  will  be
will be adjusted as            adjusted as required.
required.
.SA0                                This paragraph will be
.P 1                           printed flush left and ragged
This paragraph will be         right. Lines will be filled but
printed flush left and         not justified.
ragged right. Lines
will be filled but not
justified.
```

Skipping Lines .SP n

You can create blank space on a page by leaving a specified number of blank lines between segments of text. Use the .SP request, followed by a number, as shown in the following example. In this example, we'll leave three blank lines.

Original Document

```
.P 1
This paragraph will be
printed in its expected
location on the page.
.SP 3
.P 1
This paragraph will be
printed three lines
lower than the
previous paragraph.
```

Printed Result

```
 This paragraph will be
printed in its expected
location on the page.



 This paragraph will be
printed three lines lower than
the previous paragraph.
```

Highlighting Text

To allow you to highlight words in a paragraph, mm provides one request for italic text (.I), one for bold (.B), and one for returning to unhighlighted, or roman, text (.R). (Under nroff, italic means underscoring; under troff, italic means true italic.)

For more than one word, enclose the target text between a pair of requests, using three separate lines. The first line contains the highlighting request (.I or .B), the middle line contains the text to be highlighted, and the third line contains .R and nothing else. For a single word, you can issue the request on a single line. During printing, mm will restore the paragraph, which appears to be broken up by this procedure.

The following example illustrates each of the possibilities mentioned:

Original Document

```
.P 1
When you want a word to be
.I underlined
```

Printed Result

```
When you want a word to be
underlined, merely use the
```

```
, merely use the .I request.        .I request. To underline
To underline                        several words, use .I and .R
.I                                  together.
several words
.R                                      When you want a word in
, use .I and .R together.           bold, just use the .B
.P 1                                request. To make several
When you want a word in             words bold, use .B and .R
.B bold                             together.
, just use the .B request.
To make
.B
several words
.R
bold, use .B and .R together.
```

Changing Point Size   .S p v

When you are formatting mm requests with troff, you can change
the size of the characters being printed and the amount of spacing
between lines of text. The .S request can be used to change one of
these measurements, or both at the same time. Let's begin with
a description of point size and vertical spacing.

The size of a printed character is measured in *points* (1/72 of
an inch). Actually, the size is for a set of characters and is defined
as the distance from the bottom of a lowercase p to the top of any
uppercase letter. For reference, 9 points equal an eighth of an
inch, 12 points equal a sixth of an inch, 18 points equal a quarter
of an inch, and so on.

Vertical spacing is the distance, also measured in points,
from the bottom of one line to the bottom of the next line. In most
books, vertical spacing is about 20% greater than point size. The
difference, in points, between the vertical spacing and the point
size is known as the *leading* (pronounced to rhyme with heading).

For troff, the default is 10-point text and 12-point vertical
spacing (2-point leading). The .S request can be used with either

one argument or two arguments: point size and vertical spacing. You can enter a pair of numbers to express absolute sizes in points, you can enter numbers to express relative sizes, or you can enter a single letter from the following list:

- C Current settings

- D Default settings

- P Previous settings (equivalent to no argument at all)

In the following example, the size is increased for a title, decreased once for a byline, and then restored to the default sizes for the main body of text:

Original Document	**Printed Result**

```
.SP 3
.DS C
.S 14 18
The Big Thrill
.S -2 -4
By Henry Harker
.DE
.S D
.P 0
```

The Big Thrill

By Henry Harker

```
It wasn't a dark and stormy        It wasn't a dark and stormy
night. It wasn't even night.       night. It wasn't even night.
It was what you might call a       It was what you might call a
bright and sunny day. In fact,     bright and sunny day. In fact,
that's just what it was.           that's just what it was.
```

Here is a detailed look at the seven mm requests used in the preceding example:

.SP 3	Leave three blank lines.
.DS C	Start a centered display.
.S 14 18	Change the point size to 14 and the vertical spacing to 18.
.S -2 -4	Reduce the point size by 2 points and the vertical spacing by 4 (equivalent to .S 12 14).

`.DS E`	End the centered display.
`.S D`	Restore the default settings for point size and vertical spacing (equivalent to .S 10 12).
`.P 0`	Begin a block paragraph.

Chapter 7 Quiz

Match the name of the program listed on the left with the description of its function on the right:

1.	`deroff`	A.		Format text for a printer with characters having a fixed width.
2.	`checkeq`	B.		Format text for a printer with characters having variable widths.
3.	`troff`	C.		Process tables.
4.	`eqn`	D.		Process equations for the `nroff` formatter.
5.	`neqn`	E.		Process equations for the `troff` formatter.
6.	`nroff`	F.		Check requests used in equations and mathematical expressions.
7.	`tbl`	G.		Remove formatting requests from a file.

Match the name of each mm request listed on the left with the description of its function on the right:

8.	`.DE`	A.	Form a block paragraph
9.	`.RL`	B.	Form a paragraph with an indented first line
10.	`.P 0`	C.	Begin a static display

11.	.SA 0	D.	Begin a floating display
12.	.DL	E.	End a text display
13.	.S	F.	Begin an indented static display
14.	.EL	G.	Begin a centered floating display
15.	.B	H.	Begin a blocked floating display
16.	.P 1	I.	Begin a bullet list
17.	.R	J.	Begin a dash list
18.	.SP *n*	K.	Begin a mark list
19.	.DS	L.	Begin a reference list
20.	.AL	M.	Begin a variable-item list
21.	.I	N.	Begin an auto-number list
22.	.DF	O.	Begin an individual item in a list
23.	.ML	P.	End a list
24.	.DS I	Q.	Begin italic (or under-scored) text
25.	.SA 1	R.	Begin bold text
26.	.LI	S.	End bold or italic text
27.	.VL	T.	Turn on justification
28.	.DF CB	U.	Turn off justification
29.	.BL	V.	Skip *n* lines
30.	.DF C	W.	Change the point size and vertical spacing

In the blank spaces provided after the numbers on the left, fill in the mm formatting requests needed to produce the printed output shown on the right:

Original Document	Printed Result
Original Document	**Printed Result**

Original Document

31.
32.
Sales 1991
33.
34.
35.
Mr. Downs was introduced
to the sales staff on
Friday morning. During
his talk, he stressed
the following points:
36.
37.
Finding prospects
38.
Reaching prospects
39.
Closing prospects
40.
41.
He stressed the value of
new referrals over and
over. At one point he was
quoted as saying,
42.
"Get those referrals, no
matter what you have to do.
43.
Get those referrals
44.
!"
45.
46.
The following Monday, sales
were up
47.   27%
. Mr. Downs was highly pleased,
and informed the staff that he
would give another talk the
following Friday.

Printed Result

Sales 1991

Mr. Downs was introduced to the
sales staff on Friday morning.
During his talk, he stressed the
following points:

+ Finding prospects

+ Reaching prospects

+ Closing prospects

He stressed the value of new
referrals over and over. At one
point he was quoted as saying,

"Get those referrals, no
matter what you have to do.
Get those referrals!"

The following Monday, sales were
up 27%. Mr. Downs was highly
pleased, and informed the staff
that he would give another talk
the following Friday.

In This Chapter

A Sample Session with X

X Terminology

A Look at OPEN LOOK

More on X Clients

To Select Items in the File Manager

1. Select one item by clicking with the left mouse button.
2. Select a set of items by clicking with the middle mouse button.
3. Open an item by double-clicking with the left mouse button.

To Copy a File

1. Drag target directory's icon to workspace to create a new File Manager.
2. Hold down left mouse button, and drag item's icon to the target directory's icon.

To Move a File

1. Drag target directory's icon to workspace to create a new File Manager.
2. Hold down `⇧Shift` and left mouse button, and drag item's icon to the target directory's icon.

The Terminal Emulator

1. Type `xterm &` to create a new terminal emulator.
2. Click on the small box to reduce a window to an icon.
3. Type `exit` or press `Ctrl`-`D` to close a window and kill its processes.

Copy text to Another Window and Location

- Mark the text to be copied.
- Move to the new window and location.
- Display Edit menu, select Copy, and then Paste.

The X Window System

The Macintosh revolution has reached the UNIX system. It has spread to just about every small computing system in use, bringing with it screen areas called *windows* that provide work spaces for programs, *icons* that represent files and programs, and *mouse* control for ease of use. The general term for this kind of computing environment is *graphical user interface* (GUI).

In a graphical environment, each application is assigned its own window. This means that a number of different applications can be active simultaneously. Windows can be stacked on the screen like papers on a desk. They can also be moved, enlarged, and shrunk. To reduce clutter, each window can be reduced to an icon. A large number of icons can be displayed on the screen without interfering with each other.

Then, to tie this all together, you have a pointing device called a *mouse*. A mouse is a hand-held device that typically has one, two, or three control buttons on the front and a cord on the back that is connected to the computer. (The name mouse comes from the similarity, however slight, between the device with its cord and a rodent with a long tail.)

As you move the mouse around on a pad, a pointer on the screen moves with it, in the same direction and at the same speed. When the pointer arrives at an object on the screen, you can use the control buttons to take some action with respect to that object. Typically, a single-click of a mouse button selects an object, while a double-click opens it for view.

A mouse can also be used to move objects around on the screen. To move an object across the screen, you can point to the object and hold down a mouse button, thereby causing the object to move with the mouse. This is known as *dragging* the object. You can also use your mouse in conjunction with a *scrollbar* to scroll text within a window.

Finally, you can use your mouse to make selections from a window. If you point to the menu's name and hold down a mouse button, the menu will usually appear. Then you can point to an item on the menu and release the button to begin execution.

DOS users are already familiar with the concept of a graphical environment. Microsoft Windows is the most widely used GUI for DOS users. IBM's OS/2 is another example.

Similarly, the *X Window System*, or *X*, provides UNIX users with a variety of GUIs. In recent years, X has become a standard part of the UNIX system. AT&T and Sun Microsystems offer an X-based GUI called OPEN LOOK. DEC, Hewlett-Packard, IBM, and others, under the name Open Software Foundation, offer another GUI called *Motif*. In addition, Interactive Systems offers Looking Glass, the Santa Cruz Operation offers Open Desktop, and other vendors offer a number of other X-based GUIs.

Just as Windows requires much more computing power than DOS, X requires much more than an ordinary UNIX system. It requires more memory, more disk space, a more powerful processor, a high-resolution color graphics display, and, of course, a mouse. The additional computing power is needed because of the complexity of a graphical display in comparison to the simplicity of a character display. In addition, the system administrator must authorize and set up each X user.

A Sample Session with X

If your machine is powerful enough and the system administrator has given you authorization, you can begin a session with X by entering the following command:

```
$ xinit
```

The `xinit` command starts a program called X; then it executes each command line found in a file called `.xinitrc`, which is stored in your home directory. Depending on how your system is configured, the name of the command may be different. For example, to start OPEN LOOK, you would use the following command:

```
$ olinit
```

If you want to begin an X session as soon as you log in, you can place the command in your start-up file (`.profile`).

As soon as the session begins, a screen display like the one shown in Figure 8.1 will appear on-screen. The following windows should be included in the display:

- The desktop, called the *workspace*
- The File Manager
- A terminal emulator (`xterm`)
- Other tools, such as a calculator (`xcalc`), a mail notifier (`xbiff`), and a clock (`xclock`)

The Workspace

You can think of the workspace as the root window, or desktop, on which all other windows are placed. The workspace is usually in a neutral color that forms a background for other windows.

Figure 8.1
*Opening window
menu for OPEN
LOOK.*

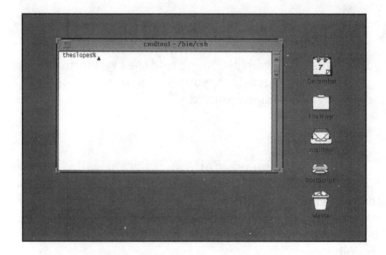

The File Manager

The File Manager displays directories and files as icons. Like its Macintosh and Windows predecessors, it allows you to move the pointer to an icon with your mouse and double-click on it to open it. Once opened, a directory or file then appears as another window on the screen. You can open several windows in this way, move them around the screen, shrink or enlarge them, and close them again. With two different directory windows open, you can move a file (or a set of files) from one directory to another by highlighting them and dragging them from one window to another.

The Terminal Emulator

By moving the pointer to the xterm window and clicking your mouse, you can activate a *terminal emulator*. Activating this window is like returning to a traditional UNIX environment. A shell prompt will appear in the upper left-hand corner of the window, where you can enter standard UNIX commands from your keyboard. Within this window, you abandon the graphical mouse-and-icon interface and return to the old-fashioned command line interface. If you are familiar with the Windows environment, the terminal emulator is similar to the MS-DOS prompt, which returns you to the DOS command line prompt when you double-click on its icon.

Other Tools

Some of the most common tools that also may appear on the workspace include the calculator (xcalc), the mail notifier (xbiff), and the clock (xclock).

The calculator allows you to operate an on-screen calculator with your mouse the way you would operate a hand-held calculator with your fingers. After activating the calculator with your mouse, you can then press the different numeric and function keys with a click of your mouse.

The mail notifier (xbiff) displays a small mailbox icon. Any time you receive electronic mail from another user, you will see a small flag rise and you will hear a beep. To read the mail that has arrived, you can either use the mail reading tool provided with your version of X or you can activate the xterm window and run the mail program. (The mail program is explained in Chapter 6.)

The clock (xclock) is just a small picture of a clock, with moving hands to indicate the current time.

Ending the Session

To end the X session, position the mouse pointer over the root window, and hold down the right mouse button to display the workspace menu. Move the pointer to Exit, and release the right mouse button. If you see a prompt requesting confirmation, click the mouse to confirm the Exit. If you started the X session from a command line, you will now return to the shell prompt. If you started the X session from .profile, you will probably terminate the entire terminal session.

X Terminology

The basic concept of the X Window System is the *display*, which typically includes:

- A graphical-display device (video)
- An input device (keyboard)
- A pointing device (mouse)
- A processing unit

Each display usually has only one video. But if a display has more than one, the individual videos are then called *screens*.

The X Window System has many application programs, and each one is assigned to a *window* of its own. When you activate a window on the screen, you are selecting an application. The active window is the one that accepts your input at any given moment.

In the X Window System, all software perform one of three basic functions, which interact with each other continuously:

- Managing the display
- Performing applications
- Managing the windows

Managing the Display

The software that manages the display is called the *display server*, or simply the *server*. Its function is to read input from the keyboard and the mouse and write output to the video. The server for an X Window System is analogous to the operating system on a non-graphical system.

Performing Applications

Programs that carry out specific application tasks are called *clients*. Several of these have already been introduced: the terminal emulator (xterm), the calculator (xcalc), the mail notifier (xbiff), and the clock (xclock).

The relationship between server and client is similar to the one between operating system and application program.

Managing the Windows

The software that generates menus, positions windows, and allows you to open new windows and close existing windows is a special client known as the *window manager*. The window manager, which can be modified, is what determines the appearance of your screen.

In the world of graphical user interfaces, a window manager is analogous to a shell program. There are various window managers available for the X Window System. The two main products are the following:

- The OPEN LOOK window manager (olwm), developed by AT&T and Sun Microsystems, is the official standard for System V, Release 4.

- The Motif window manager (mwm), developed by the Open Software Foundation (OSF), is an alternative to OPEN LOOK. It is more like IBM's OS/2 or Microsoft's Windows.

The following are designed for specific UNIX products:

- The Open Desktop window manager (odwm), developed by the Santa Cruz Operation, is available for SCO's UNIX/386 system.

- The Looking Glass window manager (lgwm), developed by Interactive Systems, is shipped with its UNIX/386 system.

The following are meant to allow you to design your own look:

- Tab window manager (twm), developed by Tom LaStrange, is fully configurable.

- The Generic window manager (gwm) is also fully configurable.

In this chapter, we'll focus on OPEN LOOK and generic X tools.

Now, we'll take a closer look at the OPEN LOOK window manager. The main areas we'll consider are:

- The file manager

- The terminal emulator

- The window manager itself

The OPEN LOOK File Manager

When you begin an X session with OPEN LOOK, the File Manager is displayed in the lower half of the screen, toward the left.

A Tour of the Menu

With the File Manager, you can use your mouse to carry out many of the same file operations you learned in Chapter 2. Let's begin by noting the different items in the File Manager window. On the top line, you will see a small box on the left side. You can click your mouse on this box to shrink the window down to an icon. In the middle of the line, you will see File Manager, followed by the name of your home directory.

On the left side of the next line, the names of four menus are shown: File, View, Edit, and Match. On the right side are the labels Directory and Pattern. You can use the open spaces to type in a directory name or a text pattern during a search.

Inside a rectangle, below the second line, you will see a list of directories, starting at root (/) and ending with the current directory. Note that the icon for a directory is a file folder.

Inside another rectangle, below the first, you will find the contents of the current directory. Subdirectories are identified by the file folder icon; ordinary files, by a sheet of paper with the upper right-hand corner folded over; program files, by another icon.

Selecting Items

When you are about to copy, move, or delete an item (or items), you begin by selecting the item (or set of items). To select an item displayed, click on the item with the left mouse button.

One way to select a set of files in the current directory is to click on each file name individually with the middle mouse button. Another way is to type a text pattern on the Pattern line, using any wild cards required, and then click on Match.

Opening Items

You open a directory to see the names of the files and subdirectories stored in the directory. You *open* a file to view or edit its contents. You open a program to begin executing it.

To open an item, double-click on the item with the left mouse button. If the item is a directory, its contents will fill the lower rectangle, and its path will fill the second line. If the item is a text file, you will be allowed to edit it in a separate window, using the editor identified by the EDITOR environmental variable. If the item is a program, it will be executed in a separate window. After execution of the program (or after you stop it by selecting Quit from the Window menu), its window will vanish.

Another way to move to a directory is to type its name on the Directory line and then click on Match.

Copying Items

To copy an item from one directory to another, follow this procedure:

1. Move the pointer to the name of the target directory.

2. Hold down the left mouse button.

3. Drag the folder across the window to the workspace, or desktop.

4. Release the left mouse button, thereby creating a new File Manager.

5. Move the pointer to the item to be copied.

6. Hold down the left mouse button.

7. Drag the item across the window to the name of the target directory.

8. Release the left mouse button.

9. Move the pointer to the small box in the upper left-hand corner of the target File Manager, thereby closing the new File Manager.

If the item is a file, a copy of the file will be placed under the target directory. If the item is a directory, a copy of the directory and every file within the directory will be placed under the target directory.

Moving Items

To move an item from one directory to another, follow this procedure:

1. Move the pointer to the name of the target directory.

2. Hold down the left mouse button.

3. Drag the folder across the window to the workspace, or desktop.

4. Release the left mouse button, thereby creating a new File Manager.

5. Move the pointer to the item to be moved.

6. Hold down the ⬆Shift key and the left mouse button.

7. Drag the item across the window to the name of the target directory.

8. Release the left mouse button.

9. Move the pointer to the small box in the upper left-hand corner of the target File Manager, thereby closing the new File Manager.

If the item is a file, the file will be moved to the target directory. If the item is a directory, the directory and every file within the directory will be moved to the target directory.

The only difference between moving and copying is Step 6. In a copy, you hold down only the left mouse button; in a move, you hold down ⬆Shift and the left mouse button together.

The OPEN LOOK Terminal Emulator

The xterm (X terminal) program is the client application that places a terminal emulator window on the desktop. When you activate this window, you enter a conventional UNIX environment with a shell prompt waiting for a command line. From this shell prompt, you can enter any of the commands or scripts described in this book. You can also start any client application, including another xterm window. To open another xterm window, just enter the following command as a background process, using the ampersand character (&):

```
$ xterm &
```

Now you have two terminal emulators on your screen, the original one and the new one you just created. You can start one command in one window and another command in the other window. While the second xterm window is running in the background, it is subject to menu control (discussed below).

Window Control

You can reduce the second window to an icon by clicking on the small box in the upper left-hand corner. Any programs in progress will continue to run after the window shrinks to an icon. You can shrink or enlarge an xterm window at any time. But if a program is running, its output to the window may be affected by the change in its dimensions. To close the second window, you can type either exit or Ctrl-D after its shell prompt, or you can select Kill from its menu. Any programs that are running in the window without nohup (no hang-up) will be killed along with the window.

Working with the Menu

The xterm window has its own menu, from which you can select a number of different functions. The standard way of displaying the menu is to press the right mouse button while the pointer is inside the xterm window. When the menu appears, your screen will look something like the one shown in Figure 8.2.

Figure 8.2
*OPEN LOOK's
xterm menu.*

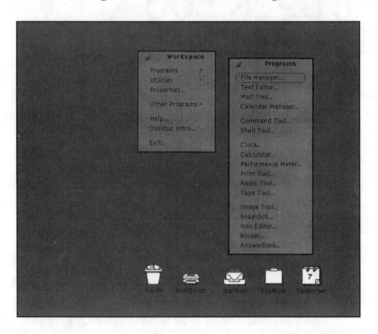

The first item on the menu, Edit, includes its own submenu with four of its own items: Send, Paste, Copy, and Cut. You can use these to move text around within the xterm window, or from one xterm window to another. The target window can be either an xterm window or another client window, provided that the other client also supports these Edit functions.

Each xterm window allows you to copy or move text from one location to another. To copy text, follow this procedure:

1. Move the pointer to the beginning of the text to be copied.

2. Hold down the left mouse button.

3. Move the pointer to the end of the desired text.

4. Release the left mouse button.

5. Move the pointer to the target window.

6. Press the right mouse button to display the menu.

7. Select Edit, and then Copy.

8. Move the pointer to the target location.

9. Select Edit, and then Paste.

The text selected will be copied to the target window and location.

To *move* text, follow this procedure:

1. Move the pointer to the beginning of the text to be moved.

2. Hold down the left mouse button.

3. Move the pointer to the end of the desired text.

4. Release the left mouse button.

5. Move the pointer to the target window.

6. Press the right mouse button to display the menu.

7. Select Edit, and then Cut.

8. Move the pointer to the target location.

9. Select Edit, and then Paste.

The text selected will be moved to the target window and location.

The OPEN LOOK Window Manager

As noted earlier in this chapter, vendors offer a number of different window managers for the X Window System, each with its own conventions and rules. To avoid confusion and maintain consistency, we'll confine our discussion here to the OPEN LOOK Window Manager (olwm), the standard for System V, Release 4.

The window manager allows you to create windows, move them around the screen, enlarge or shrink them, select one or more of them, display a help menu, and so on. We'll discuss some of these procedures now.

The Workspace Menu

The workspace, which is also called the desktop or the root window, as noted earlier, is the background screen area on which all other windows are placed. Any open space on the screen that is between windows belongs to the workspace. If you move the pointer to any part of the workspace and press the right mouse button, you will display the workspace menu in the upper left-hand corner of the screen. The workspace menu includes four items that you can select:

- Programs

- Utilities

- Properties

- Exit

The first three of these names are followed by triangular symbols, which indicate that they have their own submenus.

Programs The submenu for this menu includes all application programs that you can run right from this menu. You can also run any X client program from an xterm menu, but the Programs menu is a little simpler and more convenient. To run a program listed here, follow this procedure:

1. Move the pointer to any area of the workspace.

2. Hold down the right mouse button to display the workspace menu.

3. Move the pointer to the triangle to the right of Programs.

4. When the submenu appears, move the pointer to the name of the desired program.

5. Release the right mouse button to start the program.

A new window will appear on the screen, with the program running in it. You can kill the process by pressing Kill, Quit, or Exit in the new window's menu.

Utilities The submenu for this menu includes a number of handy tools that you will probably use often. The utilities will vary from system to system, but here are a few of the most likely candidates: Screen Refresh, Print Screen, Lock Screen, File Manager, and Network Administration.

Properties The submenu for this menu allows you to change the fonts, screen colors, locations of icons, assignment of key functions, and so on. The tools to make these changes may be found here in this menu or in an X client application.

Help Windows

On most X screens, you can move the pointer to a window and press F1 to display a help window (see Figure 8.3). The help window will usually partially overlay the window you need information about, providing a discussion of the application and how to use it. If the explanation is lengthy, you can use the scrollbar on the right side of the help window to scroll through the text. To close the help window, move the pointer to the push pin in the upper left-hand corner, and press the right mouse button. The help window will vanish, and you can return to the application window.

Figure 8.3
*The OPEN LOOK
Help screen.*

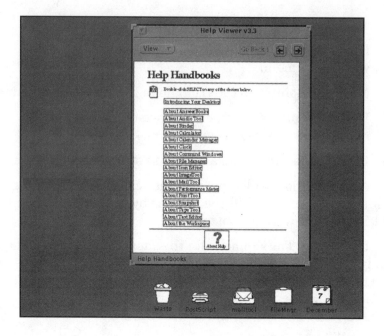

Scrolling Through a Window

If a window contains more text than the window can display at once, the window will have *scrollbars* to allow you to scroll through the text. It is common to find a scrollbar on the right side of a window, but in some instances you will find one scrollbar on the right side and another along the bottom of the window.

A vertical scrollbar looks like an elevator, with a pair of rectangular anchors above and below and the elevator car suspended in between on a pair of cables. The elevator car has an up arrow on top, a down arrow below, and a blank rectangle in the middle.

The relative position of the elevator car between the two anchors indicates where you are in the text. If it's at the top, you're at the beginning of the text; if it's at the bottom, you're at the end of the text; if it's at the halfway point, you're halfway through the text; and so on.

One way to use the scrollbar is to move the pointer to the blank area in the middle of the elevator car, hold down the left mouse button, and drag the car up or down to the desired location. Other ways of scrolling are summarized in Table 8.1.

To Scroll	Click the Left Mouse Button On
To the start of text	The top anchor
To the end of text	The bottom anchor
Up one full screen	The upper cable
Down one full screen	The lower cable
Up one line of text	The up arrow
Down one line of text	The down arrow

Table 8.1
Scrolling Techniques for OPEN LOOK

Controlling Windows

When a window first comes to the screen, it appears in a given size and location. It may be large or small. It may be near one of the four corners or in the middle of the screen. It may be on top of other windows or underneath them. It may be normal size or it may be reduced to an icon. But the size and location of a window is not fixed; you can change any of these factors.

Size   At each of the four corners of any window you will find an L-shaped blank space. If you move the pointer to one of these spaces and hold down the left mouse button, the two sides of the window than come together and the L will become flexible. You can drag the L inward to shrink the window or drag it outward to expand the window. As soon as you release the mouse button, the window's dimensions will freeze at the new size you have selected.

Location   To move a window from its current location to somewhere else on the screen, move the pointer to any of its borders (but not a corner), and hold down the left mouse button. You can now drag the window in any direction on the screen. When you reach the desired destination, release the mouse button. The window will stay in its new location.

Selection   If you have a lot of windows on the screen, you may find a number of them piled up in a stack. The window you want to work with may be covered up by other windows. To send a window to the top of the stack, where it will be in plain view, move the pointer to any of the desired window's borders, and click on the left mouse button. The window will jump to the top, activated and ready to receive input from you.

You can send only one window to the top of the stack, but you can select more than one at a time. After selecting one window (and sending it to the top of the stack), you can then proceed to select as many others along with it for a group operation. Just move the pointer to the border of each additional window, and press the middle mouse button. If you select three windows in this way, you could now move all three of them as a unit to another location, or perform some other operation.

The middle mouse button acts as a toggle. So if you want to deselect any window already selected, move the pointer to its border, and press the middle mouse button. Now that window is deselected, but all other selected windows remain selected.

Icon mode   Each window has a small box in its upper left-hand corner that contains an upside down triangle. To reduce the window to an icon, move the pointer to the small box, and click on the left mouse button. Any application in progress will continue to run. To restore the icon to full window size, move the pointer to the icon, and double-click on the left mouse button. The window will reappear in its original size and location.

More on X Clients

I'll conclude this chapter with a discussion about arguments you can add to X command lines and the initialization file. These are related because you can use arguments in the command lines you place in your initialization file.

Commands and Options

A standard set of options, shown in Table 8.2, is available to most X command lines. When the full name of the option can be abbreviated, the abbreviation will be shown in parentheses on the right. For example, -bg for -background.

Option	Use
-background *color*	Set background color for a window (-bg).
-bordercolor *color*	Set border color for a window (-bd).
-borderwidth *width*	Set border width for a window, in pixels (-bw).
-display *name*	Names display server.
-font *name*	Set font (-fn).
-foreground *color*	Set foreground color for a window (-fg).
-geometry *cxr+x+y*	Set size and location of a window (-geom).
-help	List available options for this client.
-iconic	Start as an icon instead of a full window.
-reverse	Turn on reverse video (-rv).
-title *name*	Set title for a window (-tl or -T).

Table 8.2
*Options for X
Command Lines*

Most of the options listed in Table 8.2 are self-explanatory. However, a few of them need further explanation.

If you are dissatisfied with the default fonts you see in your windows, the -font (or -fn) option allows you to select other fonts from the hundreds that may be available in your X system. To list all the fonts available, use the xlsfonts command. Here is an example with abbreviated output:

```
$ xlsfonts

-adobe-courier-bold-o-normal- -14-140-75-75-m-90 iso8859-1
-adobe-courier-bold-o-normal- -14-100-100-100-m-90-iso8859-1
-adobe-courier-medium-o-normal- -12-120-75-75-m-70-iso8859-1
-adobe-courier-medium-o-normal- -14-140-75-75-m-90-iso8859-1
-adobe-helvetica-bold-r-normal- -14-140-75-75-p-82-iso8859-1
-adobe-times-bold-i-normal- -14-140-75-75-p-77-iso8859-1
-bitstream-charter-bold-r-normal- -19-180-75-75-p-119-iso8850-1
```

```
-bitstream-charter-bold-i-normal-  -19-180-75-75-p-117-iso8850-1
-bitstream-charter-medium-i-normal-  -19-180-75-75-p-103-iso8850-1
6x10
6x13
8x13
8x13bold
9x15
9x15bold
fixed
variable
...
$ _
```

The long names earlier in the list give specifications for full identification of the fonts. The shorter names later in the list are abbreviations of the longer names.

To find out what a font looks like, you can use the **xfd** (X font display) command, followed by the name of the command. You can use wild cards to shorten longer names. For example,

$ xfd -font *courier-medium-r-normal-*120* &

If you decide to use this font in one of your windows, say your xterm window, you can select the font when you start the window, as shown in the following command line:

$ xterm -font *courier-medium-r-normal-*120* &

If you control the size and location of a window, the -geometry (or -geom) option allows you to set the dimensions and to place the window at a certain location on the screen. The option uses a specifier of the form *cxr+x+y*,

where

c is the number of columns

r is the number of rows

x is the horizontal offset of the upper left-hand corner

y is the vertical offset of the upper left-hand corner

The *c* and *r* values may be in pixels or in characters, depending on the type of window, while the *x* and *y* values are always in pixels. For example, to set up an xterm window that contains 24 rows and 80 columns, offset 200 pixels across and 100 pixels down, you could enter a command line like the following:

```
$ xterm -geom 80x24+100+200 &
```

In the command line shown above, the size of the window is in characters because it will contain only text. However, window size for most other windows is expressed in pixels.

If you want to specify the colors used in the window, you can use the -fg and -bg options on a single command line.

```
$ xterm -fg white -bg green &
```

For a text window, the -fg option specifies the color of the text, while the -bg option specifies the color of the background field.

With a lot of windows on the screen, it may become difficult to distinguish one from another. If you want to specify a name for the window (and its icon), you can use the -title (-tl) option (along with the corresponding icon title (-in) option). For example, to call the xterm window "Terminal Window 1," enter a command line like the following:

```
$ xterm -tl "Terminal Window 1" &
```

To call the xterm window "Terminal Window 1" and its icon "Trm Win 1," enter a command line like the following:

```
$ xterm -tl "Terminal Window 1" -in "Trm Win 1" &
```

This covers command line options. Now you are ready for the next subsection.

Initialization

Earlier in this chapter, we discussed the use of a file called
.xinitrc to initialize your X Window System. In this section, we'll
describe .xinitrc in greater detail.

As noted earlier, the xinit program first starts the X server
and then executes each command line found in .xinitrc in your
home directory. You can place a set of command lines in .xinitrc
that will determine exactly which windows you want to appear on
the screen at the beginning of an X session. For example, you
could include the following lines in your .xinitrc file:

```
xterm -geom 80x24+100+200 -fg white -bg blue &
xcalc -geom 240x120+900+10 &
xclock -geom 120x120+900+900 &
exec olwm
```

When you execute xinit, it first starts the X server, and then
the four lines in your .xinitrc file. These four lines place four
windows on the screen: a terminal emulator, a calculator, a clock,
and the OPEN LOOK window manager. The first three are
entered as background processes; the fourth, as a foreground
process. When you exit from the window manager, you end the X
session.

You have specified a 24x80 terminal emulator window, at
the location indicated (100 pixels across, 200 down), with white
characters against a blue background; a calculator window at the
size and location indicated; a clock window at the size and
location indicated; and the OPEN LOOK window manager.

You can close your background terminal emulator, calculator, or clock windows at any time, and the X session will keep
going. But closing the foreground window manager window will
end the X session.

Chapter 8 Quiz

Match each name on the left with a description on the right:

1. Workspace

    A. The software that determines the look of your X screen display.

2. File Manager

    B. Another name for the root window, or desktop.

3. terminal emulator

    C. The software that provides you with a traditional UNIX environment.

4. Window Manager

    D. Something that displays information about an application window on the screen.

5. help window

    E. The software that allows you to copy and move files and directories with your mouse.

Match each client name on the left with a description of its function on the right:

6. `xterm`

    A. Notifies you when mail has arrived.

7. `xcalc`

    B. Provides a graphical calculator on the screen.

8. `xbiff`

    C. Provides a terminal emulator on the screen.

9. `xclock`

    D. Generates the over-all look of the screen for OPEN LOOK.

10. `olwm`

    E. Provides a graphical time keeper on the screen.

Other questions:

11. An application program in the X Window System is called a(n) _____.

12. A pointing device that allows you to select items on the screen and move them around is called a(n) _____.

13. Each application under X has its own _____.

14. The combination of a video, keyboard, mouse, and processor is called a(n) _____.

15. The software that reads input from the keyboard and writes output to the screen is called the _____.

In This Chapter

What the System Administrator Does

Backing Up Files

Setting Up Terminals

Shutting the System Down

What the System Administrator Does

- Opens and closes user accounts.
- Installs, mounts, and troubleshoots hardware.
- Provides disk space and eliminates errors.
- Formats disks, starts the system, and shuts it down.
- Protects the system from unauthorized entry.
- Monitors system usage.
- Sets up connections to other systems.
- Logs in as the super user, has a special prompt (#), and has a special directory (/etc).

Backing Up Files

- Use ls ¦ cpio -oB > /dev/mt/2 to back up all files in the current directory on tape (drive 2).
- Use cpio -iB < /dev/mt/2 to restore all files on tape (drive 2) to the current directory.
- Use ls ¦ cpio -pv ../archive to back up all files in the current directory to another directory called archive.

Setting Up Terminals

- Use the stty command to display the current setting for your terminal or to change any of those settings.
- Descriptions of all terminals on the system may be found in one of two places:

  /etc/termcap on older systems

  /usr/lib/terminfo/* on newer System V systems

- You must include the name of your terminal in the .profile (Bourne or Korn shell) or .login (C shell) file.
- Establishing an X environment is similar to setting up a new user on the system.

The System Administrator

This chapter explains the basic operations needed for administering a UNIX system. Each larger UNIX system has one person assigned as a full-time system administrator. A smaller system, however, may not have one, and you may have to become your own system administrator. If so, this chapter will help you through the most elementary functions of system administration.

If you have been using DOS for any length of time, you probably know that you must perform certain housekeeping tasks in order to use your system effectively. You have to format disks, make backup copies of files, prune directories from time to time, and maintain the integrity of files.

With UNIX, your administrative tasks are quite a bit more complex. You have user accounts to administer; terminals, printers, and disk and tape drives to set up; file systems to maintain; and permissions to grant or revoke. We won't be able to cover all these tasks in this chapter, but we will take a look at the most common and least technical of these. Let's begin with a quick look at the responsibilities of a system administrator.

What a System Administrator Does

When you work with DOS, you are both the user and the system administrator. You run your programs and back up your own disk files. In a UNIX system with many users, someone is usually assigned the task of supporting these users in their day-to-day work by handling the administrative tasks for everyone. This system administrator is responsible for the following:

Opening and closing user accounts on the system.

Installing, mounting, and troubleshooting terminals, printers, plotters, disk drives, and tape drives.

Providing sufficient disk space and keeping file systems free of errors.

Formatting disks, starting the system, and shutting it down.

Protecting the system from unauthorized entry and destructive actions.

Monitoring system usage to guard against attacks, to optimize the performance of the system, and to handle billing.

Setting up connections to other UNIX systems.

Now, let's examine the tools available to the system administrator for carrying out these responsibilities.

Logging In as System Administrator

If you are currently logged into your system as an ordinary user, then you can switch to system administrator by logging in again with the su (substitute user) command:

```
$ su
Password:
# _
```

If you are not currently logged in, you can log into the root account, which is reserved for the system administrator:

```
login: root
Password:
# _
```

In either case, the shell displays a special prompt (#) to remind you that you are no longer logged in as an ordinary user. You are now logged in as the system's *super user*. (That's much like the transformation that takes place when Clark Kent emerges from a telephone booth as Superman.)

The super user has complete access to every directory, every subdirectory, and every file in the system, without having to worry about permissions. There is nothing to stop you from entering any directory and creating or deleting any file. If you make a mistake, you can damage a system beyond repair. Therefore, only one person should be allowed to log in as super user, and only when required to perform system maintenance. In no instance should super user status be given to someone who is likely to misuse the privilege. Select a super user who is diligent and knowledgeable, and who maintains the highest standards of professional ethics.

The System Administrator's Directory /etc

Most administrative files and commands are stored in a separate directory called /etc. Separating administrative commands from the ordinary commands in /bin, /usr/bin, or /usr/sbin keeps these special commands out of the hands of other users. You can always type the full pathname of any command; however, if you want to be able to use only the command name, place one of the following in your start-up file .profile (Bourne shell) or .login (C shell):

Bourne shell:

```
PATH=/etc:/bin:/usr/bin:$HOME/bin:.:
export PATH
```

C shell:

```
set path = (/etc /bin /usr/bin $HOME/bin .)
```

With one of these lines in your start-up file, you will be free to enter commands by their basename, without having to type full pathnames.

Working with Users

One of the important jobs of a system administrator is to interact with system users. In this section, you will learn how to communicate with users, how to set up new user accounts, and how to determine who is logged in at any given moment.

Reaching Users

Because the users on your UNIX system may not be in the same room, or even in the same building, you need an efficient way to get information to them at various times. The mail command may be a little too slow, so UNIX offers three other possibilities: the wall (write-all) command, the news command, and the /etc/motd (message of the day) file.

The wall (write-all) command is similar to the write command, in that it immediately sends a message to each terminal. Although this is the fastest way to reach users, your message will be seen only by users who are currently logged in. So, another possibility is to use the news command, which displays the contents of files stored in /usr/news.

Another option is the /etc/motd (message of the day) file. Any announcement placed in this file will be displayed each time a user logs in. Here is an example of a typical message of the day:

```
The system will be shut down
Friday night at 10:00 pm.
```

To display this message, simply change to the directory /etc, use vi to begin an editing session with the file motd, replace the current message of the day with the new message, and save the text.

Users can reply to messages from the system administrator or send their own messages to the system administrator by mailing them to root, as shown in the following example:

```
$ mail root < lost.files
$ _
```

Setting Up New User Accounts

Information about each user authorized to log into a UNIX system is summarized as a one-line entry in a file called /etc/passwd. Each entry contains seven fields, separated from each other by colons (:):

Login name

Password (encrypted)

User identifier

Group identifier (optional)

Comments, such as full name (optional)

Home directory

Login program (usually a shell)

The system will associate the user identifier and the group identifier (if any) with each file that the user creates. A typical /etc/passwd file looks something like this:

```
root:uR@pwCyI5z:0:1:super user:/:
daemon:x:1:1::/:
cron:x:1:3::/:
sys:nQ3vB*eJ4:2:2:/sys:
bin:k8S(oL7gYb:3:2::/bin:
paul:Z.u3)qKf9:15:62:Paul Stafford:/usr/paul:/bin/sh
...
```

The sixth entry can be broken down in this way:

Field	Entry	Description
1	paul	Login name
2	Z.u3)qKf9	Password (encrypted)
3	15	User identifier
4	62	Group identifier
5	Paul Stafford	Comment (full name)
6	/home/paul	Home directory
7	/bin/sh	Login program (Bourne shell)

Each working group on the system is described as a one-line entry in a file called /etc/group. With only four fields, this file is a little simpler than /etc/passwd:

Group name

Password (encrypted)

Group identifier

List of members

A typical /etc/group file looks something like this:

```
root:uR@pwCyI5z:1:root,daemon
sys:nQ3vB*eJ4:2:sys,bin
family:jYp4+sK&m:61:archie,edith,gloria,mike
...
```

The third line can be broken down as follows:

Field	Entry	Description
1	family	Group name
2	jYp4+sK&m	Password (encrypted)
3	61	Group identifier
4	archie,edith,gloria,mike	List of members

To add a new user account to the system, you must perform the following operations as super user:

- Add a line to /etc/passwd
- Add a line to /etc/group (if necessary)
- Provide the user with a home directory
- Construct a start-up file

Here are the steps in detail:

Add a Line to /etc/passwd

QUICK STEPS

1. # vi + /etc/passwd   Begin editing at the end of /etc/passwd.

NOTE: Use a plus sign between a vi command and a file name to begin a session at the end of the file.

2. a
   paul: *[password]*:15:62:
   Paul Stafford:/usr
   /paul:/bin/sh
   Esc

   Append a line for the new user.
   For the C shell, make the last field /bin/csh instead of /bin/sh.

3. :wq
   #_

   End this editing session and return to the shell.

Provide the User
with a Home Directory

1. # **cd /usr**
   # **mkdir paul**
   # _

   Create the home directory in /usr.

2. # chown paul paul
   # _

   Change the name of the directory's owner from root to paul.

3. # **chgrp 62 /usr/paul**
   # _

   Assuming the user belongs to group 62, change the owners group identifier to 62.

Create a Start-Up File
in the New Directory

1. # **login paul**
   Password:
   # _

   Log into the new directory.

2. $ **vi + .profile**
   [Bourne shell]

   Begin an editing session with vi and the start-up file.

   For the C shell, use .login instead of .profile, and use the appropriate corresponding lines.

3. **a**
   PATH=:/lbin:/usr/bin:/usr/paul/bin:

   MAIL=/usr/mail/paul

   Specify pathnames for commands and mail.

```
 4. TERM=tv950              Identify and set the
    stty erase ^h kill ^u   user's terminal.

 5. export PATH, MAIL, TERM  Export the variables
    [Esc]                    (Bourne shell only).

 6. :wq                      End this editing session,
    # _                      and return to the shell
                             prompt.
```

Finding Out Who Is
Logged In   who

One of the simplest security measures you can perform is to check
periodically to find out which users are currently logged in. To do
so, use the who command, as illustrated here:

```
$ who
root            tty00           May  2    08:59
alexis          tty05           May  2    09:23
ted             tty21           May  2    11:15
bill            tty02           Apr 29    04:26
paul            tty20           May  2    10:21
nancy           tty03           Apr 30    10:37
toad            tty26           May  2    11:42
$ _
```

The who command reads login information from a file called
/etc/utmp and displays it as shown above. Each line of the who
display specifies the login name of a user, the name of the
terminal, and the date and time when the user logged in.

If you would like more information, you can use the -u
argument to obtain a long listing:

```
$ who -u
root        tty00      May 2     08:59      .       19457
alexis      tty05      May 2     09:23     2:09     22344
ted         ttym1      May 2     11:15      .       26510
bill        tty02      Apr 29    04:26     1:22        44
paul        ttym0      May 2     10:21     2:01     26322
nancy       tty03      Apr 30    10:37     1:48      1155
toad        ttym6      May 2     11:42      .       26755
$ _
```

This long listing includes two additional columns at the right: the amount of time since the user's last activity and the process identifier (PID) of the user's shell. In the time column, each value is given in hours and minutes; two other notations include a dot (.), indicating activity within the last minute, and old, meaning no activity in the past 24 hours.

If you would like a complete listing of lines currently available on your system (not currently in use), you can include the -1 argument, as follows:

```
$ who -1
LOGIN       tty01      May 2     22:21     1:22     26362
LOGIN       tty07      Apr 29    16:25     old        49
LOGIN       tty08      Apr 29    16:25     old        50
LOGIN       tty09      May 2     10:13    13:29     22338
LOGIN       tty10      Apr 29    20:16     old       913
LOGIN       tty06      Apr 29    16:25     old        48
LOGIN       tty11      Apr 29    20:16     old       912
LOGIN       tty12      Apr 30    21:30     old      6438
LOGIN       tty24      May 2     23:38     5:23     26746
LOGIN       tty27      May 2     23:39    15:12     26756
LOGIN       tty25      May 2     23:40     0:03     26764
LOGIN       tty04      Apr 30    21:31     old      8428
LOGIN       tty16      May 2     20:01     3:42     25722
$ _
```

Checking Disk Space

Two similar commands allow you to find out how much space is being used (or remains) on disk. The du command tells you how much space each file in the current directory is using; the df command tells you how much space is left on your disk.

Checking Space Used by Files   du

The du command tells you the number of blocks used by each subdirectory in the current directory. To include files in the display also, you must include the -a option.

If du encounters a file that it cannot read or open, by default it just ignores it and proceeds to the next file. To display a message on each file that cannot be read or opened, include the -r option.

Here is an example of the du command with no options:

```
$ du
7               ./mktg
4               ./eng
5               ./plans
9               ./ltrs
31              .
$ _
```

If you are interested only in summary information, you can also include the -s option with the du command. Here is an example:

```
$ du -s /usr
2387            /etc
$ _
```

Checking Free Disk Space   df

The df command, which is considerably more complex than the du command, tells you how many blocks are available for use in the current file system. Numerous options allow you to display information about devices, inodes, and percentages. Here is an example without options:

```
$ df
/           (/dev/dsk/c0d0s0):    1547 blocks    1089 inodes
/dev        (/dev/dsk/c0d0s2):   13456 blocks    9732 inodes
/etc        (/dev/dsk/c0d0s5):   10942 blocks    7328 inodes
/lib        (/dev/dsk/c0d0s9):   17403 blocks   12847 inodes
...
$ _
```

The first column gives the name of the directory; the second (in parentheses) gives the device location of the directory; the third gives the number of free blocks; and the fourth gives the number of inodes. Since there is one inode for each file, the number of inodes indicates how many files and directories are already in use.

For disk locations, c indicates controller number, d indicates disk number, and s indicates slice (or partition) number.

To display total values, include the -t (total) option with the du command, as shown here:

```
$ df -t
/           (/dev/dsk/c0d0s0):    1547 blocks    1089 inodes
                     total:       2195 blocks    1427 inodes
/dev        /dev/dsk/c0d0s1):   13456 blocks    9732 inodes
                     total:      22476 blocks   15205 inodes
/etc        (/dev/dsk/c0d0s5):   10942 blocks    7328 inodes
                     total:      28734 blocks   16428 inodes
/lib        (/dev/dsk/c0d0s9):   17403 blocks   12847 inodes
                     total:      42163 blocks   21056 inodes
...
$ _
```

You can determine how full each disk area is by dividing the number of blocks in use by the total number of blocks. For example, the root area in the example above is 70% full (1547/2195).

To see a difference display, which uses kilobytes instead of blocks, you can include the -k (kilobyte) option.

Backing Up Files

One task that you have to perform whether you are using DOS or UNIX is file backup. UNIX provides several commands for backing up files, but we'll focus on only one of them: the cpio (copy input/output) command.

The Copy I/O Program   cpio

You can use the cpio command to perform three basic functions:

- Copy files (out) to a disk or tape drive
- Copy files (in) from a disk or tape drive
- Copy files from one directory to another

You use the first function to back up your files; you use the second to recover files from backup; and you use the third to copy files to a different directory. You select these three functions of cpio by including one of the three *keys* in Table 9.1 as an argument to the cpio command.

Table 9.1
cpio *Keys*

Keys	Function
-o	Output: Copy files form a directory to a backup device.
-i	Input: Copy files from a backup device to a directory.
-p	Pass: Copy files from a source directory to a target directory.

Options for the `cpio` Command

You can specify several options for `cpio`. Merely bundle the option with the key. Table 9.2 lists the most common options:

Table 9.2
`cpio` *Options*

Option	Function
t	Table of contents: Don't copy any files; simply display file names.
v	Verbose: Display the name of each file as it is being copied.
B	Block: Write to tape in blocks of 5,120 bytes (output and input only).
d	Directory: Create any directories required (input and pass only).
l	Link: Link rather than copy (pass only).

Copying Files Out   cpio -o

Part of Paul's home directory is shown in Figure 9.1. For the sake of simplicity, let's assume that the subdirectory called `active` contains two ordinary files and two subdirectories, and that each subdirectory in turn contains three more files.

Suppose you want to back up these files on a tape drive that is identified by the file name `/dev/rmt/2`. Because you are copying from the file system out to a device, you must use the `-o` (output) key. Because you are copying to tape, you should use blocks, which require the `B` (blocks) option.

To copy only the files in one directory, you can pipe the file names to the `cpio` command with the `ls` command. In the following example, you will copy the two ordinary files in `/usr/paul/active` (`plan.master` and `memo.sales`) to tape:

```
$ pwd
/usr/paul/active
$ ls ¦ cpio -oB > /dev/mt/2
6 blocks
$ _
```

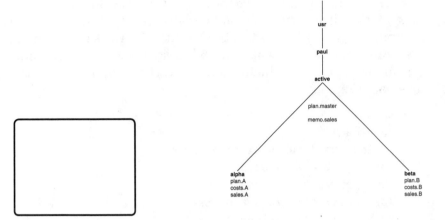

Figure 9.1
A directory to be backed up.

In the preceding example, the ls command provides the names of the files in the directory. The cpio command receives the names through a pipe (¦); it then sends the contents out in blocks (-oB), with the output redirected to the desired tape drive (> /dev/ rmt/2). On the following line, the message tells you that six blocks were written.

The preceding command copies ordinary files, but it excludes subdirectories. If you want to copy files, subdirectories, and the files within those subdirectories, use find rather than ls, as shown in the following example:

```
$ pwd
/usr/paul
$ find /usr/paul/active -print ¦
cpio - oB > /dev/rmt/2
25 blocks
$ _
```

NOTE: In UNIX, print means display or list. In the find command, -print means the same thing.

In this example, the `find` command provides the names of all files in the directory `/usr/paul/active` as input for the `cpio` command (`-print`). The rest of the command is the same as in the preceding example, except that 25 blocks are written this time. The following example includes the v (verbose) option to list the files being copied:

```
$ pwd
/usr/paul
$ find /usr/paul/active -print |
cpio - ovB > /dev/mt/2
/usr/paul/active/alpha/plan.A
/usr/paul/active/alpha/costs.A
/usr/paul/active/alpha/sales.A
/usr/paul/active/alpha
/usr/paul/active/alpha/plan.B
/usr/paul/active/alpha/costs.B
/usr/paul/active/alpha/sales.B
/usr/paul/active/beta
/usr/paul/active/plan.master
/usr/paul/active/memo.sales
25 blocks
$ _
```

A thorough backup, like the preceding one, includes the entire contents of the directory. If you have to recover from errors, you can restore directory `/usr/paul/active` exactly as it was.

Copying Files In   cpio -i

The input key (`-i`) is used to recover files that have been previously backed up using the output key (`-o`), which is described in the preceding subsection. Suppose an error has occurred in the file system and you must recover the files that you backed up on tape in the preceding example. You can use the following command line to copy the files back into `/usr/paul/active`:

```
$ pwd
/usr/paul/active
```

```
$ cpio -iB < /dev/rmt/2
$ _
```

In this example, the cpio command takes its input from the tape drive (< /dev/rmt/2) and copies it into the current directory with blocking retained (-iB).

If your original backup was to a disk drive, you would not have used blocks. Therefore, when you restore the files, you can omit the B option. Here is an example of restoring files from a disk drive:

```
$ pwd
/usr/paul/active
$ cpio -i < /dev/rdsk/c0d2s1
$ _
```

This example is nearly the same as the preceding example. The only two differences are the absence of the block option (B) and the name of the disk device (/dev/rdsk/c0d2s1). The name of the special file that represents the disk device incorporates the identifiers for the disk controller (c0), the disk (d2), and the slice (s1). Together, they form the name (c0d2s1). (Note that slice is another name for partition.)

Passing Files   cpio -p

You can use the -p (pass) key to copy files from one directory to another. You probably wouldn't use this third function of cpio for a backup, but it does give you an additional choice. Passing files is similar to copying files out, except that the target is a directory in the file system instead of a device.

Suppose you want to copy files from /usr/paul/active to /usr/paul/archive. If you want to copy only ordinary files, not subdirectories or the contents of subdirectories, you can use a command like this:

```
$ pwd
/usr/paul/active
```

```
$ ls ¦ cpio -pv../archive
/usr/paul/active/plan.master
/usr/paul/active/memo.sales
6 blocks
$ _
```

In the preceding example, cpio receives its input from ls through a pipe and passes it to the directory /usr/paul/archive. The v (verbose) option causes the names of the files to be displayed.

If you want to include all files in the current directory and all its subdirectories, you can use something like the following:

```
$ pwd
/usr/paul/active
$ find . -print ¦ cpio -pv ../archive
/usr/paul/active/alpha/plan.A
/usr/paul/active/alpha/costs.A
/usr/paul/active/alpha/sales.A
/usr/paul/active/alpha
/usr/paul/active/alpha/plan.B
/usr/paul/active/alpha/costs.B
/usr/paul/active/alpha/sales.B
/usr/paul/active/beta
/usr/paul/active/plan.master
/usr/paul/active/memo.sales
25 blocks
$ _
```

In the preceding example, the find command provides a list of names in the current directory (.) and pipes the list to cpio. This time, all files in the directory and its subdirectories are copied to /usr/paul/archive.

Other Backup Programs

In this section, we've restricted our discussion of backup and recovery to cpio. However, there are also several other programs that you can use. Table 9.3 offers a brief summary of these other programs.

Program	Comments
dd	A copy program that allows you to convert files from one format or standard to another.
tar	Tape archive: the predecessor of cpio, which is a little easier to use, but less versatile.
dump	A backup program that allows nine dump levels from 0 (entire system) to 9 (most recently changed files). Caution: dump is incapable of detecting end of tape.
restore	Counterpart of dump, used to restore from backup. Caution: it is difficult to select individual files with restor.
volcopy	Volume copy: copies an entire file system, but not individual files, to disk or tape.

Table 9.3
Backup and Recovery Programs

The cpio command is probably your best choice for backup and recovery because of its flexibility and versatility. When you use find to filter file names for it, cpio can pinpoint the files to be copied with great precision.

Setting Up Terminals

In this section, we'll take a look at the methods for describing the behavior and functions of a terminal to UNIX. UNIX must have a description of each terminal that is connected to the system.

Basic Terminal Settings   stty

Intercommunication between a terminal and a computer depends on agreement between the two on several communication traits: transmission speed, parity, word length, and so on. Default settings for these traits are stored for each terminal in a file called /etc/gettydefs. You can display the settings for your terminal by using the stty (set terminal) command. Much of what you will see displayed is beyond the scope of this book, so we'll confine our discussion to a few important items. If you use the stty command without any arguments, you will see something like this:

```
$ stty
speed 1200 baud; -parity
erase = ^h; kill = ^u;
...
$ _
```

Here is a summary of the four items displayed above:

speed 1200 baud   The terminal transmits and receives at 1200 bits per second.

-parity   Turn off parity detection, or error-checking, and set character size to 8 bits.

erase = ^h   The key combination for erasing the character behind the cursor is Ctrl-H (abbreviated as ^h).

kill = ^u   The key combination for erasing a command line is Ctrl-U (abbreviated as ^u).

By executing stty with arguments, you can change any of the settings for your terminal. For example, to change the speed, or transmission rate, to 2400 bits per second, use the following command:

```
$ stty 2400
$ _
```

The valid rates for this command are 50, 75, 110, 134, 150, 200, 300, 600, 1200, 1800, 2400, 4800, 9600, and 19200. The rate for your terminal must always match the rate for the host computer or modem.

If you want to enable parity detection for your terminal, you can use the following:

```
$ stty parity
$ _
```

If necessary, you can change more than one setting on a single command line, as illustrated in the next example:

```
$ stty 2400 parity
$ _
```

Keep in mind that stty does not change the settings of your terminal; it just informs UNIX of these settings. On older terminals, you change actual terminal settings by flipping DIP switches. On newer terminals, you make actual changes by selecting items from a screen menu. In any event, the host computer settings remain constant. You must change the settings on your terminal to match those of the computer.

As illustrated in the preceding examples, certain settings can be turned on (parity) or turned off (-parity) with a pair of similar arguments. The hyphen, or minus sign, indicates that the feature is off. Here's an example:

raw   Allow raw input

-raw   Allow cooked input

These options affect the way the system accepts information that you enter from your keyboard (the input device for your terminal). *Raw* means the system accepts exactly what you type, corrections and all; and *cooked* means that the corrections are incorporated before the system sees them. For example, suppose you begin a command line by typing sotr, back up and erase tr, and then correct the name by typing rt. Now you see sort on the command line, but what does the system see? Here is the answer:

```
sotr^h^hrt                   If you have selected raw
                             input, the system sees this.

sort                         If you have selected cooked
                             input, the system sees this
                             (the default).
```

NOTE: Most users need the cooked, or -raw, option. However, the raw option is also available for system programmers and troubleshooters.

Describing Full-Screen Features

Any time you see a program like vi, which requires a full-screen display, the system must have a description of your terminal in another file. Until a few years ago, that file was called /etc/ termcap. However, AT&T introduced a replacement for /etc/ termcap when it released System V: a directory called /usr/share/ lib/terminfo. The description of your terminal must be in one of these two places.

In the termcap (terminal capability) file, all terminal descriptions are in a single, large file. However, terminfo (terminal information) is a directory, which contains subdirectories named after letters of the alphabet. A subdirectory named a contains all the descriptions for terminals with names that begin with the letter a; b contains the entries for terminals whose names start with the letter b; and so on. Let's examine a sample entry for termcap; and then, let's look at the corresponding entry for terminfo. One of the simplest terminals to describe is the Lear Siegler ADM-3. This is what the description of the ADM-3 looks like in termcap:

```
13¦adm3¦3¦lsi adm3:bs:am:li#24:co#80:cl=^Z
```

The first four items, which are separated from each other by vertical bars (¦), are the four names that you can use to identify this terminal:

```
13 (el three, not thirteen)
adm3
3
lsi adm3
```

The remaining five items, which are separated by colons (:), are the codes that are used to identify the terminals capabilities:

bs	Backspace: it can move the cursor back and erase the previous character.
am	Automargins: when the cursor reaches the right side of the screen, the terminal can wrap it to the next line.
li#24	Number of lines: 24
co#80	Number of columns: 80
cl=^Z	Clear the screen: you can clear the screen by pressing Ctrl-Z (^Z).

Next, let's look at the entry for the same terminal (the ADM-3) in /usr/share/lib/terminfo/a/adm3. (Your system will have one of these entries, but not both.) Note that you won't actually be able to display the terminfo entry, because it has been compiled from an original entry that looks like this:

```
13¦adm3¦3¦lsi adm3, cub1=^H,
am, lines#24, cols#80, clear=^Z,
cud1=^J, ind=^J, cr=^M, bel=^G
```

The first four items, mnemonic names for the terminal, are exactly the same as the first four items in the termcap entry. The next five, which are separated from each other by commas, are similar to the corresponding entries in termcap, but not identical. Here is a closer look at them:

cub1=^H	Backspace: you can move the cursor back and erase the previous character by pressing Ctrl-H (^H).
am	Automargins: when the cursor reaches the right side of the screen, the terminal can wrap it to the next line.
lines#24	Number of lines: 24
cols#80	Number of columns: 80
clear=^Z	Clear the screen: you can clear the screen by pressing Ctrl-Z.

On the second line, the terminfo entry contains four additional items not found in the termcap entry:

cud1=^J	Cursor down: press Ctrl-J to move the cursor down.
ind=^J	Index: equivalent to the previous item.
cr=^M	Carriage return: Press Ctrl-M to perform a carriage return.
bel=^G	Bell (beep): Press Ctrl-G to sound the beeper.

Now, let's compare the two entries side by side:

tc termcap	terminfo	Description
13	13	First name
adm3	adm3	Second name
3	3	Third name
lsi adm3	lsi adm3	Fourth name
bs	cub1=^H	Backspacing
am	am	Automargins
li#24	lines#24	Lines: 24
co#80	Cols#80	Columns: 80

cl=^Z	clear=^Z	Clear the screen: [Ctrl]-[Z]
	cud1=^J	Cursor down: [Ctrl]-[J]
	ind=^J	Index: [Ctrl]-[J]
	cr=^M	Carriage return: [Ctrl]-[M]
	bel=^G	Bell (beeper): [Ctrl]-[G]

If you are using an ADM-3 terminal, and you are planning to use vi, then you must first execute one of the following command lines:

Bourne shell   **C shell**

```
$ TERM=adm3; export TERM     % setenv TERM adm3
$ _                          % _
```

Of course, you can also use any of the other three names for the terminal in place of adm3 (13, 3, or lsi adm3). Better yet, you can place one of these command lines in your start-up file. Then it will be executed automatically every time you log in. Here is the procedure:

Bourne shell   **C shell**

```
$ cd                         % cd
$ vi + .profile              % vi + .login
a                            a
TERM=adm3; export TERM       setenv TERM adm3
Esc                          Esc
:wq                          :wq
$ _                          % _
```

The terminal used in the preceding examples, the ADM-3, is one of the simplest terminals you can find. Some entries in termcap or terminfo can go on for thirty or forty lines for powerful, intelligent terminals. A sophisticated terminal, such as the DEC VT320 has extensive capabilities for handling text-editing, graphics, and international character sets.

Remember, you can't use vi on your terminal until you've done the following:

- You have located an entry for your terminal in termcap (or terminfo).

- You have identified your terminal to the system by assigning its name to the shell variable TERM.

On many UNIX systems, the system administrator handles these details for each user. However, on a system that has no system administrator, you may have to carry out these steps yourself.

Preparing for the X Environment

Before a user can use the X Window System, the system administrator must add the user's name to the list of authorized X users. The command for doing this for OPEN LOOK is called oladduser. To set up a user with login id steve, use the following command:

```
# oladduser steve
```

Once the system administrator has executed this command, this user can begin an X session by entering the following command:

```
$ olinit
```

Since the display server may be running on one machine and clients on another, each user must identify the machine on which the display server is running. If the name of the machine on which the display server is running is called xet and the display and screen numbers are both zero, you will have to execute one of the following command lines:

Bourne shell

```
$ DISPLAY=xet:0.0; export DISPLAY
$ _
```

C shell

```
% setenv DISPLAY xet:0.0
% _
```

Better yet, you can place one of these command lines in your start-up file. Then, it will be executed automatically every time you log in. Here is the procedure:

Bourne shell

```
$ cd
$ vi + .profile
a
DISPLAY=xet:0.0; export DISPLAY
 End

:wq
$ _
```

C shell

```
% cd
% vi + .login
a
setenv DISPLAY xet:0.0
 End

:wq
%
```

Shutting Down the System

Here is a brief description of the general steps required to shut a UNIX system down.

The Shutdown Script
/etc/shutdown

Many systems run around the clock. However, if you should ever have to shut down your system, all you have to do is run the shell script that is stored in directory /etc in a file called shutdown. The command line is as follows:

```
# shutdown
```

The details of this script vary from one installation to another. However, when you activate this script, it will perform the following operations for you:

- Make sure that the person running this script is in fact logged in as root.

- Determine whether or not any other users are still active on the system

- Notify such users of the shutdown with the wall (write all) command.

- Stop daemons, such as process accounting, error-logging, and the lp spooler.

- Complete all pending disk updates with the sync command.

- Unmount all devices with the umount (unmount) command.

- Terminate multiuser mode and return to single-user mode with the init s command.

Chapter 9 Quiz

1. What is the system administrator's login name?

2. What is the command for logging in as system administrator when you're already logged in as an ordinary user?

3. What is the name of the system administrator's directory?

4. What is the name of the file that identifies users who are authorized to use the system?

5. You suspect that an unauthorized user has just logged into the system. What command do you use to find out who is currently logged in?

6. What is the name of the directory that contains the names of the system's device files (such as disk and tape drives)?

7. What is the name of the file that contains information for the system timer?

8. What is the command for changing file permissions?

9. Write a command line to accomplish each of the following tasks:

10. Back up files from the current directory (without subdirectories) to a tape drive (/dev/rmt/3) with blocking.

11. Back up files from the current directory (without subdirectories) to a disk drive (/dev/rdsk/c0d1s0).

12. Restore the files backed up in Exercise 7 Assume you are now in the target directory.

13. Restore the files backed up in Exercise 8 Assume you are now in the target directory.

14. Copy the files in the current directory (/usr/willy/work) to a directory called /usr/willy/hold (Display the name of each file being copied.)

15. Change the speed of your terminal to 1200 bits per second.

16. Change your terminals erase character to Ctrl-H and change its kill character to Ctrl-E.

17. Make sure that all corrections on each command line are processed before the host computer receives them from your terminal.

Other questions:

18. What is the name of the original file that contains descriptions of terminals?

19. What is the name of the directory that will eventually replace the file named in Exercise 17?

20. What is the name of the shell variable that identifies your terminal type, as described in the file named in Exercise 17 (or the directory named in Exercise 18)?

21. Suppose your terminal type is wyse50. How would you make this known to your system if you're using the Bourne shell?

22. How would you do Exercise 20 if you were using the C shell?

23. Referring to Exercises 20 and 21, name the file in which you would place each statement.

Glossary

absolute pathname A pathname that explicitly identifies all directories from the root directory to an individual file. For example, pathname /home/albert/info/test refers to a file named test in directory info, which belongs to directory albert, which belongs to directory home, which belongs to the root directory /.

access As a noun, the ability to read, write, or execute files within a UNIX system. As a verb, to use that ability. Access to files in a UNIX file system is controlled by a set of permissions established by the system administrator. As super user, the system administrator has unlimited access within the system.

account A home directory and a set of access privileges assigned to a user to allow that user to carry out tasks in a UNIX system. Each new user is typically assigned a login name and a password by the system administrator, which allow the user to log in and begin using the resources of the system.

address In computer usage in general, the location at which something is stored in a computer system. Text, data, and computer programs are stored in memory and on disk at addresses, which are usually expressed as numeric values.

alias An alternate name, or abbreviation, used in place of a command or a sequence of commands in the C shell and the Korn shell.

append   To place after, or at the end of, a character, a line, or a file. In the vi editor, certain commands let you append text in a document. In the Bourne and C shells, the symbol >> allows you to append output to an existing file (or create a new file if the file does not yet exist).

append mode   In vi, the mode that allows you to type new text after existing text in a file; terminate this mode by pressing (Esc).

argument   On a command line, a name or code that is included with a command to modify the output of the command. For example, the command line ls -l has a single argument (-l). The shell identifies the command name with the notation $0, the first argument with $1, the second argument with $2, and so on.

ASCII   Acronym for American Standard Code for Information Interchange. A coding scheme for characters that appear on most keyboards, along with a set of control codes for operating terminals and printers. UNIX, DOS, and other operating systems for smaller computer systems use ASCII characters for input, output, and control. In Europe, the set of 128 7-bit codes is known as the ISO (International Standards Organization) character set. To accommodate accented characters in Europe and oriental character sets in Asia, UNIX is moving toward expanding the original 7-bit set into 8-bit extensions, which include 256 characters.

assign   To give a value to a variable in a programming or configuration statement. For example, in the Bourne shell statement TERM=vt100, you assign the value vt100 to the environmental variable TERM, which identifies your terminal type (VT100) to the UNIX system.

background   Processing that a system performs without requiring interaction with the user. In UNIX, append an ampersand (&) to the command line to request background processing.

background process   A process that runs without interacting with a terminal. Because each user in a UNIX system is allowed to have a number of background processes running simultaneously, UNIX is called a *multitasking* system.

backslash   A character (\) that is used in shell statements to *quote* another character (that is, to remove its special meaning to the shell). For example, if you want to use a dollar sign as a dollar sign, rather than as a symbol for end of line, enter \$.

backup   A copy of a file (or a group of files) that is stored off-line in the event that a computer system fails, losing or damaging the original file or files.

basename   The name of a file minus any extension that may be included in the full name. For example, if the full name of the source file for a C program is combine.c, its basename is combine.

batch processing   The opposite of *interactive processing*; work that is collected at a peripheral site, then forwarded to a central computer at the end of a fixed period. Such work may be forwarded at the end of each hour, each day, or each week.

baud rate   See *data rate*.

Berkeley UNIX   The versions of UNIX that were first developed at the University of California in Berkeley in the mid-1970s. Many features that were originally part of Berkeley UNIX, such as the vi editor and the C shell, have since been incorporated into XENIX and AT&T UNIX.

bin   A directory that contains executable programs, the majority of which are stored in binary files. Most programs are found in directories /bin and /usr/bin; however, users often keep additional programs in private bin directories, such as /home/charles/bin.

bit   Acronym for *bi*nary dig*it*, the basic atomic unit of a digital computer. There are eight bits in each *byte*, which contains one character.

block   A set of data (typically 256, 512, or 1,024 bytes) that is stored as a unit on a tape or disk.

bold   In printing, a font style that uses heavier strokes than the standard font (which is called *Roman*).

boot   To begin the operation of a computer system, using a bootstrap program that copies the operating system from disk to memory. In UNIX, the booting process includes one phase to initiate single-user operation and another phase to carry out a transition from single-user to multiple-user operation. A shell script called /etc/rc aids in the booting process by running many programs and processes automatically.

Bourne shell   The original command processor for the UNIX system, which is still the most widely used. The Bourne shell lacks the more sophisticated features of the C shell and the Korn shell, but it runs faster.

braces   A pair of symbols ({ and }) that are used to group items in a statement. In the Bourne shell, braces surround commands that are to be executed together; in the C shell, braces indicate variable names and cause a list of items to be expanded.

brackets   A pair of symbols ([and]) that are used to group items in a statement. In all shells and in editors, square brackets are used to identify a set of characters.

BSD   Berkeley Software Distribution, used to identify various versions of Berkeley UNIX, such as BSD 4.2 and BSD 4.3.

buffer   In computer technology in general, an area in memory where information is stored temporarily, usually for an intermediary step in a process. When you use a text editor, you first enter the text in a buffer, and then you store it in a disk file.

bug   A hardware or software error. According to tradition, the term originated when an early computer failure was found to be the result of a dead insect.

bus   An internal communication network in a computer system. A typical system includes an address bus, a data bus, and a control bus. The width of the address bus determines the amount of memory that can be addressed by the system.

byte   A unit of eight bits, which contains a single character of text. The capacity of memory and disks is measured in bytes, kilobytes, and megabytes.

carriage return   A character, abbreviated as CR, that is used in most ASCII systems to terminate a line of text. The key that generates the character, Ctrl-M is labeled either Enter or Return on most keyboards. In UNIX, newline (NL) is used instead of carriage return (CR) to terminate lines.

case The capitalization or noncapitalization of a character. Capitalized characters are called uppercase; noncapitalized characters are called lowercase. In DOS, case is ignored in file names; in UNIX, case is considered.

character The basic unit of textprocessing, which can be any of the following: a letter of the alphabet, a number, a symbol, a blank space, or a control character. Most control characters are typed by holding down the Ctrl (control) key and pressing another key on the keyboard.

child process A process spawned from another process. The original process is called the parent, and the new process is called the *child*. To create, or spawn, a new process, the UNIX system duplicates an existing process and then changes the recently created duplicate to the process desired. This is known as *forking*.

chip A tiny piece of semiconductor material, usually silicon, onto which has been etched a set of electronic circuits. A hundred or more chips can be sliced from each silicon wafer, which is two or three inches in diameter. Because each chip is housed in a package with metallic leads, people often refer to the entire package as a chip. Dozens of chips can be plugged into a circuit board, and a set of circuit boards form a computer system.

C language A computer programming language that combines the ease of use of a high-level language with the system-control features of a low-level language. About 90 percent of the UNIX system is written in C. During the 1970s, UNIX and C were closely related, but now C has become a separate tool in its own right and is used widely outside UNIX.

client In a UNIX-based network, a UNIX system that uses the file systems provided by another UNIX system. In the X window system, it is an application program which depends on the display server.

command A request to have something accomplished by a computer system using a computer program. The program can be as simple as date, which merely displays the date and time, or as complex as vi, which offers a sophisticated set of editing tools.

command line   A line of input, usually from a keyboard, that includes at least one command, along with any accompanying arguments and connectors. Commands can be grouped together on a command line or connected by a pipe. In addition, the input and output of commands can be redirected. In the following example, the ls command, modified by the -1 argument, is piped to the pg command: $ ls -1 ¦ pg

command name   A name for a program that you can type at your keyboard to execute the program. The name of the command can usually be followed by arguments on a command line.

command processor   A program that interprets command lines and provides for carrying out the tasks requested in command lines. In the UNIX system, the command processor is also known as the shell. There are three command processors used on UNIX systems: the Bourne shell, the C shell, and the Korn shell. See also *Bourne shell*, *C shell*, and *Korn shell*.

communication speed   See *data rate*.

compile   To translate the high-level symbolic notation used in a computer program into the low-level coding required to run the program on the computer.

compiler   A computer program that translates high-level programs, called source files, into low-level programs, called object files.

computer   An electronic machine that can perform a variety of high-speed tasks under the direction of a *program* or a set of programs. A program that handles the basic functioning of the computer is called an operating system; a program that is used to carry out a specific task for a user is called an application program. UNIX is an example of an operating system.

concatenate   To join two or more files or segments of text to form a single unit. The cat command, which is an abbreviation of this word, concatenates files.

configure   To adjust the hardware or software components of a system to certain specifications. A particular arrangement of devices or programs is called a *configuration*.

console   A computer system's main terminal, from which system administration is performed. Recent releases of UNIX allow any terminal to be designated as the console, which is identified by device file /dev/console.

constant   An assigned value that remains unchanged, as opposed to a *variable*.

control character   A character, usually generated by holding down the Ctrl key and pressing another key, that is used to control the operation of the terminal or the printer. For example, Ctrl-I causes an advance to the next tab stop on terminals and printers that support this feature. A key control character in the UNIX system is Ctrl-D, which indicates end of file (and end of session).

controller   A machine that handles the flow of data to and from a peripheral device, such as a disk or tape drive.

cooked mode   A mode in which input is accepted command line by command line rather than character by character. Cooked mode, the default for the UNIX system, is the opposite of *raw mode*.

core   An obsolete term for computer memory.

core dump   A recording of the contents of computer memory at the moment when an error occurred. Unfortunately for ordinary users, core dumps are left in working directories in ordinary files named core. The contents of these files are of value only to those who are familiar with the internal workings of the UNIX system.

cpio   A UNIX program that is used to copy files in one of three different ways: from a working directory to a backup device, from a backup device to a working directory, or from one directory to another.

crash   A major hardware or software failure, which interrupts the functioning of a computer system.

cron A UNIX daemon that periodically checks the contents of a file called /var/lib/crontab and carries out any tasks due to be performed.

crontab A short name for file /var/lib/crontab, which contains a list of UNIX commands to be performed at specific times. A system administrator can use crontab as an automatic timer to trigger the initiation of important jobs.

CRT Abbreviation for cathode-ray tube, which provides the screen display for most terminals.

C shell The command processor that was designed at the University of California by William N. Joy and others. This command processor allows you to retrieve previous command lines (which are called *events*) and re-execute them, either with or without modification.

cursor The symbol that appears on your video screen to indicate the location of the next character that you type from your keyboard.

daemon A program that, once activated, starts itself and carries out a specific task. The UNIX system uses daemons extensively to handle jobs that have been queued, such as printing, mail, and communication.

data Information that is to be, or has been, processed by a computer. Strictly speaking, *data* is the plural of *datum*, but it is often used collectively as if it were singular.

data rate In all forms of communication, the rate at which data is sent or received, measured in bits per second. Also referred to as *communication speed*, *bit rate*, and *baud rate*.

debug To rid hardware or software of errors, or bugs.

decimal With reference to numbers, base ten.

default A selection or value that is provided by computer hardware or software when you don't make an explicit choice.

delete To remove a segment of text, a file, or a directory. The vi editor has several commands, including x and d, to delete text. The UNIX rm command is used to delete a file; the rmdir command is used to delete a directory.

device In computer usage in general, any piece of equipment that is connected directly to a computer, such as a terminal, printer, modem, disk drive, or tape drive. Also called a *peripheral device*, an *input/output device*, or an *I/O device*. In UNIX, a file system becomes a logical device, eliminating the need to refer to disk drives by name.

device file A file that represents a physical device that is mounted on a UNIX system. All device files, also known as *special files*, are stored in directory /dev.

directory In operating systems in general, a file that contains the names of other files. UNIX has a primal directory that is called *root* (represented by /), along with subdirectories organized in a hierarchy. When you log into a UNIX system, you start in your home directory. You can change to another directory with the cd command, display the name of the current directory with the pwd command, create a directory with the mkdir command, display the contents of a directory with the ls command, and remove a directory with the rmdir command. You can use a single dot (.) to represent the current directory and a pair of dots (..) to refer to the parent directory.

display server In the X Window System, the software that manages the display. The display server reads input from the keyboard and the mouse and writes output to the video. Also called the *server*.

disk A mass storage medium that employs a magnetic coating on a round, flat substance that holds electrical charges. If the underlying substance (called the *substrate*) is plastic, it is a floppy disk, or a diskette; if the substrate is metallic, it is a hard disk.

document Another term for a file that contains text.

DOS An operating system developed for microcomputers in the early 1980s (the version that runs on the IBM Personal Computer is called PC DOS). Originally patterned after CP/M, more recent versions of MS-DOS have been heavily influenced by UNIX concepts.

drive A mechanical device that spins a storage medium (disk or tape), reads data from it, and writes data to it.

driver   A software program that handles the details of interface between a computer and a peripheral device.

echo   To repeat on the screen characters that are entered at the keyboard. You can use the echo command to explicitly display a string of characters.

ed   The original UNIX text editor that preceded vi. The ed program is a primitive line editor that lacks the full-screen capabilities of vi.

edit   To make changes to a file, such as moving, copying, inserting, and deleting text.

editor   A program that is used to make changes to a file. The two programs used most often on UNIX systems are the ed line editor and the full-screen vi visual interpreter. The programmable emacs editor is also used at many UNIX installations.

environment   A set of shell variables and their assigned values provided for each process that is called. The default environment for your terminal is stored in your home directory in a file called either .profile (Bourne or Korn shell) or .login (C shell). You can modify the environment by reassigning shell variables.

eqn   A preprocessor for troff that lets you format mathematical expressions. The corresponding preprocessor for nroff is called neqn.

erase character   The character that is used to erase the character just typed on a command line—usually either the number symbol (#) or backspace (Ctrl-H).

Esc   The escape key (Esc), which is used in vi to leave text-entry mode and return to command mode.

ex   An enhanced version of the ed line editor. The vi editor is the visual interpreter of ex.

execute   To run a program. On a chmod command line, you can add or remove permission to execute a file using the x symbol. You must have execute permission for a directory to be able to change to that directory or to be able to include that directory's name in a pathname given on a command line.

expression   A representation of a number or text that can vary, depending on how individual values are interpreted. Expressions are often used to match text in a file or match file names in a directory. An example of an expression is `memo.*`, which may be used to match `memo.402`, `memo.TKL`, `memo.old`, and so on.

extension   That part of a file name that follows a period (also known as a *suffix*). For example, each source file for a C program has an extension of `.c`.

field   In text-processing, a segment of a line of text that may be named and processed by a program. The `sort` program can use fields when it sorts lines in a file. In UNIX, fields are usually separated by spaces or tabs.

field separator   A character, also called a *delimiter*, that is used to separate one field from another. The default field separator for many programs, such as `sort`, is a blank space (or a tab).

file   A collection of characters that has a name and may contain text, a program, data, the names of other files, or information about a device. A file that contains the names of other files is called a *directory*; a file that contains information about a device is called a *device file* (or *special file*); and a file that begins with a period is called an *invisible file* (because the `ls` command without an argument won't display it).

file name   The name given to a file, which must be unique within any given directory. In UNIX, you can use as many as 14 characters in a file name, including hyphens, periods, and plus signs.

File Manager   In the X Window System, the software that allows you to select, copy, move, and open files and directories in a graphical environment.

file system   A set of files on a disk, together with the information required to manage the files. The directories within a UNIX file system form a hierarchy.

file type   A description of the function of a file. These types include ordinary files, directories, and special files, which represent devices in the system.

filter   A program that takes a set of data (usually in a file) as input, processes the data, and makes the processed data its output. Some examples of filters include `grep`, `sort`, `awk`, and `sed`.

foreground   A conceptual location in a computer system where interaction takes place between a user and a process initiated by the user; the opposite of *background*.

format   To prepare a document for printing by filling and aligning lines of text, by marking bold and underlining, and by making other enhancements to a printed page.

full-duplex   A communication mode that allows data to flow in both directions simultaneously.

global   From the beginning of a file to the end. This term is often used to describe an operation such as a search; the opposite of *local*.

graphical user interface (GUI)   In computer usage in general, a user interface that features screen windows, icons, and mouse control. The X Window System provides a variety of graphical user interfaces for UNIX.

grep   A program that allows you to search for occurrences of text in a file (or in a group of files).

group   A collection of users on a UNIX system who have something in common and share a group identifier. All those working on a particular project or all members of a certain organization may belong to a group. Group identifiers are listed in the `/etc/group` file.

half-duplex   A communication mode that allows data to flow in only one direction at a time.

hardware   The electronic components of a computer system, as opposed to *software*, the programs that run on the system.

hardwired terminal   A terminal that is connected to a host computer via a dedicated line (that is, a line that is not shared with any other terminal).

hexadecimal   With reference to numbers, base sixteen. To express hexadecimal numbers, the following digits are used: 0, 1, 2, 3, 4, 5, 6, 7, 8, 9, A, B, C, D, E, F. For example, the decimal number 26 would be represented in hexadecimal notation as 1A.

high-level language   A computer language that can be used on many different computer systems. By contrast, a *low-level language* refers to specific hardware locations and is inseparable from a specific hardware architecture. Another name for low-level language is *assembly language*.

history   In the C shell and the Korn shell, a list of command lines (or events) previously executed by a user.

home directory   The directory that a user enters after logging into a UNIX system; also called the *login directory*.

host   A central computer, also known as a *host computer*, which provides processing for terminals and other peripheral devices (and, in some instances, other computers).

indent   To offset text from the margin. You can indent either the first line of a paragraph or all lines.

input   Data entered into a computer system to be processed by a program.

insert mode   In vi, the mode that allows you to type new text in front of existing text in a file; terminate this mode by pressing Esc.

install   To connect a piece of hardware to a computer system; to place the program files of a piece of software in a directory, where they can be executed.

interactive processing   Performance of tasks on a computer system that involves continual exchange of information between the computer and a user; the opposite of *batch processing*.

I/O   Abbreviation for input/output: the transfer of data between a computer and its peripheral equipment, or devices.

italic   In printing, a font style that uses slanted strokes and rounded corners. Also called oblique.

justify   In text-formatting, to align text flush left or flush right (or both) against a margin.

kernel   The program that interacts between a UNIX system and computer hardware. The kernel occupies approximately 10% of the UNIX system.

kill character   The key that you use to erase a command line, often either the at sign (@) or Ctrl-U.

Korn shell   The most recent command processor, named after David G. Korn, which combines the advantages of the earlier Bourne shell and C shell.

laser printer   A printer that employs the technology of a photocopier and is capable of printing text (in varied fonts) and graphics together on the same page.

link   Attachment of an existing file to a directory (usually a different directory) that allows file-sharing. You can use the ln command to form a new link.

local   Restricted to only part of a file; the opposite of *global*.

login name   The name by which a user logs into a UNIX system; any files owned by the user are identified by this name.

logout   Termination of a UNIX session. Merely turning off your terminal isn't always enough; sometimes you must end a session by logging out.

low-level language   A computer language that deals with hardware registers by name; also known as *assembly language*. A program written in a low-level language can be used only on a computer system that uses one type of main processor (or possibly a member of a family of processors). Assembly language, which uses symbolic addressing, is one step above machine language.

macro   A command that incorporates a set of other commands. You custom design a command, called a macro, from existing commands. Both the vi editor and the nroff and troff formatters use macros. The mm macro package described in this book is an example of a large collection of nroff and troff macros.

magnetic tape   A storage medium that allows you to archive a large amount of data relatively inexpensively. Files stored on magnetic tape, unlike those stored on disk, cannot be retrieved by random access. You can back up files to magnetic tape using several different programs, such as dd, tar, and cpio.

mainframe   The largest and most powerful type of computer system that is widely used. A mainframe typically occupies many cabinets and fills an entire room. Amdahl's UTS is a UNIX-derived operating system that runs on mainframes.

man   A program that lets you display pages from the UNIX reference manual. For example, if you want detailed information about the who command, you enter man who at the shell prompt. (The man program may or may not be available at your particular UNIX site.)

-man   An nroff/troff macro package that is specifically designed to handle pages from the UNIX reference manual.

mass storage device   A piece of equipment, such as a disk or tape drive, that stores large amounts of data relatively inexpensively. Although these devices cost less than the main memory in a computer system, they are much slower to access. The UNIX system is designed to be stored on disk, while those files needed at a particular moment are copied to memory for processing. Mass storage devices are also used for daily and weekly backups.

-me   An nroff/troff macro package, developed for Berkeley UNIX systems, that formats documents.

medium   A disk, tape, or other object on which information is actually stored. Most media used today employ a metallic substance, such as iron oxide, to capture magnetic charges. However, a newer technology involving plastic discs and optical scanning (CD-ROM) will eventually supersede today's magnetic methods.

memory   The electronic work area of a computer where actual processing takes place. Today's state-of-the-art desktop computer has at least one megabyte of memory. During the first twenty years or so of the computer age, memory was constructed using tiny magnetic rings called cores and was referred to as *core memory*. This terminology has survived in the UNIX system; a recording of memory contents at the moment of a failure is still called a *core dump*.

metacharacter   A character that is used to carry a special meaning, such as a caret (^, beginning of line), a dollar sign ($, end of line), or an asterisk (*, match any character). To use one of these characters without special meaning, you must either precede it with a backslash (\) or enclose it within quotation marks. Bypassing the special meaning of a metacharacter is called *escaping* or *quoting* the character.

microcomputer   A small desktop computer, also called a personal computer (PC), that is usually used by one person at a time.

microprocessor   A main processor (or CPU, central processing unit) that is usually contained on a single chip.

minicomputer   An intermediate-size computer, typically about the size of a refrigerator. The UNIX system was originally developed in the late 1960s and early 1970s on a minicomputer, the PDP-7 of Digital Equipment Corporation.

-mm   An nroff/troff macro package for formatting manuscripts; the standard macro package of UNIX System V. It is the most extensive macro package available.

modem   Abbreviation for modulator/demodulator, a device that translates digital codes into tones (that is, modulates them) and translates tones into digital codes (that is, demodulates them). The purpose of a modem is to allow you to send information from a digital computer system across telephone lines to another computer system. In the twenty-first century, when analog telephone lines are replaced with optical fiber lines capable of carrying audio, data, and video signals, there will no longer be a need for modems.

mount   To connect a device to the UNIX system and thereby integrate it into the system.

mouse   A pointing device with control buttons that allows you to point to, select, and maneuver items on the screen in a graphical display.

-ms   An nroff/troff macro package for formatting manuscripts; the standard macro package for the UNIX system before System V.

Multics   The predecessor of the UNIX system; an experimental operating system developed by MIT and Bell Laboratories in the 1960s. The UNIX system derived much of its technology (and its name) from Multics.

multiplex To interleave signals or data from different sources. The UNIX system employs multiplexing of memory.

multitasking Running more than one process at once by relying on time-sharing techniques.

multiuser Supporting more than one user. UNIX is a multiuser, multitasking operating system.

network A system of hardware and software that connects a group of computers and allows them to transmit information back and forth to each other. Networks are usually classed as either local area networks (LAN) or wide-area networks (WAN).

neqn An nroff preprocessor that lets you format mathematical expressions for character printers. (The corresponding troff preprocessor is called eqn.)

nroff The UNIX text formatting program that handles text that is to be printed on character printers. The program handles text to be printed on laser printers and phototypesetters. Otherwise, the two programs are nearly identical.

octal With reference to numbers, base 8. The octal digits are 0, 1, 2, 3, 4, 5, 6, and 7.

operating system A program that manages the details of operating a computer system. These details include managing memory, keeping track of directories and files, scheduling processes, and handling input/output operations. Application programs rely on the operating system to perform tasks.

option An argument on a command line, usually preceded by a minus sign, that modifies the functioning of the command—also known as a *flag* or a *switch*. For example, the -x option on the command line vi -x allows the vi editor to read an encrypted file.

ordinary file The most common type of file in a UNIX file system; it contains text, programs, or data. When you display a list of files with the command ls -l, ordinary files are identified by hyphens (-).

output Data that has been processed by a computer program.

owner   The user who creates a file and therefore has privileged access to it.

parent directory   The directory above the current directory. In the hierarchy of a UNIX file system, every directory except root has a parent. You can refer to the parent directory using the double dot notation (..).

password   A personal identifier used to validate a user's authorization to log into a UNIX system. A password may consist of one to fourteen characters, but an effective password should be at least six characters long. It should contain a combination of upper- and lowercase letters, numbers, and symbols that you can easily memorize. However, it should not contain a sequence that is easy to guess, such as the name of a relative, spouse, or pet, your telephone number, or your license number.

password file   A file, /etc/passwd, that contains basic information about each user authorized to log into a given UNIX system. For each user, the file contains a line that gives the user's login name, encrypted password, user identifier, group identifier (if any), home directory, and login program.

pathname   A sequence of directory names that indicates the location of a file in a UNIX file system. A *relative pathname* gives the location relative to the current directory; an *absolute pathname* gives the location with respect to the root directory. Each directory name is separated from the next name lower in the hierarchy by a slash (/), while the root directory is denoted by a slash (/) and nothing more. Suppose you are currently in directory /usr/albert/plans and want to refer to another directory under albert called letters. The absolute pathname would be /usr/albert/letters (the same from any directory); the relative pathname would be ../letters.

peripheral device   See *device*.

personal computer   A computer intended for use by one person; also called a *microcomputer*. The most widely used personal computers today are the IBM Personal Computer (along with its derivatives and compatibles) and the Apple Macintosh. A personal computer can be used as a terminal in a UNIX system. The most powerful personal computers, such as those that are based on the Pentium microprocessor, are capable of running UNIX itself.

phototypesetter An expensive, high-quality, high-resolution printer that produces printed output for professional work. Like a much lower-resolution laser printer, a phototypesetter is capable of generating a variety of typefaces in different sizes. In UNIX, the troff program formats text that is intended for laser printers and phototypesetters.

pica A unit of measure in typography (1/6 of an inch), commonly used to indicate the length of a line of type. For example, a column that is three and a half inches wide is 21 picas wide. Picas are often combined with *points* for more precise measurements. For example, you could express 7/12 of an inch as 3,06 (3 picas and 6 points). See also *point*.

pid See *process identification number*.

pipe A programming device that lets you use the output of one process as the input of another. You must use a vertical bar (¦) between two command invocations to indicate piping. For example, to display the contents of the current directory one screenful at a time, you can pipe the ls -l command through the pg command, as follows:

```
$ ls -l ¦ pg
```

The result of this command line is that the pg command uses the file display generated by ls -l as its input. The output is the file display in 24-line segments that will fit on your screen.

pipe line a sequence of commands connected by pipes. For example, to display the lines of a file called entries in alphabetical order, you could construct the following command line:

```
$ cat entries ¦ sort ¦ pg
```

When you execute this command line, the cat command retrieves the file, the sort command arranges the lines in order, and the pg command displays the result in 24-line segments.

point   A unit of measure in typography (1/72 of an inch), used to indicate the size of a typeface. Most ordinary text is set in 10, 11, or 12 points; headings are usually set in approximately 12 to 24 points; and chapter headings are generally 24 points or larger. There are 12 points in a *pica*, and the two units are often combined in typographic measurements. For example, you could express a quarter of an inch as 1,06 (1 pica and 6 points).

port   To modify software so that it will operate in a different environment. For example, a programmer could modify a DOS program to allow it to run under UNIX, or modify a UNIX system designed for a minicomputer so that it will run on a microcomputer.

A *port* is also an input or output data path on a microcomputer (called a *channel* on a mainframe).

portable   Pertaining to software that can be ported, or modified to run in another environment. UNIX is an example of a portable system. Because all the programming that is hardware-specific is restricted to the *kernel*, a programmer can port UNIX to a new computer system by changing only the kernel (about 10 to 15% of the total UNIX code).

preprocessor   A program that manipulates data before the primary processing program goes to work. Examples are the eqn and tbl programs that handle equations and tables before troff performs general-purpose formatting on a text file.

process   The computer activity that takes place while a command is being executed. In the UNIX system, there can be many processes that represent different invocations of the same program. The kernel assigns a unique process identification number (*pid*) to each process active in the system.

process identification number   Usually abbreviated *pid*, a number that the kernel assigns to a process active in a UNIX system. The pid is especially important for background processes, because you must know the number to terminate the process (kill). If you start a background process, you can determine the pid in two ways: (1) note the number when the shell displays it on the screen; or (2) display it by using the ps command.

program   A sequence of instructions to a computer system, which directs the operation of the system. The concept of a program is what distinguishes a computer from nearly every other type of machine. To operate a lawn mower or a bicycle, you manually direct the operation of the machine with your hands and feet. To operate a computer, you have to provide the machine with a detailed list of instructions, which the machine appears to perform on its own.

Programs are referred to collectively as *software* and are classed as either those that aid the computer in its basic functioning (operating systems) or those that are designed to carry out a specific task (application software). Application software performs the work that people use computers for; an operating system carries out the administrative tasks that allow applications to function smoothly.

When writing programs, programmers use a *programming language* to facilitate the job. Such a language lets the programmer work with a set of notational conventions that lend themselves to human usage. However, before the program can be used by the computer, it must be translated into a set of codes that lend themselves to machine operation. For a high-level language (such as FORTRAN, Pascal, or C), the process of translating the program is called *compiling*; for a low-level assembly language, the process is called *assembling* the program. A program that compiles other programs is called a *compiler*; a program that assembles other programs is called an *assembler*. Another type of high-level language (such as BASIC) is interpreted line-by-line by a program called an *interpreter*. Programs written in low-level languages run the fastest of all types of programs; programs written in interpreted languages run the slowest.

programming language   See *program*.

prompt   Text or symbols that appear on the screen to solicit input from a user. The most common prompt in the UNIX system is the one that informs you that the system is ready to accept a command line. The default for this prompt on most systems is a dollar sign ($) for the Bourne or Korn shell, a percent sign (%) for the C shell, and a pound sign (#) for the super user.

pwd   A UNIX command that displays the name of the current directory (*print working directory*).

queue   A list of jobs awaiting execution (from the French word for line). Queues in a UNIX system are nearly always processed by *daemons*. See also *daemon*.

quoting   Preventing special characters from being interpreted as special characters, often using quotation marks. To quote a string of characters, you can surround them with either double quotes ("*string*") or single quotes ('*string*'); single quotes are used more extensively. To quote a single character, precede it with a backslash (\). For example, to read a dollar sign as a dollar sign (rather than as a symbol for end-of-line), enter \$.

raw mode   A mode in which characters entered into the UNIX system are read and interpreted one at a time. See also *cooked mode*.

real-time processing   Processing by a computer system that takes place inside the computer while events related to the processing are taking place outside the computer. An example is the processing used to determine a missile's position during a missile launch; the processing must keep pace with external events. Earlier versions of UNIX were not suitable for real-time applications; however, efforts are under way to correct this deficiency in newer releases.

record   In database applications, a complete set of information for one item. Each individual piece of information is contained in a *field*; a given number of fields form a record. Some files, such as /etc/passwd, /etc/group, and /var/lib/crontab, contain one-line records; others, such as /etc/termcap and /usr/share/lib/terminfo/* contain multiple-line records.

redirection   The act of either accepting input from a source other than the standard input (the keyboard) or sending output to a destination other than the standard output (the video screen). The symbols used are the less than sign (<) for redirection of input and the greater than sign (>) for redirection of output. For example, to send Paul a message already typed and stored in a file called news, use the following command line:

```
$ mail paul < news
```

To store the contents of the current directory in a file called files, use the following command line:

```
$ ls -l > files
```

To append text to an existing file, you can use the double greater than sign (>>), as in the following example:

```
$ ls -l >> files
```

regular expression A set of symbols, including text and metacharacters, used to search for text. The most common components are the period (.), which matches one character; the asterisk (*), which matches any number of characters; and brackets ([*string*]), which list a set of characters to be matched.

relative pathname See *pathname*.

request An nroff/troff command. Most of these include a period, followed by two lowercase letters. Many requests also include a numeric argument, such as the page offset request, .po *n*.

restore To retrieve data that has been previously backed up from a computer system. If your computer system fails, you might have to restore data to resume use of the system.

Roman In typesetting, the normal font, which is neither bold nor italic.

root The primary directory in the UNIX system; the login name for the superuser. A system administrator who is just logging in can log in as superuser by typing root; one who is already logged in as an ordinary user can enter the su (substitute user) command. Either way, the next step is to enter the superuser password.

RS-232C A standard for serial communication that is used to connect computers, terminals, printers, and modems. The complete standard calls for 25 wires, but many configurations use as few as three (send, receive, and ground). A typical RS-232C connector is enclosed in a trapezoidal case about two inches wide and one-half inch high.

scroll bar   In graphical displays in general and in the X Window System in particular, a vertical or horizontal screen display that allows you to scroll through text in a window.

scrolling   The act of shifting a screen display up or down one line at a time.

search path   A list of directories in which a given user's commands may be found. Each time the user enters a command at the keyboard, the shell searches the list to find the command. You can execute only those commands that belong to the directories in your search path. The search path is usually found in the initialization file (`.profile` for the Bourne shell or `.login` for the C shell).

security   Measures taken to keep intruders out of a computer system. The UNIX system uses login names and passwords to maintain security, and these provide a fairly good defense against unauthorized entry. However, sophisticated intruders have devised a number of clever schemes for bypassing ordinary UNIX security.

server   In networks in general, a station that provides some service to other stations on the network. See *display server*.

session   One complete interaction between a user and the UNIX system, from login to logout. It is possible for a given user to carry on more than one session at a time using either windows or several different terminals.

shell   A command processor for the UNIX system, which includes its own programming language. As command processor, the shell interprets command line and arranges to have the requested tasks performed. As programming language, the shell supports variables, logical control, and conditional statements. The original command processor is called the Bourne shell; an enhanced version developed at the University of California is called the C shell; and a more recent version that combines the features of both is called the Korn shell. The Bourne and Korn shells are named for their originators; the C shell is named after the C programming language, from which it borrows many features. The word shell conveys the sense of something that houses something else within it. You can think of the shell as a process that surrounds the kernel and conceals it from the ordinary user.

sleep   Pertaining to a UNIX process, to suspend execution until some event takes place or for a specific period of time. Processes automatically sleep while waiting for results from peripherals. In addition, you can request a general suspension with the `sleep` command.

software   A collective name for the programs that run on a computer system, as opposed to *hardware*, the electronic components.

sorting   The process of rearranging a list of items in a prescribed order. The UNIX `sort` command lets you sort information in a variety of different ways.

special character   A character used to form a *regular expression* for the purpose of carrying out a search; also called a *metacharacter*.

special file   A file that represents a hardware device; also known as a *device file*.

standard input   The expected source of input to a process (the keyboard is the default).

standard output   The expected destination of output from a process (the video screen is the default).

string   In computer usage in general, a sequence of characters.

su   A UNIX command (substitute user) that allows a user to use a different login name. If you have more than one account on a UNIX system, you can change from one to the other with the `su` command. By issuing this command without an argument, a system administrator can change from ordinary user to superuser.

subdirectory   A directory that is directly below another in the hierarchy of the UNIX file system. In a pathname, the slash (/) separates the name of each subdirectory from its parent. For example, /home/chet/files is a subdirectory of /home/chet.

super user   A term used to describe the system administrator as a user of a UNIX system, particularly the system administrator's freedom of access without regard to permissions.

sync   A UNIX command that updates files by writing from memory to disk. You can think of this command as the one that synchronizes disk space with memory.

tab   A control character (Ctrl-I) that causes either a cursor to advance to a predetermined horizontal location (terminal) or a printhead to advance (printer).

tape drive   A machine that reads from and writes to magnetic tape. Because the data is stored sequentially on the tape, this kind of mass storage device is best suited for full system backups.

tar   A UNIX program (tape archive) that lets you copy files to and from magnetic tape, using a variety of options. (In XENIX, the program is also used to copy to and from diskettes.)

tbl   An nroff/troff preprocessor that lets you format tabular material.

tee   A UNIX program that allows you to send text to a file and display the text on the screen simultaneously. As shown in the following example, the tee command is always preceded by a pipe symbol (¦):

```
$ ls -l ¦ tee files
```

The list of file names is displayed on the screen and also stored in files. Now you can retrieve the information using cat, pg, or more, or edit it using vi.

TeleType   A type of terminal, in use until about the mid-1970s, that employed printing on a roll of paper rather than a video display. The prevalence of this type of terminal during the period when UNIX was being developed made the words terminal and teletype nearly synonymous in UNIX terminology. The abbreviation tty is used to this day to represent terminal, even though teletype machines are now obsolete.

$TERM A shell variable that identifies the type of terminal you are using. The name assigned to this variable must be defined in the UNIX system's terminal definition file (termcap or terminfo).

termcap A file (pathname /etc/termcap) that describes the capabilities of each terminal that can be used on a given UNIX system. The termcap file (terminal capability) is gradually being superseded by a newer terminfo file in System V.

terminal An interactive device that enables you to use a computer system. Modern video terminals include a keyboard, a monitor, and possibly a microprocessor. The printing terminals of the 1960s included a keyboard and a printer.

terminal emulator In the X Window System, the software, called xterm, that provides you with a traditional terminal with a shell prompt and command line.

terminfo A directory that contains descriptions of the functions of all the terminals that can be used on a UNIX system. The full pathname of the directory is /usr/share/lib/terminfo. This feature of UNIX System V is designed to replace termcap eventually.

text Written material that has been generated by a computer system. Memos, letters, reports, articles, and books all consist of text. Within a computer system, text is made up of codes that represent letters, numbers, symbols, punctuation, and control characters. These codes usually conform to the American Standard Code for Information Interchange (*ASCII*).

text editor A program that is used to enter and modify text. In UNIX, vi is probably the most commonly-used text editor.

text entry mode A mode in a text editor that allows you to enter text.

text file A file that contains only text; also called a *document*.

text formatter   A program that prepares text for printing, allowing you to produce indentation, margins, justification, headers, footers, pagination, and other forms of text enhancement. In UNIX, the basic text formatters are nroff (for character printers) and troff (for laser printers and phototypesetters). Other programs that handle specialized types of text include eqn and neqn (for mathematical expressions) and tbl (for tabular material). Macro packages derived from nroff and troff include ms, me, and mm. Macro packages provide ease of use for new users.

time-sharing   A method of rotating processes that allows more than one user to have access to a computer system simultaneously. Each process is allocated a small segment of time in succession so that each user appears to have the computer to himself or herself. The amount of time assigned to each process is determined by a system of priorities.

troff   A UNIX text formatting program, often mentioned together with its companion program nroff. While nroff (pronounced "EN-roff") prepares text for printing on a character printer, troff (pronounced "TEE-roff") prepares text for printing on a laser printer or phototypesetter. These general-purpose formatters are accompanied by auxiliary programs that handle specialized types of text: eqn for mathematical expressions (with troff), neqn for mathematical expressions (with nroff), and tbl for tabular material. To use one of the formatting programs, you must embed codes in a text file. These codes, most of which consist of a period followed by two letters, are interpreted by the formatters as commands. Commands for nroff and troff are called *requests*. A macro feature of nroff and troff lets you create your own custom requests. A complete set of these macros can form a macro package, which simplifies text formatting. Some of the most common macro packages include ms (the standard before System V), me (found in Berkeley systems), and mm (the standard for System V). The mm macro package is described in Chapter 7 of this book.

Trojan horse   A scheme for breaking into a UNIX system, named after the trick used to end the Trojan war. In UNIX warfare, a Trojan horse is a mock program, named after a real

UNIX command, that helps an intruder carry out a later invasion. When a user or the system administrator unknowingly invokes the Trojan horse, it collects vital information, such as passwords or permissions, for use by the intruder.

tty   An abbreviation for TeleType, which is used in UNIX to mean terminal. For example, `tty03` means terminal number 3.

typeface   In printing, a set of characters that share a common design, though often in different styles. A set of characters with a particular typeface, style, and size is called a *font*.

typesetter   See *phototypesetter*.

UNIX system   A multiuser, multitasking operating system. Originally developed by Ken Thompson and Dennis Ritchie at Bell Laboratories in 1969, it has gradually gained wider acceptance since its simple beginnings. During the 1970s, the system was distributed to many universities throughout the United States. During the 1980s, the system became a standard for the U.S. government and has been implemented by more and more computer manufacturers. One of the most attractive features of the UNIX system is its portability, which allows it to be run on computer systems of all sizes and brand names. Some of the drawbacks of the system include its cryptic command names and inconsistent rules of syntax. The name UNIX is taken from its predecessor, the Multics operating system. The UNIX system is described in this book.

Usenet   A worldwide bulletin board that is available at sites that belong to the UUCP network. The bulletin board includes news groups for those interested in computer technology, recreation, science, social issues, and general discussion.

UUCP   A set of programs and protocols that have become the basis of a worldwide network between UNIX systems; named after the UNIX-to-UNIX copy program. The version that has accompanied UNIX since System V, Release 3 goes by one of two names: HoneyDanBer or Basic Networking Utilities. The word HoneyDanBer is derived from the names of its originators, Peter Honeyman, David A. Nowitz, and Brian E. Redman. UUCP is described in Chapter 6 of this book.

variable   A symbolic name to which you can assign a value, which may vary from one instance to another.

vi   The most popular UNIX text editor, which was developed at the University of California at Berkeley by William Joy. Actually, vi is the visual interpreter of the ex line editor. Because it is a full-screen editor, vi can operate properly only after your terminal has been identified and described to the system. The vi editor is described in Chapter 5 of this book.

wild card   A character, used to search for text, that may represent any character (or any character in a set). A wild-card character is like a wild card in a card game, which may represent any other card in the deck.

window   An area of a video screen that is dedicated to a particular program or file. Many of the newer implementations of UNIX employ windows as an easy, graphical way to provide multitasking.

Window Manager   In the X Window System, the software that generates the overall look of the screen display.

word processor   A program that combines text-processing and text-formatting. In the UNIX system, text-processing and text-formatting are separate functions.

workspace   In the X Window System, the root window, or desktop, on which all other windows are overlaid.

workstation   A desktop computer system, often rich in graphical features, that is more powerful than an ordinary personal computer. While personal computers are mainly intended for business applications, workstations tend to be favored by scientists and engineers.

working directory   The directory in which you are working; also known as the *current directory*.

XENIX   An operating system, derived from UNIX, that was specifically designed for personal computers in the early 1980s. With the growing power of personal computers in the late 1980s, the need for a separate XENIX system is diminishing and AT&T and Microsoft Corporation have now merged XENIX with UNIX.

Quick Reference

This appendix summarizes the function, syntax, and some of the most common options for each command described in this book.

bc

Start the high-precision calculator

```
$ bc [options] [files]
```

Option	Function
-1	Invoke the math library

Command	Function
+	Add
-	Subtract
*	Multiply
/	Divide
sqrt	Take a square root

continues

continued

Option	Function
scale	Request decimal places
define	Define a function
quit	End a session

cal

Display a calendar for a year or month

$ cal [*month*] [*year*]

in which

month is a number from 1 to 12 (1 for January, 2 for February, 3 for March, and so on)

year is a number from 1 to 9999 (representing a year A.D.)

calendar

Send a reminder to yourself

$ calendar [-] [*year*]

Option	Function
-	Run calendar for all users who have calendar files

cat

Display the contents of a file; concatenate files

$ cat [*options*] *files*

Option	Function
-s	Suppress messages about nonexistent files
-u	Unbuffer output
-v	Display nonprinting characters

continues

Option	Function
-t	With -v only, display tab as ^I
-e	With -v only, display $ at the end of each line (Release 3)

continued

cd

Change directories (move from one directory to another)

```
$ cd [directory]
```

If you omit a directory name, move to your home directory.

chmod

Set file permissions

```
$ chmod [augo]]+-=][rwx] files
```

or

```
$ chmod number files
```

Option	Function
a	All (user, group, and others) (the default)
u	The user (or owner)
g	The user's working group
o	Other users (outside the user's group)
+	Add permission
-	Remove permission
=	Assign permissions absolutely
r	Permission to read
w	Permission to write
x	Permission to execute

cp

Copy a file (or a group of files)

$ cp *source_file target_file*

or

$ cp *files* **directory**

cpio

Back up and recover files

$ cpio -o [aBcv]   Copy out

or

$ cpio -i [Bcdfmrtuv]   Copy in
text

or

$ cpio -p [adlmruv]   Pass
directory

Option	Function
a	Update access times of input files after copying
B	Copy in block of 5,120 bytes per record
c	Include ASCII header information
d	Create directories as required
f	Copy all files except those named in text
l	Link instead of copy whenever possible
m	Retain modification times already in effect
r	Rename files interactively (using prompts)
t	Table of contents: display names only
u	Copy the files unconditionally
v	Verbose: Display names of files being copied

cu

Call another system

```
$ cu [options] system
```

Option	Function
-d	Display diagnostic messages
-e	Set even parity for sending
-lline	Select a line name (first available line if *line* is omitted)
-m	Select a direct line with modem control
-n	Number: prompt for a telephone number
-o	Set odd parity for sending
-srate	Set the data rate to *rate* (300 bits per second by default)
-t	Call an ASCII terminal
system	You can use a telephone number or a uucp name

The following commands can be used in cu sessions:

Command	Function
~!	Escape from cu to the local shell
~!command	Run *command* on the local system
~$command	Run *command* on the local system and send output to the other system
~%cd	Change directories on local system (Release 2)
~%put *file*	Copy *file* to the other system
~%take *file*	Copy *file* from the other system
~.	Disconnect the two systems

dc

Start the desk calculator

```
$ dc [file]
```

Command	Function
=	Add
-	Subtract
*	Multiply
/	Divide
p	Print (display)
q	Quit

egrep

List lines in a file that meet criteria, including compound expressions

```
$ egrep [options] text [files]
```

Option	Function
-c	Count: display the number of matching lines
-e *expr*	Match an expression that begins with a hyphen
-f *file*	Read expressions from *file*
-i	Ignore case during search
-l	Display file names only, not matching lines
-n	Display line numbers with matching lines
-v	Display nonmatching lines instead of matching lines

fgrep

List lines in a file that meets criteria (literal strings only)

```
$ fgrep [options] text [files]
```

Option	Function
-c	Count: display the number of matching lines
-e *expr*	Match an expression that begins with a hyphen
-f *file*	Read expressions from *file*
-i	Ignore case during search
-l	Display file names only, not matching lines
-n	Display line numbers with matching lines
-v	Display nonmatching lines instead of matching lines
-x	Match only entire lines

find

List file names that meet criteria

```
$ find directories options
```

Option	Function
-atime *d*	Match files accessed *d* days ago
-cpio dev	Write file to device *dev* using cpio format
-ctime *d*	Match files changed *d* days ago
-depth	List files before their directories
-exec *cmd*	Execute command *cmd* unconditionally
-group *name*	Match files that belong to group *name*
-links *n*	Match files with *n* links
-mtime *d*	Match files modified *d* days ago
-name *name*	Match files named *name*
-newer *name*	Match files newer than file *name*
-ok *cmd*	Execute command *cmd* with confirmation
-print	Display the names of all files matched
-size *b*	Match files that are *b* blocks long
-type x	Match files if x=p, directories if x=d
-user name	Match files owned by user name

grep

List lines in a file that meets criteria, searching for strings and regular expressions

```
$ grep [options] text [files]
```

Option	Function
-c	Count: display the number of matching lines
-i	Ignore case during search
-l	Display file names only, not matching lines
-n	Display line numbers with matching lines
-v	Display nonmatching lines rather than matching lines

ln

Form a link to a file

```
$ ln source_file target_file
```

or

```
$ ln files directory
```

lp

Queue a file (or a list of files) for printing

```
$ lp [options] files
```

Option	Function
-c	Make a copy of the file (or files) before printing it (or them)
-dprinter	Direct printing to printer printer
-m	Mail message to user after printing
-ncopies	Print the number of copies indicated (copies)
-tmessage	Print a message as a banner on the page that precedes the printed output
-w	Write a message to the user after printing

lpstat

Display the printing queue

`$ lpstat [options]`

Option	Function
-c[*items*]	Display classes and printers (*items*=names of classes)
-d	Display the name of the default printer
-o[*items*]	Display the status of printing requests (*items*=names of classes, names of printers, or identifiers of printing requests)
-p[*items*]	Display the status of printers (*items*=names of printers)
-r	Display the status of the request scheduler
-s	Display a summary of printing status (options -cdru combined)
-t	Display all status information
-u[*items*]	Display the status of print requests (*items*=login names of users)
-v[*items*]	Display printers with their pathnames (*items*=printers)

NOTE: In each instance, the *items* listed must be separated by commas.

ls

Display (or list) the contents of a directory

`$ ls [options] [file]`

in which

file can be the name of a file or a directory

Option	Function
-a	Display all file names (including those that begin with periods, such as .profile)
-C	Display file names in multiple columns sorted from top to bottom
-F	Display a slash (/) at the end of each directory name and an asterisk (*) at the end of the name of each executable file
-l	Display a long list in seven columns
-n	Display a long list with numeric entries for user and group
-p	Display a slash (/) at the end of each directory name
-r	Display in reverse order
-t	Display file names by time of last modification
-u	Display file names by time of last access
-x	Display file names in multiple columns sorted from left to right

mail (Release 2)

Send electronic mail to another user; receive mail

```
$ mail [options] [users]
```

Option	Function
-e	Don't show mail
-f *file*	Read from *file* instead of the default mail file
-p	Display all incoming mail without prompts
-r	Display mail in reverse order
-t	Precede your message with the names of all recipients

Code	Action
* (or ?)	List all the mail commands
p	Redisplay the current message (print)
d	Delete the current message

continues

Code	Action
m *user*	Forward the current message to *user*
s	Save the current message (with header) in file mbox
s *file*	Save the current message (with header) in *file*
w	Save the current message (without header) in file mbox
w *file*	Save the current message (without header) in *file*
Enter	Display the next message
! *command*	Execute *command* without leaving mail
q	Quit mail (leave only unexamined messages)
x	Exit mail (leave all messages)

mail (Release 3)

Send electronic mail to another user; receive mail

`$ mail [options] [users]`

Option	Send Function
-o	Don't use address optimization
-s	Don't begin with a new line at the top
-t	Add a To: line to your message
-w	For remote mail, don't wait for completion of remote transfer program

Option	Receive Function
-e	Don't show the mail
-F *user*	Forward mail to *user*s
-h	Show a numbered list of messages
-f *file*	Read from *file* instead of the default mail file
-p	Display all incoming mail without prompts
-r	Display mail in reverse order

Code	Action
?	List all the mail commands
n	Display message *n*
p	Redisplay the current message (print)
d	Delete the current message
dq	Delete the current message and quit
d *n*	Delete message *n*
m *user*	Forward the current message to *user*
s	Save the current message (with header) in file mbox
s *file*	Save the current message (with header) in *file*
w	Save the current message (without header) in file mbox
w *file*	Save the current message (without header) in *file*
-	Display the previous message
+	Display the next message
[↵Enter]	Display the next message
h	Display some headers, including the current header
h a	Display all headers
h d	Display headers for messages to be deleted
h *n*	Display header for message *n*
! *command*	Execute *command* without leaving mail
q	Quit mail (leave only unexamined messages)
x	Exit mail (leave all messages)

mailx

Send electronic mail to another user; receive mail

```
$ mailx [options] [users]
```

Option	Function
-e	Check for mail without reading it
-H	Display headers without messages

continues

Option	Function
-N	Display messages without headers
-s *hdr*	Set subject header to *hdr*
-U	Convert from uucp to mailx

Command	Action
~?	List all escape commands
~s *subject*	Enter a subject title called *subject*
~t *user(s)*	Add *users* to the To list
~c *user(s)*	Add *users* to the Copy list
~h	Display To, Subject, and Copy prompts
~r *file*	Read text into your message from another *file*
~w *file*	Write your message to another *file*
~v	Use vi to edit your message
~p	Display (print) the current message
~f *message(s)*	Read in other *messages*
~m *message(s)*	Read in other *messages* (indented to the first tab stop)
~! *command*	Run a UNIX *command* and return to mailx
~¦ *command*	Pipe the message through *command* (UNIX command)
~q	Quit mailx (save message in file dead.letter)
~x	Exit mailx (discard message)

Command	Action
?	List all commands with explanations
list	List all commands without explanations
header	Display active headers
z	Display the next page of headers
z-	Display the last page of headers
from [*list*]	Display header(s) (See Chapter 6)
top [*list*]	Display only the first five lines of message(s)
next	Display the next message

continues

continued

Command	Action
type [*list*]	Display message(s)
preserve [*list*]	Preserve message(s) in mbox
save [*list*] *file*	Save message(s) (append) to *file*
delete [*list*]	Delete message(s)
undelete [list]	Undelete deleted message(s)

Command	Action
edit [*list*]	Edit message(s)
Reply [*list*]	Reply to sender(s) only
reply [*list*]	Reply to sender(s) and to other recipient
scd [*directory*]	Change to *directory* (home if name omitted)
! *command*	Execute UNIX command and return to mailx
quit	Quit (save only unread messages in mbox)
xit	Exit (save all messages in mbox)

mesg

Determine whether or not other users can send messages directly to your screen

$ mesg y   Allow incoming messages

$ mesg n   Forbid incoming messages

mkdir

Create a new subdirectory under the current directory

$ mkdir *directory*

mm

Format text for printing

$ mm [*options*] *file(s)*

Request	Function
.P 0	Block paragraph
.P 1	Paragraph with indented first line
.DS option	Static display
.DF *option*	Floating display
.I	Indented
.I F n	Double-indented
.C	Centered
.CB	Blocked
.BL	Bullet list
.DL	Dash list
.ML *mark*	Mark list
.RL	Reference list
.VL	Variable-item list
.AL	Auto-number list
.SA 1	Justify text
.SA 0	Unjustify text
.SP *n*	Skip *n* lines
.I	make text italic
.B	Make text bold
.R	make text roman
.S p v	Change point size and line spacing

mv

Rename a file (or files); move a file (or files)

```
$ mv source_file target_file
```

or

```
$ mv files directory
```

nroff

Format text for printing (fixed width)

```
$ nroff [options] [files]
```

Option	Function
-cx	Process with macro package mx
-e	Space words equally in justified text
-opages	Print only *pages* as listed here
-Tprinter	Specify a particular *printer*
p1-p2	Print from page *p1* to page *p2*
-p	Print from beginning of file to page *p*
p-	Print from page p to the end of the file

Request	Function
.pl *n*	Page length *n* lines
.po *n*	Page offset *n* characters
.pn *n*	Page number *n*
.bp	Page break
.ll *n*	Line length *n* characters
.in *n*	Indent *n* characters
.ti *n*	Temporarily indent *n* characters
.ne *n*	Need vertical space (*n* lines)
.fi	Turn on filling
.nf	Turn off filling
.ad	Adjust text
.na	Do not adjust text
.hy *n*	Hyphenate after *n* characters
.nh	No hyphenation
.br	Break to a new page
.ls *n*	Line spacing *n*
.ce	Center a line
.ce *n*	Center the next *n* lines
.ul	Underline text
.cu	Continuously underline text
%	Place page number
\u	Superscript
\d	Subscript
.1C	Single column

Request	Function
.2C	Double column
.TS	Start of table
.TE	End of table
.EQ	Start of equation
.EN	End of equation

passwd

Change your password

```
$ passwd
Changing password for user
Old password:
New password:
Retype new password:
$ _
```

pg

Display text one screenful at a time

```
$ pg [options] [files]
```

Option	Function
-c	Home cursor and clear screen each page
-e	Do not pause at the end of a file
-f	Do not split lines wider than screen
-n	Allow one-letter commands without pressing Enter
-s	Highlight prompts and messages
+*line*	Start at line number *line*
+/*string*/	Start at the first line that contains *string*
p	Go to the previous file

continues

continued

Option	Function
n	Go to the next file
-	Move to the previous screen
+	Move to the next screen
⏎Enter	Move to the next screen

Option	Function
-nl	Move back n lines
+nl	Move forward n lines
?text?	Move to the previous line that contains text
/text/	Move to the next line that contains text

ps

Check the status of processes

```
$ ps [options]
```

Option	Function
-a	Display all processes except process group leaders and processes not started from terminals
-d	Display all processes except process group leaders
-e	Display all processes, not just your own
-f	Produce a "full" list
-l	Produce a "long" list

pwd

Display the name of your current directory

```
$ pwd
/usr/james/admin/letters
$ _
```

readnews

Read the Usenet bulletin board

```
$ readnews [options] [newgroups]
```

Option	Action
?	Help
N	Go to the next newsgroup
U	Unsubscribe from the current newsgroup
b	Back up one article in the current newsgroup
-	Return to the previous article
+	Skip the current article
e	Erase the memory of having read the current article

Option	Action
s *file*	Save the current article in *file*
r	Reply to the author of an article
f	Post a follow-up to an article
Del	Throw away the rest of an article
x	Exit

Example:

```
$ readnews -n rec.games.chess rec.pets
```

rm

Delete a file (or a group of files)

```
$ rm [options] files
```

Option	Function
-f	Remove files from directories forcibly
-i	Remove files interactively (using prompts)
-r	Used with a directory name, remove all subdirectories and files, then remove the directory itself

rmdir

Delete (or remove) existing directories

```
$ rmdir directories
```

Option	Function
-p	Remove directories along with any parent directories that may become empty (Release 3), and display the names of all directories removed
-r	Delete files from directories recursively
-s	used with -p, don't display directory names

sh

Shell (the command processor)

```
$ sh [script]
```

Shell Variables

Bourne and C shells	
HOME	Login directory
MAIL	Mail file
PATH	Command search path
TERM	Terminal type

Bourne shell only	
PS1	Primary prompt
PS2	Secondary prompt
IFS	Internal file separator
TZ	Time zone
LOGNAME	Login name

Korn shell only	
EDITOR	Full-screen editor (emacs, gmacs, or vi)
ENN	Environment file, usually called .kshrc
HISTFILE	Command history file
SHACCT	Shell accounting file
SHELL	Default shell
VISUAL	Same as EDITOR, but overrides EDITOR

Command	Function
<	Redirect command input
>	Redirect command output>
>	Redirect and append to an output file
&	Run a background process

Command	Function
echo *text*	Display *text* on the video monitor
read *var*	Receive text from the keyboard and assign it to variable *var*
ps	Display the status of background processes
nice n	Change the priority of a process
kill *pppp*	Terminate background process *pppp*
shl	Use the shell layer manager
p1 ¦ *p2*	Pipe: Use output of *p1* as the input of *p2*
p ¦ tee file	Tee: Display the output of p while it is being redirected to file

Matching Patterns	
?	Match any one character
*	Match any string of characters
[characters]	Match any of the characters enclosed

Positional Parameters	
$0	Command
$1	First argument
$2	Second argument
$3	Third argument
$n	The nth argument

sort

Sort lines in a file; merge sorted files

$ sort [*options*] [*files*]

Option	Function
-b	Ignore spaces and tabs in front of text
-c	Make sure file has already been sorted
-d	Sort in dictionary order

Option	Function
-f	"Fold" uppercase into lowercase
-m	Merge files that have already been sorted
-M	Sort items as months (Jan, Feb, Mar, . . .)
-n	Sort in numeric order
-o *file*	Place output in *file*
-r	Sort in reverse order
-u	Unique: if identical lines occur, output only one
+*n*	Begin sorting after *n* fields
-m	Stop sorting after m fields

su

Change to another login name

```
$ su name          Change to user name
Password:
$ _
```

```
$ su               Change to root
Password:
#_
```

tee

Redirect output to a file while sending it to the standard output

```
$ tee [options] [files]
```

Option	Function
a	Append to a file (similar to >>)
i	Ignore the signal from the Del key, which usually interrupts processing

uucp

Copy file(s) to another UNIX system

```
$ uucp [options] [file(s)
```

Option	Function
-m	Mail a return message upon completion of copy

uux

Execute a command on another UNIX system

```
$ command ¦ uux system! command
```

The C and Korn Shells

In Chapter 3, "Processing Commands," you learned how to use the command processors, known as the Bourne shell, the C shell, and the Korn shell. This appendix presents several features of the C shell and Korn shell that are not found in the Bourne shell:

- Using the initialization files
- Setting the shell prompt
- Retrieving previous command lines
- Creating customized commands

Initialization Files

While the Bourne shell has a single initialization file called .profile, the C shell has two initialization files named .login and .cshrc, and the Korn shell uses two files called .profile and .kshrc. The .login file is similar to .profile, but .cshrc is unique to the C shell. Let's first discuss .login.

The C Shell Login File   .login

The .login file, which is read and executed only when you log in, contains the basic information that allows your terminal to function properly. The statements placed here are similar to those placed in .profile for the Bourne shell, but the commands and syntax are slightly different for the C shell. Here is an example of a simple .login file, which contains three lines:

```
stty kill "^A" erase "^H"
setenv TERM vt100
set path=(/bin /usr/bin $HOME/bin .)
```

The first line contains a command that sets the terminal, stty. This line assigns (Ctrl)-(A) as the kill key and (Ctrl)-(H) as the erase key. (As you may recall, the kill key is the key combination that erases an entire command line, and the erase key is the one that erases the previous character.)

The second line contains a command that identifies your terminal to the system by assigning a value to the TERM variable. The value assigned on this line (vt100) must be listed in the appropriate place in the terminal information file that is used on your system (either /etc/termcap or /usr/lib/terminfo/v/vt100).

The third line sets up your command search path, using a construction that differs from the one used by the Bourne shell. Assuming that your home directory is /home/paul, the system will search for command names in the following directories:

```
/bin
/usr/bin
/home/paul/bin
```

The Korn Shell
Login File   .profile

The .profile file, which is read and executed only when you log in, is about the same for the Bourne shell and the Korn shell, but the Korn shell has three main additional environment variables, called ENV, HISTSIZE, and VISUAL.

The ENV variable gives the location of the Korn shell's environment file (.kshrc). For example,

```
$ ENV=$HOME/.kshrc
$ export ENV
```

The HISTSIZE variable corresponds to the C shell's history variable, while the VISUAL variable allows you to edit in full-screen mode, using the editor of your choice. For example,

```
$ HISTSIZE=30
$ export HISTSIZE
$ VISUAL=vi
$ export VISUAL
```

The C Shell Run Command File .cshrc

The .cshrc file is unique to the C shell; it is read and executed each time the system creates a new C shell, which occurs both when you first log in and also when you start a C shell procedure. The .cshrc file is generally used to do three things:

- Set your shell prompt
- Set the number of command lines to be saved for future reference, referred to as a *history*
- Create custom commands, known as *aliases*

The following example of a simple .cshrc file contains five lines:

```
set prompt = "\!> "
set history = 10
alias     t          cd /usr/lib/terminfo/v
alias     u          cd /usr/lib/uucppublic/paul
alias     show       cd '\!*; ls -l ¦ pg'
```

These lines would be entered in the Korn shell's .kshrc file as follows:

```
PS1="!>"
HISTSIZE=10
alias -x t="cd /usr/lib/terminfo/v"
alias -x u="cd /usr/lib/uucppublic/paul"
alias -x show="cd !*; ls -l ¦ pg"
```

The first line sets your prompt. Although you can always use the default prompt for the C shell (%) or the Korn shell ($), it can be much more convenient to use sequential numbers that count your command lines for you. Then you can refer to previous command lines by number. In the C example, the exclamation mark preceded by a backslash (\!) specifies the dynamic numbering of command lines. When you log in with this setting in your .cshrc file, your first shell prompt will look like this:

```
1> _
```

In the terminology of the C shell or the Korn shell, each command line is called an *event,* and the set of command lines stored for future reference is called the *history* list. The second line in the example .cshrc file specifies the length of the history list (10). This means that the system will save the previous ten command lines, or events, for reference. Because you have requested line-numbering, it will be easy for you to refer to events by number.

Each system limits the maximum number of events allowed in a history list. For most systems, the limit is around 25 events. You can also change the setting for the variable history on a command line, as shown here:

C Shell:

```
1> set history = 5

2> _
```

Korn Shell:

```
1> HISTSIZE=5

2> _
```

From this point on, the system will retain only five events at a time. Later, if you want to view the events stored, you can execute the history command:

```
21> history
     16  cd ../admin
     17  pwd
     18  ls -l
     19  mv letter ltr.427
     20  vi ltr.427
22> _
```

As you will learn shortly, you can retrieve any one of these events, run it again, or modify it and run it.

To permit us to retrieve a larger number of events, let's make the history list ten events long by executing another set history command. Although this setting was in .cshrc (or .kshrc), the following command makes certain it is in effect:

C Shell:

```
22> set history = 10

23> _
```

Korn Shell:

```
22> HISTSIZE=10

23> _
```

The last three lines of the sample .cshrc (or .kshrc) file contain aliases. An alias is simply an abbreviation that you can assign to an existing command (usually a long, complex command). For example, the alias shown on the third line lets you enter

```
2> t
```

rather than

```
2> cd /usr/lib/terminfo/v
```

whenever you want to change to the terminfo directory indicated. The alias saves time by allowing you to use a shorter name.

Now that we've briefly discussed the .cshrc (or .kshrc) file, let's look at some of the features in more detail.

Retrieving Command Lines

The ability to retrieve any event in the history list is a great convenience that can save you time. Some command lines are very long and easy to mistype. The most common ways you can retrieve a command line are as follows:

• Invoke the previous event

• Invoke an event by actual line number

To invoke either of these, you must first type an exclamation mark (!). Because of this special meaning, you have to use an escape (\) any time you use an exclamation mark for any other purpose in the C shell. You saw an example of this in the notation used to set up line-numbering in the .cshrc file.

Repeating the Previous Event   !!

The simplest command you can use is !!, which repeats the most recent event (re-executes the most recent command line). Suppose you are right where you left off in the previous section (checking the history list). If you enter !! now, the history command will be executed again:

```
22> !!
history
    16    cd ../admin
    17    pwd
    18    ls -l
```

```
19   mv letter ltr.427
20   vi ltr.427
23> _
```

You can display the history list a second time by entering !! rather than history. The C shell (or Korn shell) displays the command line and then the results of the command line.

Invoking an Event
by Number   !n

To illustrate this feature, let's repeat command line 17. In this instance, you won't save any keystrokes. However, in most instances, you probably will. This is how it will look on your screen:

```
24> !17
pwd
/usr/paul/admin
25> _
```

Merely type an exclamation mark, followed by the number of the event desired (in this example, 17).

TIP: To use a file name that you have just generated, type !$ (for example, vi !$).

Selecting Arguments on a Command Line

In Chapter 3, "Command Processing," you learned that the Bourne shell splits each command line into individual units and assigns them numbers. The C and Korn shells also do this. For example, consider the following command line:

```
19> mv letter ltr.427
```

This command line contains the following three units, or *words*:

mv	Word 0 ($0): the command
letter	Word 1 ($1): the first argument
ltr.427	Word 2 ($2): the second argument

The C and Korn shells allow you to select from these words when you invoke an event in your history list. Simply append a colon and a number to your repeat command. For example, to use the file name ltr.427 as an argument in another command line, you could use the following notation:

```
26> cat !19:2
```

cat ltr.427	First, the shell interprets the notation. Cat unit $2 from event 19.

May 18, 1991	
Dear Fred,	Then it displays the output.
..	
Sincerely,	
Paul	
27> _	

The command line on line 26 means, "Use the second argument on line 19 as the argument for the cat command." In the sections that follow, you will learn how to select an individual argument (as in the previous command) or a series of arguments. To make the discussion easy to follow, we'll use the following command line throughout:

```
27> echo arg-1 arg-2 arg-3 arg-4 arg-5
arg-1 arg-2 arg-3 arg-4 arg-5
28> _
```

Selecting the First Argument

You can use either the number one (1) or a caret symbol (^) to select the first argument. The following example uses the number one:

```
28> echo !27:1
echo arg-1
arg-1
29> _
```

The example that follows is equivalent to the previous example:

```
28> echo !27:^
echo arg-1
arg-1
29> _
```

Selecting the Last Argument $

The symbol for selecting the last argument ($) is much more useful that the one for selecting the first argument because you may not know exactly how many arguments there are. In the following example, the dollar sign ($) is equivalent to 5:

```
29> echo !27:$
echo arg-5
arg-5
30> _
```

Selecting a Set of Arguments   n1-n2

You can use a hyphen (-) between a pair of numbers to select a range of arguments. In the following example, we select arguments 2, 3, and 4:

```
30> echo !27:2-4
echo arg-2 arg-3 arg-4
arg-2 arg-3 arg-4
31> _
```

Selecting All Arguments   *

If you want to select every argument on the command line, you can use the wild-card character (*), as shown in the following example:

```
31> echo !27:*
echo arg-1 arg-2 arg-3 arg-4 arg-5
arg-1 arg-2 arg-3 arg-4 arg-5
32> _
```

Because you are using the same command on line 31 that you used on line 27, command line 31 could be entered more simply as follows:

```
31> !27
echo arg-1 arg-2 arg-3 arg-4 arg-5
arg-1 arg-2 arg-3 arg-4 arg-5
32> _
```

However, if you were using a different command on line 31, the wild-card notation would be very handy.

Simplified Notation

The C shell allows you to omit the colon (:) any time you are using symbols instead of numbers to select arguments. In other words, command lines 28, 29, and 31 could be entered more simply as follows:

```
28> echo !27^
echo arg-1
arg-1
29> echo !27$
echo arg-5
arg-5
30> ...

31> echo !27*
echo arg-1 arg-2 arg-3 arg-4 arg-5
arg-1 arg-2 arg-3 arg-4 arg-5
32> _
```

With numbers, however, you always must include the colon (:) when selecting arguments.

Changing a Command Line

To avoid unnecessary typing, you can modify an event when you invoke it. Merely type the appropriate modifier after the colon (:) rather than numbers or symbols to select arguments.

Making Substitutions   s

The C shell's substitute modifier s is similar to vi's substitute command s (if necessary, refer to Chapter 5, "Editing with vi"). Let's repeat event number 27 and append the modifier s/a/A:

```
32> !27:s/a/A
echo Arg-1 arg-2 arg-3 arg-4 arg-5
Arg-1 arg-2 arg-3 arg-4 arg-5
33> _
```

As the preceding example shows, the s modifier by itself replaces only the first occurrence on the line. It changed arg-1 to Arg-1, but the other four arguments were unchanged.

If you want to replace a with A everywhere on the line, you have to include the global modifier g, as shown in the following example:

```
33> !27:gs/a/A
echo Arg-1 Arg-2 Arg-3 Arg-4 Arg-5
Arg-1 Arg-2 Arg-3 Arg-4 Arg-5
34> _
```

To make a replacement only in one argument, you can include the argument number and also the s modifier, each with its own colon. In the following example, we change arg to ARG only in argument number 3:

```
34> !27:3:s/arg/ARG
echo ARG-3
ARG-3
35> _
```

Previewing an Event   p

If you want to look at an event without executing it, merely append the preview modifier p. Here is an example:

```
35> !27:p
echo arg-1 arg-2 arg-3 arg-4 arg-5
36> _
```

Using Abbreviations alias

The last three lines of the sample .cshrc (or .kshrc) file described earlier in this chapter contained alias commands. For this example, these three lines constitute an alias list. On the fourth line, we assigned to u the command line cd /usr/lib/uucppublic/ paul. Therefore you can enter

```
36> u
37> _
```

rather than

```
36> cd /usr/lib/uucppublic/paul
37> _
```

Displaying the Alias List

You can display your alias list at any time by executing the alias command alone, as follows:

```
37> alias
alias           t           cd /usr/terminfo/v
alias           u           cd /usr/lib/uucppublic/paul
alias           show        cd '\!*; ls -l ¦ pg'
38>
```

Using a Temporary Alias

The aliases stored in .cshrc go into effect each time you log in or create a new shell. If you want to set up an alias for one session, you can assign it and then remove it, as shown in this example:

```
38> alias s cd /usr/sandy/sales
39> s
...
43> s
...
```

```
47> s
...
55> unalias s
...
56> _
```

In the preceding example, you assign an alias called s on line 38, use the alias three times (lines 39, 43, and 47), and then remove the alias on line 55.

Using Dynamic Selection   \!*

The fifth line of the initialization file .cshrc includes a provision for dynamic selection. All this means is that you can enter the target directory name at the time you enter your command line. The alias line reads as follows:

C shell:

```
alias     show    cd '\!*; ls -l ¦ pg'
```

Korn shell:

```
alias -x show="cd !*; ls -l ¦ pg"
```

In this example, we assign to the name show a command line that lets us change to any directory and display a long listing of files. The -x option allows exported aliases. The notation \!* (C shell) or !* (Korn shell) simply means, "Enter any name here." This would be another way of showing the desired command line:

```
cd directory; ls -l ¦ pg
```

The following example uses the alias show:

```
56> show /usr/alfred/times
cd /usr/alfred/times; ls -l ¦ pg
total 52
```

```
drwx — x —     2    alfred   758   Jul 18   15:42   anderson
-rwxr-x —      1    alfred   292   Feb 20   09:14   archer.tmp
dwx — x — —    1    alfred   326   Nov 31   08:57   bell_sales
-rw-r — —      3    alfred   615   Aug 3    13:09   carter.new
-rw-r — —      1    alfred   961   may 11   10:38   dale_two
...
57> _
```

ANSWERS TO QUIZZES

Answers for Chapter 1

1. D	2. A	3. True	4. B	5. C
6. C	7. D	8. B	9. A	10. D

Answers for Chapter 2

1. F	2. I	3. C	4. B	5. G
6. A	7. D	8. J	9. H	10. E
11. L	12. K			

13. `cp memo.? ../MEMOS`

14. `cd ..`

15. `mv *.G ../sales`

16. `ls -l`

17. `ln /usr/paul/LETTERS/expedite expedite`

18. `mkdir news`

19. `chmod u+x,g+w,o-rwx meeting`

20. `rm interest.[KNR]`

Answers for Chapter 3

1. A   2. C   3. B   4. D   5. A

6. B   7. C   8. B   9. D   10. C

11. T   12. D   13. A

Answers for Chapter 4

1. E   2. B   3. A   4. G   5. C

6. F   7. D

8.   `cal 10 1562`

9.   `cat > test.doc`

      `This is a very,`

      `very small file.`

      `Ctrl-D`

      `$ _`

10.   `lp -m memo.101 memo.102`

11.   `find /usr -user penny -atime 30`

12.   `grep "006[0-9][1-9]" parts.*`

13.   `sort +3 parts.* > parts.price`

```
14.  sort +2 -3 parts.* > parts.partno
```

```
15.  bc
     scale = 5
     sqrt(500)
     22.36068
     quit
```

Answers for Chapter 5

1. H	2. E	3. A	4. I	5. L
6. D	7. B	8. J	9. C	10. G
11. K	12. F	13. D	14. F	15. E
16. A	17. C	18. B	19. E	20. H
21. B	22. D	23. F	24. A	25. J
26. C	27. I	28. G	29. `5dd`	30. `d$`
31. `d^`	32. `d5}`	33. `5x`	34. `/select`	
35. `p`	36. `:1,$s/select/choose/g`			

Answers for Chapter 6

1. D	2. G	3. B	4. E	5. J
6. A	7. I	8. F	9. C	10. H

```
11.  write sean < hello
```

```
12.  mesg n
```

```
13.  calendar
```

```
14.  mail linda mike paula < urgent
```

```
15.  mailx
```

16. `reply`

17. `cu gemini`

18. `cu gemini ¦ tee gemini.session`

19. `mail minverva!ken`

20. `cat sales.3Q ¦ uux - minerva!lp`

Answers for Chapter 7

1. G	2. F	3. B	4. E	5. D
6. A	7. C	8. E	9. L	10. A
11. U	12. J	13. W	14. P	15. R
16. B	17. S	18. V	19. C	20. N
21. Q	22. D	23. K	24. F	25. T
26. O	27. M	28. H	29. I	30. G
31. .DS C	32. .B	33. .R	34. .DE	35. .P0
36. .BL	37. .LI	38. .LI	39. .LI	40. .LE
41. .P 0	42. .DS I	43. .B	44. .R	45. .DE
46. .P 0	47. .I			

Answers for Chapter 8

1. B	2. E	3. C	4. A	5. D
6. C`	7. B	8. A	9. E	10. D
11. client	12. mouse	13. window	14. display	
15. server				

Answers for Chapter 9

1. `root`   2. `su`   3. `/etc`   4. `/etc/passwd`

5. `who`   6. `/dev`   7. `/usr/lib/crontab`   8. `chmod`

9. `ls ¦ cpio -oB > /dev/rmt/3`

10. `ls ¦ cpio -o > /dev/rdsk/1c0d1s0`

11. `cpio -iB < /dev/rmt/3`

12. `cpio -i < /dev/rdsk/c0d1s0`

13. `cpio -pv ../hold`

14. `stty 1200`

15. `stty erase = ^h kill = ^e`

16. `stty -raw`

17. `/etc/termcap`

18. `/usr/lib/terminfo`

19. `TERM`

20. `TERM = wyse50; export TERM`

21. `setenv TERM wyse50`

22. `.profile` (Bourne shell); `.login` (C shell)

Index

Symbols

! symbol, system name separator, 152
key, erasing characters, 15
$ _ prompt (Bourne shell), 46
$TERM shell variable, 271
% _ prompt (C shell), 46
& symbol, background processing, 57-58
(command, 110
(*) wild-card character, 35-36
(<), (>), redirection symbols, 50
(>>) appending text symbol, 53
(?) wild-card character, 35-36
+ symbol, adding permissions, 39
- symbol, removing permissions, 38-39
/, root directory identification, 22
/ command, 128
= symbol, absolute file permissions, 39
\, escape character, 89
{} (braces) command, 111
| (vertical bar), pipe symbol, 54
~ (tilde), escape command, 143, 150

A

A command, 117-118
abandoning text, 109
absolute file permissions, 39
absolute pathname, 245
access, 245
accounts, 217-221, 245
action statements in searches, 84-85
addresses, 154, 245
.AL request, mm macro package, 175
aliases, C shell/Korn shell, 245, 315

analyzers, 6
append text-entry mode, 102, 118
appending, 246
    text, 117
    to existing files, 52
arguments, 246
    commands, 48-49
    selecting C shell/Korn shell, 312
    with commands, 15
ARPANET, 157
ASCII, 246
assigning, 246
AT&T
    OPEN LOOK, 9, 188
    System V, System V/386, 7
auto-number lists, 175-178

B

B command, 110
.B request, mm macro package, 179
background processes, 56-59, 246
background processing symbol (&), 57-58
backslash characters, 247
backups, 225-231, 247
bang (!), system name separator, 152
basenames, 247
basic terminal settings in UNIX, 231-234
batch processing, 247
bc command, 96-97, 277
beginning/end of line, moving cursor to, 109
Berkeley UNIX, 247
Berknet, 157
bin directory, 247
bits, 247
bit-mapped graphic displays, 8

.BL request, mm macro package, 172
blank space on pages, 179
block paragraphs, 168
blocked display text, 171
blocks, units of measure, 84, 247
bold text, 179, 247
boot, 247
Bourne shell, 45, 63, 248
Bourne, Stephen R., Bourne shell
    creator, 45
braces ({}) command, 111, 248
brackets, 36, 248
BSD (Berkeley Software Distribu-
    tion), 248
BSD (Berkeley standard delivery)
    4.3, University of California, 8
buffers, 248
bugs, 248
bullet lists, 172-173
bulletin boards, 159-162
bundling command line options, 92
bus, 248
bytes, 248

C

-c (copy) option, printing, 78
C language, 249
C shell, 46, 252
    alias commands/lists, 315
    arguments and command lines,
        308-312
    dynamic selection, 316
    events, 306-309, 314
    history command/lists, 306-307
    .login file/.cshrc file, 63, 304-305
    simplified notation, 313
    substitute modifier, 313
CAE (Common Applications
    Environment), X/Open, 8
cal (calendar) command, 71-72,
    138-139, 278
calculators, 94-97, 191
capturing external sessions in
    files, 150
carriage returns, 248
cases, 249
cat (concatenate) command, 30-31,
    73, 278
categories of newsgroups, 157
cd command, 26, 279
CDE (common desktop environ-
    ment), 9

centered display text, 171
characters, 249
    deleting, 120
    erasing at command line, 15
    matching sets by suffix numbers
        in brackets, 36
    printing size, 180-182
    transposing, 127-128
checkeq utility, 167
child processes, 249
chips, 249
chmod (change mode) command,
    39, 279
clear screen command, 115
clients, 193, 249
clock, X Windows, 191
colors of X Windows window, 207
command lines, 15-17, 47-48, 250
    arguments (C shell/Korn
        shell), 309
    C shell/Korn shell, 308-309, 313
    environmental variables, 66
    erasing single characters, 15
    for terminal settings, 237
    X Window System, 204-207
command mode and text-entry
    mode, 104
command processors, 250
commands, 249
    (, 110
    / (slash), 128
    {} (braces), 111
    ~., 150
    A, 117-118
    aliases in C shell/Korn shell, 315
    and processes, 49
    arguments, 48-49
    B, 110
    bc, 96-97, 277
    cal (calendar), 71-72,
        138-139, 278
    cat (concatenate), 30-31, 73, 278
    cd, 26, 279
    chmod (change [access] mode),
        39, 279
    clear screen, 115
    cp, 29, 280
    cpio (copy input/output), 84,
        225, 280
    cu (call up), 146-151, 281
    cursor movement, 105
    d, 120

d), 123
d}, 124
date, 13
dc, 94-95, 282
df, 224-225
du, 223
dw, 120
Edit (xterm window menu), 199
egrep, 282
escape, 143
executing
    in files, 60-63
    on other systems, 156
export, 66
fgrep, 282
find, 81, 283
G, 112
grep, 85, 284
H, 111
history (C shell/Korn shell), 307
I, 116-117
kill, 59
L, 111
ln (link), 34, 284
logout, 17
lp (lineprinter), 76, 284
lpstat (lineprinter status),
    79, 285
ls (list), 25, 285
M, 111
mail, 139, 286-287
mail -r option, 141
mailx, 142-146, 288
mailx -f option, 146
mesg, 290
mesg -n/-Y option, 137
mkdir (make directory),
    27-28, 290
mm, 290
more, 75, 158
mv (move), 31, 291
n (next), 128
names, 250
ndd, 122
news, 216
non-UNIX, 13
nroff, 291
O, 118-119
OPEN LOOK Window Manager,
    200-201
oladduser, 238
options, 25

paging screen, 112
passwd, 14, 293
pg (page), 75, 158, 293
postnews, 160
ps (process status), 58, 294
put (p), 125-127
pwd (print working directory),
    27, 295
q!, 109
quit, 104
readnews, 159, 295
readnews -f option, 161
readnews -s option, 159
repeat, 109
rm (remove), 33, 296
rmdir, 28, 296
rn, 159
s (substitute), 130
screen display, 114
screen movement, 111-113
setenv, 66
sh, 296
sort, 90, 298
stty (set terminal), 11, 232
su (substitute user), 214, 299
talk, 137
tee, 54-56, 299
undo, 109
Utilities, workspace menu
    (OPEN LOOK Window
    Manager), 201
uucp (UNIX-to-UNIX copy),
    151-157, 300
uuname, 148
uux, 156-157, 300
vi, 102
vnews, 159
W, 110
wall (write-all), 216
who, 13, 221
who am i, 15
Window menu, Quit, 195
write, 104, 136
xfd (X font display), 206
xinit, 189
xlsfonts, 205
xp, 127
z (zero screen), 114
communications and UNIX, 135-157
compilers, 6, 250
computers, 250
concatenating, 73, 250

configuring, 251
consoles, 251
constants, 251
control characters/controllers, 251
cooked mode, 251
Copy I/O program, 225
copying
    files, 29-30
        in, 228-229
        out, 226-228
        to directories, 229-230
        to other systems, 154-156
    items in X Windows, 196
    text, xterm window menu, 199
core/core dump, 251
cp command, 29, 280
cpio (copy input/output) command,
    84, 225-226, 251, 280
crashes, 251
criteria in searches, 82-84
cron daemon, 252
crontab, 252
CRT, 252
.cshrc file (C shell), 305
Ctrl+D keys, logging out of
    system, 17
Ctrl+H keys, erasing characters, 15
cu (call up) command, 146-151, 281
current directory, 23
cursor, 104-112, 252

D

d command, 120
d) command, 123
d} command, 124
daemons, 252
dash lists, 173
data, 252
data rate, 252
date command, 13
dc command, 94-95, 282
debuggers, 6, 252
decimals, 252
defaults, 252
    fonts, 205
    printer, 76
    printing, 167
    terminal settings, 231
Del key, restoring shell prompt, 17
deleting, 252
    directories, 28
    files, 33

text, 120-125
denied (-) permissions, 38
deroff utility, 167
desk calculators, onscreen, 94
/dev directory, 24
device files, 24, 253
df command, 224-225
directories, 21-28, 253
    /dev, 24
    /etc (system administrator),
        215-216
    /home, 23
    /usr, 23
    /usr/share/lib/terminfo, 234
    copying files, 29, 229-230
    current, 23
    deleting, 28
    information, 60-61
    opening in X Windows, 195
    parent, 23
    root, 21
    working, 27
directory files, 24
disks, 253
disk space, checking, 223-225
display servers (X Window Sys-
    tem), 192, 238, 253
display text, 169-172
displaying
    alias lists in C shell/Korn
        shell, 315
    calendars, 71-72
    large files, 75-76
    printing queue, 79-80
    text onscreen, 73-76
displays, X Windows components,
    192-194
disposing of command output, 53
.DL request, mm macro
    package, 173
documents, 253
    formatting, 165-166
    previewing onscreen, 167
DOS (Disk Operating System),
    3, 253
    Microsoft Windows/dosshell GUI
        (graphical user interface), 4
    similarities/differences with
        UNIX, 4-7
drives, 253
drivers, 254
.DS request, mm macro
    package, 169

du command, 223
dw command, 120
dynamic selection in C shell/Korn shell, 316

E

echoes, 254
ed program, 254
Edit command, xterm window menu, 199
editing, 254
editing sessions, 103-104
editors, 254
egrep command, 282
electronic mail, 139-142
ending X sessions, 191
entering
    command lines, 15-17, 47-48
    text, 74, 106, 115-119
    UNIX commands, 13-14
environment, 254
environmental variables, 66
eqn preprocessor, 254
eqn program, 166
erase character, 254
erasing single characters, 15
Esc key, 254
escape character (\), 89
escape command, 143
/etc directory (system administrator), 215-216
/etc/gettydefs file, 232
/etc/group file, 218
/etc/motd (message of the day) file, 217
/etc/passwd file, 217
/etc/rc startup file, 63
/etc/termcap file, 234
/etc/utmp file, 221
events, C shell/Korn shell, 306-309, 314
ex command mode, 104, 130
ex program, 254
exclamation mark (!), system name separator, 152
execute, 254
execute (x) permissions, 38
executing commands
    in files, 60-63
    on other systems, 156
exiting X Windows, 208
export command, 66

expressions, 255
extensions, 255
external systems
    capturing sessions in files, 150
    communication with, 146-157
    logging out with
        ~. command, 150

F

fgrep command, 282
fields, 255
    separators, 255
    sorting by, 90-91
File Manager (X Window System), 12, 190, 194-195, 255
file names, 23, 255
file permissions, 37-41
file system, 255
file types, 255
files, 21-24, 29-36, 255
    appending to, 52
    backing up, 225-231
    concatenating, 73
    copying, 29-30, 154-156, 226-230
    .cshrc (C shell), 63, 305
    deleting, 33
    devices as, 24
    directory information, 60-61
    displaying large, 75-76
    /etc/gettydefs, 232
    /etc/group, 218
    /etc/motd (message of the day), 217
    /etc/passwd, 217
    /etc/termcap, 234
    /etc/utmp, 221
    executing commands in, 60-63
    initialization, 63-66
    .kshrc (Korn shell), 305
    linking, 33-35
    .login (C shell), 63, 304
    math functions, 97
    multiple, sorting, 93
    naming, 23
    .newsrc, 161
    opening in X Windows, 195
    passing, 229
    paths of, 23
    .profile (Korn shell), 63-66, 304
    searching, 80-89
    selection with wild-card characters, 35-36

sending sort output to, 93-94
sharing, 33-35
shutdown, 240
sorting lines, 90-94
startup
   command lines for terminal
    settings, 237
   /etc/rc, 63
uucp network systems
   access, 148
viewing and storing data, 54
.xinitrc, 189, 208
filters, 256
find command, 81, 283
finding/replacing text, 128-131
fonts, defaults (X Windows), 205
foreground, 256
formatting, 256
display text, 169-172
documents, 165-166
lists, 172-178
paragraphs, 168-169
formatting programs/utilities,
  165-167
free disk space, checking, 224-225
full pathnames, 23
full-duplex, 256
full-screen displays, 234

G-H

G command, 112
Generic window manager, 194
global, 256
grep command, 85, 256, 284
group, 256
GUI (graphical user interface), 4,
  187-188, 256
guidelines for editing sessions,
  103-104

H command, 111
half-duplex, 256
hardware, 256
hardwired terminal, 256
headers, mailx command, 144
help window (OPEN LOOK
  Window Manager), 201
hexadecimal, 256
high-level language, 257
high-precision calculators, 96-97
highlighting text, 179-180
history command (C shell/Korn
  shell), 307

history
  command line, 257
  lists (C shell/Korn shell), 306
/home directory, 23, 257
HOME variable, 64
host, 257
hyphens in lists, 173

I-J

I command, 116-117
.I request, mm macro package, 179
I/O, 257
IBM OS/2, 188
icons, 187, 204
IEEE (Institute of Electrical and
  Electronic Engineers) Posix, 8
indents, text and paragraphs,
  168-169, 257
initialization files, 63-66
initializing X Windows, 208
input
  options from terminal, 233
  redirecting, 50-51
insert mode, 257
inserting text, 116-119
installing, 257
interacting with external
  systems, 148
interactive processing, 257
internal communication, 135-146
italic text, 179, 257

Joy, William, C shell, 46
justifying text, 178, 257

K-L

kernel, 57, 257
keystrokes, repeating/undoing,
  107-109
kill character, 258
kill command, 59
kill key, erasing characters, 16
Korn shell (David Korn), 46, 258
  arguments, 311-312
  command lines, 308-309
  commands
    alias, 315
    history, 307
  displaying alias lists, 315
  dynamic selection, 316
  events, 306, 309
  history lists, 306

.kshrc file, 305
previewing events, 314
.profile files, 304
repeating events, 308
temporary aliases, 315

L command, 111
laser printer, 258
lines, deleting, 122
linking files, 33-35, 258
lists, formatting, 172-178
ln (link) command, 34, 284
local, 258
.login file (C shell), 63, 304
login, 9-11, 214-215, 258
login:_ prompt, 11
logout, 17, 150, 258
Looking Glass (Interactive Systems), 188, 193
low-level language, 258
lp (lineprinter) command, 76, 284
lpstat (lineprinter status) command, 79, 285
ls (list) command, 25, 285

M

-m (mail) option, printing, 78
M command, 111
macros, 166, 258
magnetic tape, 258
mail command, 139-141, 146, 286-287
mail notifier (X Windows System), 191
MAIL variable, 65
mailbox window (X Window System), 12
mailx command, 142-146, 288
mainframe, 258
man program, 259
mark lists, 173-174
mass storage device, 259
math function files, 97
mathematical expressions, 166
mathematical library, 97
me program, 166
medium, 259
memory, 259
menus
    File Manager (X Windows System), 194-195
    workspace (OPEN LOOK Window Manager), 200-201

xterm windows, 198-199
mesg command, 137, 290
messages
    clearing from screen, 115
    routing through other systems, 153
    sending to users, 135
    terminal-to-terminal, 136-138
metacharacters in regular expressions, 88, 259
microcomputer, 260
microprocessor, 260
Microsoft
    System V/386, 7
    Windows, 4, 188
    XENIX, 7
minicomputer, 260
mkdir (make directory) command, 27-28, 290
.ML request, mm macro package, 173
mm command, 290
mm macro package, 167-168
mnemonic codes (mail command), 140
modem, 260
modes
    append text-entry, 118
    ex command, 104, 130
    insertion text-entry, 116
    text-entry, 102-104
    vi command, 103
more command, 75, 158
Motif (Open Software Foundation), 9, 188
Motif window manager, 193
mount, 260
mouse, 187, 260
moving
    cursor, 104-112
    files, 31-33
    items in X Windows, 196
    paragraphs at a time, 111
    sentences, 125
    text, 125-128, 199
    windows (OPEN LOOK Window Manager), 203-204
ms program, 166
Multics, 260
multiple files
    searching, 86-88
    sorting, 93
multiplex, 261
multitasking, 4, 56-59, 261

multiuser, 261
mv (move) command, 31, 291

N-O

n (next) command, 128
-n (numeric) option, sort
   command, 92
naming files in directories, 23
naming windows in X Windows, 207
ndd command, 122
negn program, 166
neqn preprocessor, 261
networks, 147, 151-154, 261
news command, 216
newsgroups, 157-161
.newsrc file, 161
non-UNIX commands, 13
not found error message, 14
nroff program, 6, 165, 261, 291

O command, 118-119
onscreen desk calculators, 94-95
Open Desktop (Santa Cruz Operation), 188, 193
OPEN LOOK (AT&T/Sun
   Microsystems), 9, 188
OPEN LOOK Window Manager,
   193-197, 200-204
Open Software Foundation,
   Motif, 188
opening directories/files/programs
   in X Windows, 195
operating systems, 3-4, 261
options, 261
   as arguments in commands, 48
   bulletin board commands, 159
   cpio command, 226
   letters/numerals, formatting
      auto-number lists, 176-178
   mailx command, 144-145
   printing, 77-78
   sorting, 92-93
   terminal input, 233
   with commands, 25
ordinary files, 24, 261
OS/2 (IBM), 188
OSF (Open Software Foundation),
   Motif, 9
output, 261
   of commands, disposing of, 53
   redirecting, 49-53
   sort, sending to files, 93-94

P

.P requests, mm macro
   package, 168
pages, blank space, 179
paging screens, 112-113
paging commands, 112
paragraphs
   deleting, 124
   formatting, 168-169
parent directory, 23, 262
parentheses, moving a sentence at
   a time, 110
parity detection for terminals, 233
passing files, 229
passwd command, 14, 293
password file, 262
passwords, 9-11, 14-15, 262
PATH variable, 65
pathnames, 262
paths of files, 23
permissions, file, 39-41
personal computer, 262
pg (page) command, 75, 158, 293
phototypesetter, 263
pica, 263
PID (process identifier), 58,
   222, 263
pipe line, 263
pipes, 53-54, 263
point sizes, 180-182, 264
ports, 264
portable, 264
positional parameters, 62
Posix (portable operating system
   environment standard), IEEE, 8
postnews command, 160
prefixes for newsgroups, 159
preprocessors, 166, 264
previewing
   documents onscreen, 167
   events in C shell/Korn shell, 314
printers
   default, 76
   specific, 78-79
printing, 76-80
   changing character size, 180-182
   defaults, mm macro
      package, 167
   job queues, 77-80
   options, 77-78
processes, 264
   and commands, 45, 49

background, 58-59
connections, 53-56
.profile file, 63
Korn shell, 304
shell variables, 63-66
programming tools, 6
programs, 265
backup, 230-231
Copy I/O, 225
eqn, 166
formatting, 165-167
kernel, 57
man, 259
negn, 166
nroff, 6, 165
opening in X Windows, 195
stty (set terminal), 11
tbl, 166
troff, 6, 165
utility, 71-98
uucp, 7
vi (visual interpreter), 6
xterm (X terminal), 197
Programs command, workspace
menu (OPEN LOOK Window
Manager), 200-201
prompts, 265
$ _ (Bourne shell), 46
% _ (C shell), 46
login:_, 11
Properties command, workspace
menu (OPEN LOOK Window
Manager), 201
ps (process status) command,
58, 294
put command, 125-127
pwd (print working directory)
command, 27, 266, 295

Q-R

q! command, 109
queues for printing jobs, 77, 266
quit command, 104, 195
quitting
text, 109
X Windows, 191, 208
quoting, 266

-r (reverse order) option, sort
command, 92
.R request, mm macro package, 179
ranges of arguments, C shell/Korn
shell, 312

raw mode, 266
read (r) permissions, 38
reading
bulletin boards, 159-160
file permissions, 37-39
readnews command, 159-161, 295
real-time processing, 266
records, 266
redirection of input/output,
50-53, 266
reference lists, 174
regular expressions, wild card
characters, 88-89, 267
removing file permissions
with - symbol, 39
renaming files, 31-33
repeat command, 109
repeating
events, C shell/Korn shell, 308
keystrokes, 107-109
replacing text, 128-131
request command, 267
requesting background processing,
57-58
responsibilities of system administrator, 214
restore, 267
revoking permissions, 40
RFS (Remote File Sharing), 7
right margin text justification, 178
Ritchie, Dennis, UNIX creator, 273
.RL request, mm macro
package, 174
rm (remove) command, 33, 296
rmdir command, 28, 296
rn command, 159
roff program, 165
roman text, 179, 267
root directory, 21-22
routing messages through other
systems, 153
RS-232C standard, 267

S

s (substitute) command, 130
s command, 130
.S request, mm macro package, 180
.SA 0 requests, mm macro
package, 178
Santa Cruz Operation, Open
Desktop, 188
screen display, 112-115

screens
    clearing system messages, 115
    displaying text, 73-76
    movement commands, 111
    paging, 112-113
    scrolling, 113-114
scripts, variable names, 62-63
scroll bar, 268
scrolling, 268
    screen, 113-114
    windows (OPEN LOOK Window
        Manager), 202-203
search action statements, 84-85
search criteria, 82-84
search path, 268
searching
    files, 80-89
    for text, 128
security, 268
selecting arguments, C shell/Korn
    shell, 312
selecting items in X Windows, 195
sending messages to users, 135
sentences
    deleting, 123
    moving, 125
server, 268
sessions, 189-191, 268
setenv command, 66
sh command, 296
sharing files, 33-35
shell, 268
    programs, 45-46
    prompt, 17, 46-47
    scripts, 61
    variables, .profile file, 63-66
Shift+3 keys, erasing characters, 15
shrinking/enlarging xterm
    windows, 198
shutdown file, 240
simplified notation in C shell, 313
sizing windows (OPEN LOOK
    Window Manager), 203-204
skipping lines in text, 179
slash (/), root directory identifica-
    tion, 22
/ (slash) command, 128
sleep, 269
software, 192-194, 269
sort command, 90, 298
sort output, sending to files, 93-94

sorting, 269
    by fields, 90-91
    lines in files, 90-94
    multiple files, 93
    options, 92-93
.SP request, mm macro
    package, 179
special characters, 269
special files, 24, 269
specific printers, 78-79
standard input/output, 269
starting
    UNIX, 9-17
    vi editor, 101-104
    X sessions, 189-191
startup file
    /etc/rc, 63
    terminal settings, 237
strings, 269
stty (set terminal) command,
    11, 232
su (substitute user) command, 214,
    269, 299
subdirectory, 270
subscription lists, 159-162
substitute modifier, C shell, 313
Sun Microsystems, OPEN LOOK,
    9, 188
super user, 270
symbols
    appending text (>>), 53
    background processing (&),
        57-58
    pipe (|), 54
    redirection, 50
sync command, 270
system
    administration, 6-7
    hang ups, 17
    logging into, 11-12
    logging out, 17
system administrator, 213-216
    adding users to X Windows,
        238-239
    /etc directory, 215-216
    file permissions, 37
    login, 214-215
    login names/passwords, 9
    new user accounts, 217-221
    responsibilities, 214
    working with users, 216-222
system messages, clearing from
    screen, 115

System V (AT&T), 7
System V/386 (AT&T/Microsoft), 7

T

tabs, 270
Tab window manager, 194
talk command, 137
tape drives, 270
tar program, 270
tbl preprocessor, 270
tbl (table) program, 166
tee command, 54-56, 270, 299
TeleType, 270
temporary aliases, C shell/Korn
  shell, 315
TERM variable, 65
termcap file, 271
terminal descriptions, 234-238
terminal emulator (X Window
  System), 190, 197, 271
terminal-to-terminal message,
  136-138
terminals, 271
  communicating with UNIX, 10
  in UNIX systems, 231-239
  input options, 233
  parity detection for, 233
  settings in UNIX, 231-234
  transmission rates, 232
terminating background
  processes, 59
terminfo directory, 271
text, 271
  abandoning, 109
  appending, 117
  copying, 199
  deleting, 120-125
  display, 169-171
  displaying onscreen, 73-76
  entering, 74, 106, 115-119
  finding/replacing, 128-131
  formatting point sizes, 180-182
  highlighting, 179-180
  inserting, 116-119
  justifying, 178
  moving, 125-128, 199
  searching for, 85-89, 128
  skipping lines, 179
  styles, 179
text editors, 101-112, 271
text entry mode, 102-104, 271
text files, 271

text formatter program, 272
text runoff programs, 165
text-formatting/processing, 6
Thompson, Ken, UNIX creator, 273
tilde (~), escape command, 143
time-sharing, 272
transmission rates for
  terminals, 232
transposing characters, 127-128
troff program, 6, 165, 272
Trojan horse, 272
TTY (current terminal number),
  58, 273
typeface, 273

U

undo command, 109
University of California BSD 4.3, 8
UNIX system, 273
  commands, 13-14
  compatibility of versions, 7-9
  communication, 135-157
  file system, 21-24
  GUI (graphical user interface),
    X Window System, 4
  multitasking system, 4
  quitting, 239-240
  shell prompt, 12, 17
  similarities/differences with
    DOS, 4-7
  standard five directories, 21-22
  starting/logging into system,
    9-17
  system administrator, 213-216
  terminals, 231-239
  wastebasket, 53
Usenet, 157-162, 273
users
  adding to X Windows, 238-239
  new accounts, 216-221
  sending messages, 135
/usr directory, 23
/usr/share/lib/terminfo
  directory, 234
utilities, 71-98, 167
Utilities command, workspace
  menu (OPEN LOOK Window
  Manager), 201
uucp (UNIX-to-UNIX copy)
  command, 151-157, 300
uucp addresses, 154

uucp networks, 147-148,
    151-154, 157
uucp program (System V), 7, 273
uuname command, 148
uux command, 156-157, 300

V

variable-item lists, 175
variables, 274
    environmental, 66
    HOME, 64
    MAIL, 65
    names in scripts, 62-63
    PATH, 65
    shell, .profile file, 63-66
    TERM, 65
variations in command lines, 47-48
vertical spacing, 180
vi (visual interpreter) text editor
    program, 6, 101-104, 274
vi command, 102-103
viewing and storing data in
    files, 54
.VL request, mm macro
    package, 175
vnews command, 159

W

W command, 110
wall (write-all) command, 216
wastebasket, UNIX version, 53
who am i command, 15
who command, 13, 221
wild card characters, 274
    (?), (*), 35-36
    regular expressions, 88-89
    using in file names, 35-36
    uucp command, 156
Window Manager, 274
window managers, 193-197
Window menu commands, Quit, 195
windows, 187, 274
    OPEN LOOK Window Manager,
        201-204
    X Windows, 198, 206-207

word processor, 274
words, deleting, 120
working directory, 27, 274
working groups in systems, 218
workspace, 274
    menu, OPEN LOOK Window
        Manager, 200-201
    X Windows, 189
workstation, 274
write (w) permissions, 38
write command, 104, 136
writing to bulletin boards, 160-161

X-Z

x (execute) permissions, 38
X.25 network, 157
X/Open CAE (Common Applica-
    tions Environment), 8
XENIX (Microsoft), 7, 274
xfd (X font display) command, 206
xinit command, 189
.xinitrc file, 189, 208
xlsfonts command, 205
xp command, 127
xterm (X terminal) program
    (X Window System), 197
xterm windows (X Window
    System), 12
    menus, 198-199
    shrinking/enlarging, 198
X Window System, 4, 9, 12,
    187-188
    adding users, 238-239
    command line options, 204-207
    copying/moving/selecting items,
        195-196
    display components/software,
        192-194
    File Manager, 190
    initializing, 208
    selecting fonts, 205
    starting/quitting sessions,
        189-191, 208
    terminal emulator, 190

z (zero screen) command, 114